METASKILLS

Other books
by Marty Neumeier

The Designful Company
Zag
The Brand Gap

META SKILLS

FIVE TALENTS FOR
THE ROBOTIC AGE

MARTY NEUMEIER

METASKILLS: FIVE TALENTS FOR THE ROBOTIC AGE
by Marty Neumeier

New Riders
New Riders is an imprint of Peachpit, a division of Pearson Education
www.newriders.com

Copyright © 2013 by Marty Neumeier

Project Editor: Michael J. Nolan
Designer and Illustrator: Marty Neumeier
Design Team: Beryl Wang, Lisa Lin, Jameson Spence, Kelly Kusumoto
Production Editor: Cory Borman
Copyeditor/Proofreader: Jennifer Frye Needham
Indexer: Joy Dean Lee

For Eileen

CONTENTS

PREFACE

What happens when a paradigm shifts? Do we simply wake up one day and realize that the past seems irreversibly quaint? Or do financial institutions fail, governments topple, industries break down, and cultures crack in two, with one half pushing to go forward and the other half pulling back?

This is a book about personal mastery in a time of radical change. As we address our increasing problems with increasing collaboration, we're finding that we still need something more—the bracing catalyst of individual genius.

Unfortunately, our educational system has all but ruled out genius. Instead of teaching us to create, it's taught us to copy, memorize, obey, and keep score. Pretty much the same qualities we look for in machines. And now the machines are taking our jobs.

I wrote this book to cut cubes out of clouds, put our swirl of societal problems into some semblance of perspective, and suggest a new set of skills to address them. While the problems we face today can be a source of hand-wringing, they can also be a source of energy. They can either lead to societal gridlock or the most spectacular explosion of creativity in human history.

One thing's for sure: There's no going back, no secret exit, no chance of stopping the clock. The only way out is forward. Our best hope is that once we see the shape of our situation, we can turn our united attention to *reshaping* it. It won't require a top-down strategy or an international fiat to get the transformation going. Just a relative handful of people—maybe people like you—with talent, vision, and a few modest tools.

I've divided the book into seven parts. The first is about the mandate for change. The next five are the metaskills you'll need to make a difference in the postindustrial workplace, including *feeling, seeing, dreaming, making*, and *learning*. The last is a set of suggestions for educational reform, written from the perspective of a hopeful observer.

As you read about the metaskills, take comfort in the knowledge that no one needs to be strong in all five. It only takes one or two talents to create a genius.

—*Marty Neumeier*

ACKNOWLEDGEMENTS

I'm deeply indebted to a number of people who gave their time freely to help with some of the technical aspects of the book. Among them is Dr. Carolyn M. Bloomer, an anthropologist whose understanding of human evolution, psychology, and culture was critical to the accuracy of my argument. Also Dr. Paul Pangaro and Hugh Dubberly, who generously shared their cybernetics-eye view of how we think and learn. Thanks to Gene Bellinger, who was patient and supportive as he helped me shape my presentation of systems thinking. And, finally, Andy Vineyard, my go-to guy for everyday technology, who explained in delightful detail how plumbing works.

I'm grateful to my publishing team at Peachpit, including Nancy Aldrich-Ruenzel, Michael Nolan, and Sara Jane Todd. This is our fourth book together in ten years, which speaks volumes about our working relationship.

Many thanks to my team at Liquid Agency, who have been remarkably creative and encouraging in their support of the project. In particular, I'd like to call out Alfredo Muccino, Scott Gardner, Dennis Hahn, Mariah Rich, Bill Zabit, and Mark Shaw. Thanks also to those who helped bring the book into being with their excellent design skills, including Beryl Wang, Lisa Lin, Jameson Spence, Miles Ryan, Kelly Kusumoto, and Cya Nelson.

I'm very fortunate to have an inner circle that includes Alina Wheeler, a fellow author who continually sends me links to articles and ideas she thinks I might find useful; Martin Lindstrom, another author who was generous with his trade secrets; my oldest friend, Paul Polito, who introduced me to the North County Trade Tech High School and who read through my first draft not once, but twice; my second-oldest friend, Gordon Mortensen, whose eye for design is second to none; Gary Peattie, valued in-law and seasoned book publisher; and my younger and wiser brother, Peter Neumeier, who offered sage advice on the flow of ideas.

Finally, and with much love, I'd like to thank my wife Eileen, who encouraged me to write the book, and whose insights grace every page of it.

PROLOGUE

The Midi-Pyrénées, southern France. A spray-painted silhouette of a prehistoric hand, positioned low on the wall at Pech Merle, seems at odds with the other images in the cave—the fluidly stylized drawings of horses, mammoths, reindeer, and other herd animals of the prehistoric hunt. In fact, the hand stencils are the only naturalistic references to human beings at all, and the only subjects of any kind shown actual size. You could place your own hand over the stenciled hand of a cave painter, and even after 25,000 years of human evolution, your hand would fit.

The stencils are highly mysterious. Why would artists with enough skill to conjure magnificent animals in full motion, and who entered the caves to make paintings only after practicing outside the caves, bother to tag the wall with a simple stencil that a kindergartener could make on the first try? Were the hands the equivalent of personal signatures, or perhaps clan symbols? Or were they examples of ancient graffiti, painted by nonartists after the "real" artists had left? Why were there no images of human beings drawn in the same style? And what exactly were the cave paintings for?

No one can say for sure, but here's a theory that fits the facts: The paintings were designed as a kind of magical mystery show to inspire greatness in the hunt. The caverns were prehistoric cathedrals, special places of elevated consciousness where the hunters could psych themselves for the coming hunt. Animals, not humans, were the subjects, because animals were what the hunters revered. They respected their immense power and beauty in a world where humans were lower on the food chain.

When Pablo Picasso came to view the caves of southern France, he couldn't help notice a particular nuance. The ancient artists had deftly arranged their two-dimensional images over the natural bumps and fissures of the stone, giving them a subtle depth. When viewed in the flickering light of a candle, *voilá!* the dimensionalized animals came to life, appearing to fly across the walls. The caves, in this construction of the facts, were nothing less than the ancient version of our 3D cinemas. On a good night (or with the right drugs) they were probably much *better* than our 3D cinemas.

And the hand silhouettes? Poignant symbols of gratitude for a unique and surprising gift. No other animal of their acquaintance could fashion tools, hunt with weapons, or cast motion pictures onto cave walls. The human hand, with its sensitive fingers and opposable thumb, made all this possible. So for about ten thousand years our ancestors enshrined their thanksgiving in hundreds of caves, from Africa to Australia, to remind us of who we are and where we came from. They're reaching out as if to say: "This hand made this drawing."

8.7 million homes, North America. "It's a poor workman who blames these" was the clue that Alex Trebek read from the television monitor. It was February 16, 2011, in the very last round of a three-day *Jeopardy!* marathon that pitted IBM'S "Watson" computer against two human champions, Ken Jennings and Brad Rutter. Ken was the biggest money winner of all time. Brad held the record for the longest winning streak. To rack up a score, a contestant must be the first to hit the buzzer with the right answer, or more precisely, the right question, since the game begins with the answer.

Even before Alex finished reading the clue, Watson's 2,880 parallel processor cores had begun to divvy up the workload. Who or what is "workman"? What does poor mean in this context? Is workman penniless? Maybe out of a job? Meanwhile, other processors got busy parsing the sentence. Which word is the subject? Which is the verb? If this word is a noun, is it a person or a group? Making the task more tricky, *Jeopardy!* clues are displayed in all capital letters, so Watson had to figure out if "WORKMAN" was a proper noun or a common noun.

Despite knowing almost nothing, at least in the human sense of knowing, Watson's massively parallel processing system held a distinct advantage over its human counterpart. It was fast. At 33 billion operations per second, it could search 500 gigabytes of data, or the equivalent of one million books, in the blink of an eye. It could also hit the buzzer in less than eight milliseconds, much faster than a human hand.

Yet Watson was programmed not to hit the buzzer unless it had a confidence level of at least 50 percent. To reach that level, various algorithms working across multiple processors returned hundreds of hypothetical answers. Another batch of processors checked and rechecked these answers against the stored data, assigning probabilities for correctness. During the three seconds that these operations took, Watson's onstage avatar, a color-shifting globe with expressive lines fluttering across its face, gave the distinct impression of someone thinking deeply.

Then the buzzer.

"What are tools?" answered Watson in a cheerful computer voice. The confidence rankings for the top candidates had been "tools" at 84 percent, "Yogi Berra" at 10 percent, and "explorer" at 3 percent. So tools it was.

"You are right for $2,000," said Alex.

By the end of the game Watson had passed Ken's $19,200 and Brad's $21,600 to win with $41,413, becoming the first nonhuman champion of *Jeopardy!*

Below Ken's written answer to the Final Jeopardy question he had scrawled the footnote: "I, for one, welcome our new computer overlords."

TEN QUESTIONS

WHY DO WE CREATE?

Expressions of human creativity dating back more than 40,000 years
have been found in hundreds of caves from Europe to Australia.

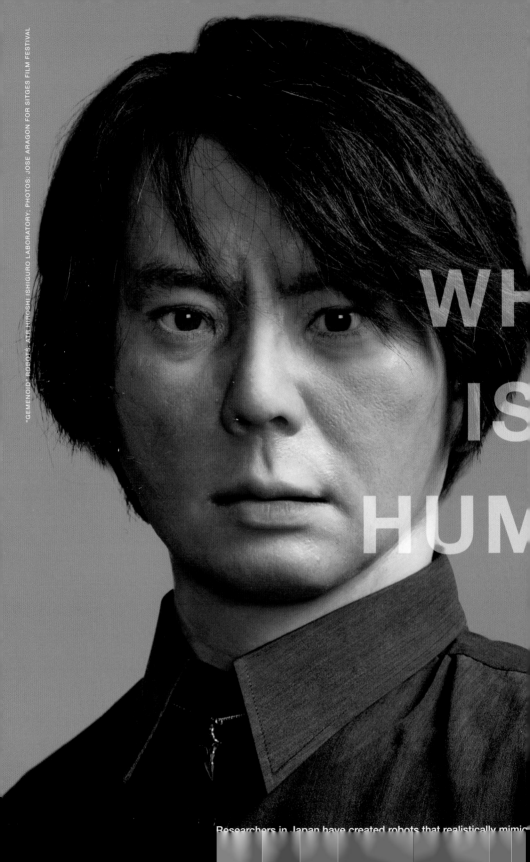

WH
IS
HUM

Researchers in Japan have created robots that realistically mimic

AT
A
AN?

ch, movement, and facial expressions of their human operators.

WHY DO W

The Great Recession has triggered a widespread debate about

E WORK?

political leaders haven't offered a compelling vision for the future.

WHAT IS A SIN?

Every day, Americans generate 4.4 pounds of trash per person,
totaling more than 250 million tons every year.

WHAT IS BEAUTY?

Every year, beauty pageants such as Little Miss America show off
more than 100,000 children under 12 years of age.

WHO WILL WE WORSHIP?

Lady Gaga amassed more than fifty million Facebook fans in 2012,
only to be topped by Eminem the same year.

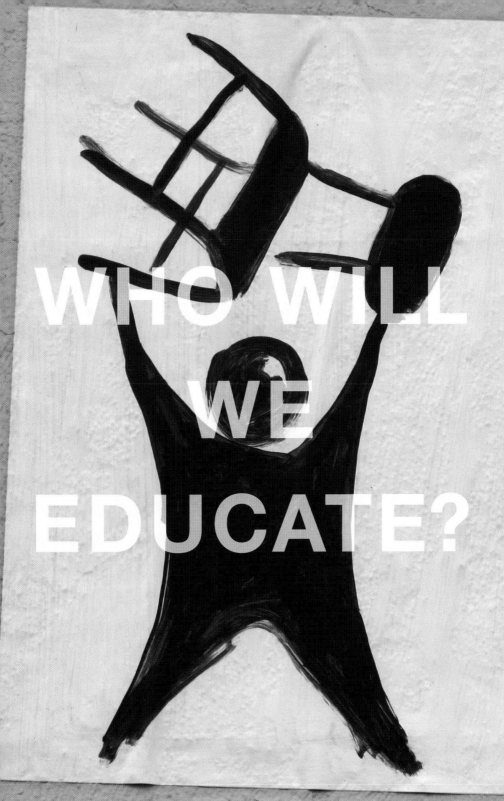

WHO WILL WE EDUCATE?

In 2011, more than 10,000 Chilean students took to the streets to protest a lack of affordable education.

HOW WILL

Alarmed by the increasing desctruction of sea life from toxic dump

WE EAT?

...signer proposed a sewer grate that sends a clear message.

WHERE WIL

By 2050 the world popluation is expected to top 9 billi

WE LIVE?

which nearly 7 billion will end up in cities.

WHAT MAKES US HAPPY?

German artists created a 16-foot, neon "feel-o-meter" that uses surveillance

THE MANDATE

THE ARC OF HUMAN TALENT. Over the last 13 billion years or so, the universe has been under the thumb of entropy. *Entropy* is the force that causes energy in a system to decrease over time. It's a tendency for things to become disorderly, lose their purposeful integrity, and finally die or simply become meaningless. Think of decaying orbits, dying suns, rotting plants, rusting iron, forest fires, old newspapers, or the destructive path of war.

Standing in opposition to entropy is life. Life is the impulse to fight against entropy. Remember Victor Laszlo in *Casablanca?* "If we stop breathing, we'll die. If we stop fighting our enemies, the world will die." Our common enemy is entropy; the impulse to resist entropy is called *extropy.*

The battle between entropy and extropy is literally a life-and-death struggle. Creatures are born, fight for life, and die in huge numbers year after year. Yet considering the enormous power of entropy, the battle is going pretty well. Individual lives end, but important life lessons are passed down through DNA. In the case of humans, additional learning is passed down through various forms of culture. Since the day *Homo erectus* first fashioned a stone blade, around two-and-a-half-million years ago, the human race has evolved into the most awesome entropy-fighting species on Earth.

If evolution continues on its path towards increasing order, complexity, and beauty, entropy will slowly recede into the shadows. At least that's the theory. Whether it happens or not will depend a great deal on what humans do in this very century. At seven billion strong, we're now the most populous mammals on the planet with the possible exception of rats. And since the rats aren't likely to be game changers, it's up to us. We're the ones that will make or break the future.

The arc of human evolution is really the arc of human talent. For our purposes, we can define talent as an inherited and learned ability to create beautiful things—whether they're tools, objects, experiences, relationships, situations, solutions, or ideas. If the outcomes are not beautiful, the maker is demonstrating creativity, but not necessarily talent. Talent works on a higher level than creativity. It requires highly developed "making" skills. And making skills can only be learned by making things.

The name *Homo erectus* means upright man, but the real evolutionary advantage of erectus was not walking. It was working. When our hominid ancestors came down from the trees, their hands were finally freed to do other things. This, in turn, encouraged evolutionary changes to their hands. The human hand, with its articulate fingers and opposable thumb, turned out to be the lever that launched what we now call technology.

Our long history matters because it tells us what evolution designed us to do. If our evolutionary purpose were only to eat and reproduce, we wouldn't have needed large brains or opposable thumbs. We wouldn't have needed technology or art. We wouldn't have developed an interest in social networking or space travel. We wouldn't have changed our biology as much as we have—more than any other mammal in history. Therefore we must be designed for something else.

Does this mean we're born with a purpose?

While some might say yes, I say no. I think we come into this world with a set of evolution-derived capabilities that both suggest and limit what we can do. If any of us have a guiding purpose, it's only because we've chosen one. Which, as I'll go into later, might not be a bad idea.

If you're looking for a ready-made purpose, the *transhumanists* have a breathtaking one for you. They believe that humankind's purpose is to accelerate evolution beyond its current biological limitations, so that increasing levels of intelligence, complexity, and love will spread throughout the universe. They see modern-day humans as midwives in this process. The life forms that will take it from here, in the transhumanist view, will be human-machine combos and human-made biological beings. The exact point at which machines will supercede humans is called the Singularity, a term coined by information theorist John von Neumann. They predict this to occur sometime between 2030 and 2050.

Why would someone believe this? Hard to say. But the underpinnings of this notion are rational, and worthy of serious consideration no matter what conclusions you draw from them.

Think about this: The world's ability to store, communicate, and compute information has grown at annual rates of at least 23% since 1986. The total amount of digital information is now increasing tenfold every five years. A total of five exabytes of data existed in 2003. Today the world is generating the same amount every two days. If we could put this data on CD-ROMS and pile them up, the stack would extend past the moon. The amount of information in existence is around 1.27 zettabytes, or 1,000 exabytes, each of which is equivalent to 4 billion books.

In a recent two-month period, more videos were uploaded on YouTube than have been aired since 1948 on the big three networks. Wikipedia has generated over 13 million articles in more than 200 languages over a single decade. This is what can happen when technology is open to everyone.

The democratization of knowledge is a profit platform, too. Amazon has a goal of making every book ever printed available in any language in under 60 seconds. Google's mission is to organize all the world's information, not just book information, and make it universally accessible.

Ten years ago, former IBM chief Lou Gerstner noted that complexity was spiraling upward faster than the capability of humans to handle it. "Therefore," he said, "the infrastructure itself—from end to end—will have to be reengineered to have the ability to perform many tasks that require human intervention today. What is coming is a kind of computing that will take its cue from the human autonomic nervous system." He characterized this as a "self-awareness" that would allow systems to defeat viruses, repel attacks, and repair themselves on the fly. Today our electronic networks are so rich and complex that they're beginning to behave like biological systems.

We come into this world with a set of evolution-derived capabilities that both suggest and limit what we can do.

In John von Neumann's day, computing was a simple, step-by-step affair that precluded any humanlike abilities such as pattern recognition, learning, or self-awareness. Yet only a half century later, IBM and the US government are investing in "cognitive computer chips" that can perform massively parallel processing—the same kind that occurs in the human brain. These new chips consume very little power and have a fundamentally different design, using an arrangement of 256 neuron-like nodes to make a "neuro-synaptic core."

Watson was a jury-rigged version of a massively parallel computer chip. Some critics dismissed IBM's accomplishment on the premise that a room-sized computer is not a viable alternative to a three-pound human brain. But keep in mind that today's iPhone has as much processing power as a whole Cray supercomputer had only 25 years ago. In 25 more years it will be the size of a blood cell.

Growing computer power is enabling four interconnected technologies, which in turn are driving exponential change. These are: information technology, nanotechnology, genetics, and robotics. Kevin Kelly, in his excellent book *What Technology Wants*, has labeled this ever-growing community of tools the *technium*. Speaking of computer chips he says that "tiny synthetic minds no bigger than an ant's know where on Earth they are and how to get back to your home (GPS); they remember the names of your friends and translate foreign languages [and] unlike the billions of minds in the wild, the best of these technological minds are getting smarter by the year."

The math behind the technium is similar to Moore's Law, the 1965 prediction that the amount of computing power you can buy for a dollar will double every 18 months. Gordon Moore's formula has surprised everyone with its consistency. Looking back, if Apple had invented the iPod in 1961 instead of 2001, each unit would have cost $3 billion and required a trailer to haul it around. Now the device costs only $50 and can fit on a watchband.

"We're up to something like the 28th doubling of computing power," says Joel Garreau, author of *Radical Evolution*. "Doubling is an amazing thing. It means that each step is as tall as all the previous steps put together." This amounts to an exponential increase of about 100 million times. "You've never seen a curve like that in all of human history."

Inventor and author Ray Kurzweil calls this phenomenon the Law of Accelerating Returns, which he defines as the speed-up in the rate of evolution, with technical evolution picking up the slack for much slower biological evolution. He notes, as one example, that the resolution and bandwidth of brain scanning have been doubling in accordance with Moore's Law. He predicts that in a couple of decades we'll be able to reverse-engineer the brain and apply its principles to machines, and maybe even use machines to alter the brain.

Meanwhile, the human brain is evolving on its own. By studying mutations in our DNA, researchers have concluded that our genes are evolving considerably faster than they were in preagricultural times. Yet the rate of technological evolution is a billion billion times as fast as the evolution of DNA.

Kelly sees human evolution as a play in four acts. The first was the invention of language about fifty thousand years ago, which shifted the burden of evolution away from a total dependence on genetic inheritance. The second was the invention of writing about ten thousand years ago, which allowed ideas to travel across time and territory. The third was the development of science, which is a metainvention—an invention that spawns more invention. Now, he says, evolution has evolved a fourth manner of evolution. "We are reaching deep within ourselves to adjust the master knob. We are messing with our source code, including the code that grows our brains and makes our minds." With advances in gene splicing, genetic engineering, and gene therapy, "we are ending a four-billion-year-old hegemony of Darwinian evolution."

Kurzweil believes that the future will be far more surprising than most of us realize, because we haven't internalized the fact that the rate of change itself is accelerating. He says: "There will be no distinction, post-Singularity, between human and machine and between physical and virtual reality. If you wonder what will remain unequivocally human in such a world, it's simply this quality: ours is the species that inherently seeks to extend its physical and mental reach beyond current limitations."

Is this really our future? Not neccessarily, says Joel Garreau.

The future
looks more like
a vertical takeoff
than a gentle rise.
But what are we
racing towards?

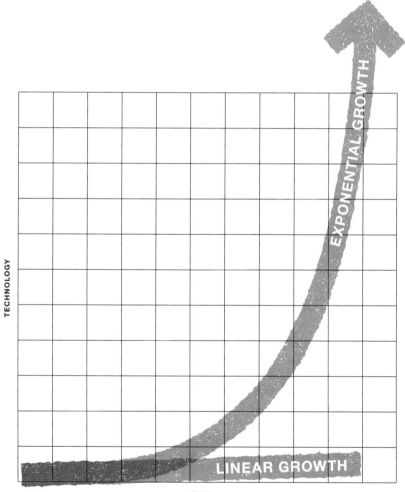

He lays out three possible scenarios, each with its own poster child. The first is the *heaven scenario*, in which we become godlike through the continuing evolution and collaboration of man and machine. The poster child for this scenario is Kurzweil. The *hell scenario* predicts that the growing power of technology might be used by miscreants (humans, no doubt) to extinguish or at least harm life on Earth. The proponent of this scenario is venture capitalist Bill Joy, cofounder of Sun Microsystems. Finally, the *prevail scenario* says that humanity is not a slave to growth curves, and somehow we'll muddle through. The poster child for this scenario is virtual reality pioneer Jaron Lanier, author of *You Are Not a Gadget.*

There's something reassuringly human in Lanier's view of the future. It suggests that we shouldn't (and probably won't) drive recklessly at ever-accelerating speeds; that we shouldn't (and probably won't) drive at ten miles an hour with the brakes on; and that we shouldn't (but probably will) drive slightly faster than the speed limit, gripping the wheel nervously as we glance at the accident on the side of the road. It suggests that there are limits to exponential growth that we simply have yet to encounter. We can only hope they're not the catastrophic kind.

In the meantime, we have every right to marvel at our evolutionary progress. Michael Eisner, the former head of Disney, observed that we've come a long way "from paintings on cavemen's walls to the ability to digitally beam movies, television, news, information, and music into every cave in the world." That ability—the skillful application of art and science—is what we call talent.

THE INNOVATION MANDATE. Economic gloom. Dwindling resources. Growing pollution. Failing schools. Why do we have so many huge, hairy problems? Are these the natural by-products of exponential change? Will the weight of our problems grow larger as the world becomes more complex? Maybe, but here's another way to look at it: The weight seems too large because the lever is too small.

The tools and skills we've developed for the *last* era are inadequate to address the challenges of the *next* era. We find ourselves caught in the middle between two incompatible paradigms: The old industrial platform is collapsing, but we can't quite make out the new platform. We're not sure which way to jump.

As a descriptor, the "Information Age" doesn't really capture the spirit of where we're headed. While an explosion of information is certainly a key driver of change today, we could also say that petroleum was a key driver in the Industrial Age. Yet we didn't call it the Oil Age; we called it the Industrial Age. Our shared vision of machinery, factories, and magnificent mass production was both palpable and inclusive. It fired our collective imagination.

Today, gushing flows of information are not only fueling vast networks of knowledge, they're allowing us to tinker with the very building blocks of life, exposing biology to advances in machinery, and machinery to advances in biology. We're entering a period of increasing human-machine collaboration, made possible by information, but also transcending it.

We're entering what I'll call the Robotic Age.

This chaotic shift from one platform to the next is likely to create massive amounts of both obsolescence and opportunity for years to come. As business strategists can tell you, threats can also be framed as opportunities. The dying city core can be transformed into a vibrant Old Town. The rising cost of oil can pave the way for alternative fuels. The increase in Alzheimer's can focus the search for profitable new drugs.

At the same time, opportunities, if not addressed, can turn into threats. The company that ignores the struggling startup with a different idea can suddenly find its customers deserting in droves. The government that denies the wishes of its people can find that public opinion has galvanized against it. Clearly, the window of opportunity operates both ways—it can open up to the fresh air or slam down on our fingers.

Innovation is the discipline that decides which it will be. In a time of rapid change, success favors those who can make big leaps of imagination, courage, and effort. With innovation, people and institutions have the means to escape a dying past and make it safely to the other side. Without it, they can lose their momentum, abandon their uniqueness, and wander off course as they drift back to the status quo. Innovation is the antidote to entropy: If we stop breathing we'll die.

In the Robotic Age, the drumbeat of innovation will only grow louder. The urge to march will be felt from top to bottom—from the societal level to the company level to the individual level. But it's mostly at the company level that the future will be forged, because business has the motive and the means to drive large-scale change.

Whenever a paradigm shifts, three kinds of people emerge: 1) those who resist change because they've been so successful with the previous paradigm; 2) those who embrace change because they *haven't* been successful with the previous paradigm; and 3) those who embrace change *despite* their success with the previous paradigm. This third group is the serial innovators, the entrepreneurs, the iconoclasts who embody the principle of creative destruction.

Creative destruction was a term popularized by economist Joseph Schumpeter in the 1940s. It refers to a process of radical innovation in which new business models destroy old ones by changing the entire basis for their success. This applies to products, services, processes, and technologies. For example, the telephone destroyed the telegraph, the automobile destroyed the horse-drawn carriage, and the smartphone destroyed the cell phone. In an age of rapid change, markets tend to change faster than any one company, since markets have nothing to lose by changing. Only companies who get good at creation and destruction can consistently turn discontinuity to their advantage.

The payoff for radical innovation can be huge. During a period when cell phone maker Nokia earned $1.1 billion on a 35% market share, smartphone maker Apple earned $1.6 billion on a 2.5% market share. Within 13 years under Steve Jobs, Apple surpassed Microsoft to become the most valuable technology company in the world, giving its shareholders a 100-times return on their investment during that period.

When people hear the word innovation, they usually think of technology-based products—the iPad, the Prius, the Wii, Tesla, and others. But this only is the tip of the iceberg. The Doblin Group, a think tank in Chicago, has identified ten areas where innovation can deliver an advantage to companies:

1. The business model, or how the enterprise makes money.
2. Networking, including organizational structure, the value chain, and partnerships.
3. Enabling processes, or the capabilities the company buys from others.
4. Core processes, or the proprietary methods that add value.
5. Product performance, including features and functionality.
6. Product systems, meaning the extended system that supports the product.
7. Service, or how the company treats customers.
8. Channels, or how the company connects its offerings to its customers.
9. Branding, or how the company builds its reputation.
10. Customer experience, including the touchpoints where customers encounter the brand.

In each of these areas, innovation can be employed as a booster rocket to leave competitors in the dust. Business leaders are beginning to see, sometimes through the dust of market changers, the wealth-generating power of originality. They're learning what Rudyard Kipling knew a century earlier:

> *They copied all they could follow,*
> *but they couldn't copy my mind.*
> *So I left 'em sweating and stealing,*
> *a year and a half behind.*

Almost everything can be copied these days, given enough time and motivation. The only thing that can't be copied is originality. By definition, the original stands alone. Every category has leaders and followers, and thanks to greater transparency and the growing power of social media, customers are rewarding the former and devaluing the latter. The same principle now applies to nonprofits, educational institutions, and even cities, countries, and governments. Change is in the air.

WHERE ARE THE JOBS? A persistent topic in political circles is the "trickle-down theory" of job creation. It goes like this: If we make the right people rich enough, they'll give us jobs. Conversely, if we *fail* to make them rich, they'll lose interest in building big companies, and jobs will disappear.

Trickle-down economics was a popular theme of the Reagan administration during the 1970s. But because the "optics" of jobs and other benefits merely trickling down to the masses was less than inspiring, the administration retitled the idea *supply-side economics*. Reagonomics, as it came to be known, was similar to the *horse-and-sparrow theory*, a concept from the 1890s. If you fed a horse enough oats, it went, some would surely pass through to the road for the sparrows.

Concepts like these have considerable appeal at the top of the food chain, as you might imagine. But the feudal system of the Middle Ages was abandoned for a reason—it didn't work for the serfs. This made it difficult for feudal lords to hold onto their power, and over time the system was replaced with democracy. Yet the feudal system is always lurking in the wings, ready to sweep back onto history's stage. It happened again in the United States during the late 1970s when the government deregulated Wall Street and at the same time insured it against significant losses. In doing so, says economist Robert Reich, "It allowed finance—which until then had been the servant of American industry, to become its master, demanding short-term profits over long-term growth."

By 2007 financial companies accounted for over 40 percent of corporate profits and nearly as much of corporate pay, up from 10 percent during the Great Prosperity between 1947 and 1997. During periods like this, when the rich took home a smaller percentage of total income, the economy grew faster and median wages soared. "We created a virtuous circle in which an ever-growing middle class had the ability to consume more goods and services, which created more and better jobs, thereby stoking demand."

Today we have the flip side. The rich are getting richer while the poor are getting poorer. To be more precise, members of the middle class are being squeezed downward into the ranks of the poor, creating what Citigroup calls the "consumer hourglass effect," in which there are only two worthwhile markets left, the highest income and the lowest income. The middle-income market is now stagnant. Procter & Gamble has noticed the same phenomenon. "It required us to think differently about our product portfolio and how to please the high-end and lower-end markets," says group president Melanie Healey. "That's frankly where a lot of the growth is happening."

Now the top one percent of Americans takes home 25 percent of total income. In terms of wealth, the top one percent controls 40 percent of the total. Meanwhile, executive compensation is rising beyond prerecession levels with no end in sight. Surely, if the benefits were going to trickle, they would have trickled by now. So where are the jobs?

The nearly universal opinion of economists is that the engine for job creation is growth. If we grow the economy, they say, we can put everyone to back to work. Yet in the last 20 years this has not been strictly true; a lot of growth in developed countries has come from information-based businesses, which have created enormous shareholder wealth, but relatively few jobs. In 2011, software giant SAP reported revenues of $16 billion, but only 53,000 employees. Google is now a $29 billion company, but only employs 29,000 people. Facebook has revenues of $4 billion with only 2,000 people.

If you look at where banks, hedge funds, and venture capitalists are investing most heavily, it's in software companies and financial instruments where the returns are the quickest and most sizable. Even our manufacturing companies are becoming information companies, keeping the design and marketing here, sending the manufacturing where labor is cheapest. As manufacturing jobs have moved overseas, the middle class has had nowhere to go but down, while the "ruling" class—those at the top who control the business models, strategies, and policies—have enjoyed a greater and greater share of the pie.

The pie-eating contest is almost over. Starving the middle class to feed the upper class hasn't been good for anyone. Instead, it's led to the Great Recession—an economic cul-de-sac in which the

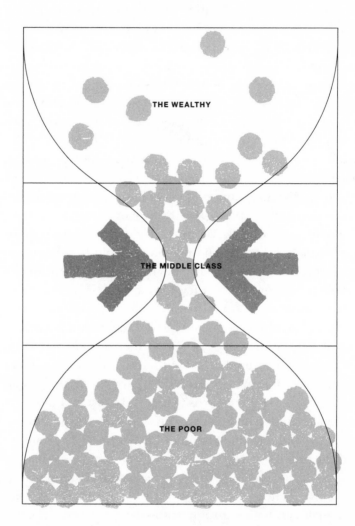

A concentration of economic power at the top has been squeezing the middle to the bottom.

THE WEALTHY

THE MIDDLE CLASS

THE POOR

HOURGLASS EFFECT

middle and the bottom no longer have the financial means to support the top. Any marketing strategy that targets the top and the bottom of the hourglass and ignores the middle is not a solution but an act of desperation.

According to Reich's figures, the average hourly pay of Americans has risen only 6 percent, adjusted for inflation, since 1985. Contrast this with the Germans, whose average pay has risen nearly 30 percent. At the same time, the top one percent of German households takes home 11 percent of total income, while the top one percent of American households takes 25 percent of the pie. Germany has managed to avoid the hourglass effect by supporting manufacturing and education.

But do we really want to bring back the bad old days—the dirty factories, the punch clocks, the mind-numbing repetitive work? Of course not. What we want is a new kind of industry that encourages the growth of talent. We want jobs that demand our best ideas, that respect our unique skills, that engage our minds as well as our muscles. Rather than bring creative work down to the level of factory work, we need to bring factory work up to the level of creative work.

THE ROBOT CURVE. Over time, there's consistent downward pressure on the value and cost of work. The job market is more than willing to shell out good money for original thinking and unique skills. But because business is competitive, creative processes tend to become routinized, moving step by step from original work down to skilled work, from skilled work down to rote work, and from rote work down to robotic work. At each step along the way, the value and the price decrease, with the value staying higher than the price.

Let's call this the Robot Curve.

At the top of the Robot Curve is creative work, where there's less routine and a lot of experimentation. Since this work is fairly original, maybe even unique, the cost is high and so is the value, as long as the work addresses a significant need. Creative work might include scientific discoveries, technological breakthroughs, new business ideas, product invention, organizational leadership, and all manner of creativity in the arts and entertainment fields. How much should Oprah be paid? Who knows? But if you want Oprah, there's little choice but to pay her fees.

One step down is skilled work, which includes the work of professionals. The techniques used by skilled workers and professionals were once original, but have now become best practices. There's still an element of creativity, but much of the expertise is shared by other professionals in the same discipline. This shared knowledge offers clients and employers a degree of interchangeability in the people they hire, albeit on a sliding scale of talent. I may not know which heart surgeon is the best, but I can at least be confident that my own doctor has a modicum of training and experience.

As skilled work becomes more standardized, or as technology can transform it, it turns into rote work and can be outsourced to lower cost producers. Writing a decision-tree script for a phone operator requires the creativity and experience of a skilled worker. But it standardizes the work so employees don't need the same high level of experience or education. The cost goes down, the value stays higher than the cost, and the work can be scaled up. The outsourcing mills of Bangalore are examples of rote work in action.

When rote work can be done more cheaply or more consistently with machines, it quickly becomes automated. That same decision tree designed for a phone operator may lend itself to a software application with voice simulation. The welding operation that was once done by a human worker can now be done even better by a robotic arm. The professional photograph that once would have cost $4,000 and two days' time can now be rented instantly online for $25. While automation puts people out of work, it also opens up new opportunities at the top of the curve for the originators and professionals who invent and manage these systems.

As the 21st century deepens, robots and algorithms will move into every area of our lives, and even into our bodies and brains. The current obsession with drugs and plastic surgery shows a willingness—even eagerness—to alter our biology with technological interventions. But the main reason this trend is likely to continue is that at every stop on the Robot Curve, new value is unlocked. In fact, you could argue that the Robot Curve has been the engine

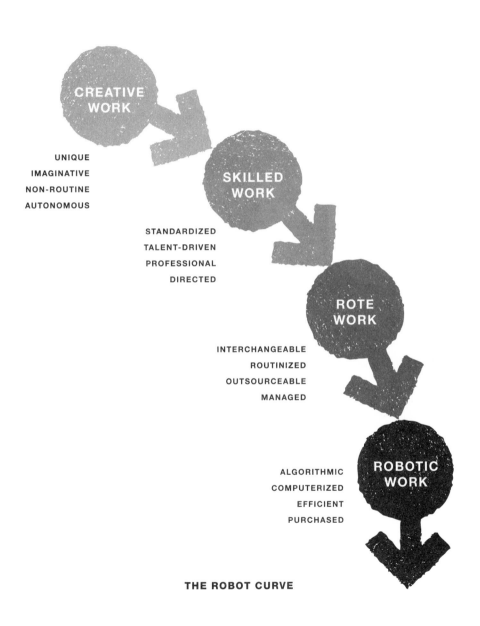

The value and cost of work decreases as its mechanization increases.

CREATIVE WORK

UNIQUE
IMAGINATIVE
NON-ROUTINE
AUTONOMOUS

SKILLED WORK

STANDARDIZED
TALENT-DRIVEN
PROFESSIONAL
DIRECTED

ROTE WORK

INTERCHANGEABLE
ROUTINIZED
OUTSOURCEABLE
MANAGED

ALGORITHMIC
COMPUTERIZED
EFFICIENT
PURCHASED

ROBOTIC WORK

THE ROBOT CURVE

for growth over the whole course of evolution. Today, the company that doesn't get ahead of the curve is the one that's stranded on the wrong side of the innovation gap.

So what does the Robot Curve say about jobs? Not surprisingly, it says that the best jobs will be at the top of curve. The top jobs determine all the other jobs down along the curve. The lower you are on the curve, the less autonomy you have, the less money you make, and the less adaptable you are when the marketplace demands new skills. In the jargon of the jobs world, lower-level skills are "brittle."

The Robot Curve also shows that pushing capabilities down the curve produces profits. Every time a new idea becomes a professional practice, or a professional practice becomes a rote procedure, or a rote procedure becomes a robotic operation, there's a chance for someone to profit. For example, the IBM Watson experiment led to a large contract with WellPoint, giving its doctors a powerful new tool for analyzing symptoms and choosing the best treatments. When stock photography began to take business from custom photography, it opened up a vast online market for commercial photographers who could figure out which images the media most needed. Where most photographers saw only doom, some saw opportunity.

After his *Jeopardy!* experience, contestant Ken Jennings shared his fears: "Just as factory jobs were eliminated in the 20th century by new assembly-line robots, Brad and I were the first knowledge-industry workers put out of work by the new generation of 'thinking' machines. 'Quiz-show contestant' may be the first job made redundant by Watson, but I'm sure it won't be the last."

True. And this continuing pattern of destruction and creation is exactly the way the world evolves. The Robot Curve is a waterfall of opportunity that flows endlessly from the creative to the automated. If we can't find valuable work, it's not because we're in a recession; we're in a recession because we can't find valuable work. We've been confusing cause and effect. We're still trying to apply Industrial Age ideas to Robotic Age realities, and the result has been a creative and economic vortex.

According to research by ManpowerGroup, 52 percent of companies in the US report difficulty in filling jobs. Yet even when when we worry that twenty million jobs are missing, three million jobs are going unfilled. The talent vaccuum is not confined to America, the company says. One in three employers around the world say they can't find skilled workers to fill their jobs. Meanwhile, a record 210 million people are out of work.

Kathy Smith, human resources manager at a manufacturer of airplane parts, said: "A tremendous gap exists between the workers that are available and the jobs we have open. Before, you could be a sheet metal mechanic and all you had to know was how to shoot rivets. Today, you need to do that, but also know how to inspect for quality, understand lean business principles, be able to do repairs, and be willing to continuously improve your processes and keep on learning." In other words, workers who offer more than clock time.

The Robot Curve is a waterfall of opportunity that flows endlessly from the creative to the automated.

Where will the best jobs come from? Not from rich people. Giving rich people more money will not produce the jobs we need. Instead, the best jobs will come from creative people—rich or not—who put societal contribution ahead of salary and stock options.

Employers in the Robotic Age don't want employees to be robots. They have robots. What they want are people who think for themselves, use their imagination, communicate well and can work in teams, and who can adapt to continuous change.

We have an unfounded fear that machines will someday start thinking like humans. What we should really fear is that humans have already started thinking like machines. Machines can be tremendously useful for storing and recalling billions of facts, for repeating complex operations at high speed, or for working tirelessly for little money and no praise. Humans who try to compete with machines will find themselves, like Ken Jennings, out of a job.

For Final Jeopardy, the category is "Evolution." This creature's three-pound, massively parallel processing computer will always search for deeper answers.

Question: What is a human?

A CRISIS OF HAPPINESS. Sometime during the Great Depression, Americans began to blame their unhappiness on a lack of manufacturing growth. Sound familiar? If we could only get the factories moving again, we could put people back to work and our incomes would go back up. Then surely we'd be happy.

So the government enlisted a panel of economists to put metrics in place to gauge our progress toward this all-important goal. The result was the national income and products account, which had as its chief feature an indicator called Gross Domestic Product. GDP measures in dollars the market value of all products and services produced during a given period, and it soon became the yardstick for the national "standard of living." With this new measurement in place, the nation could simply focus on making money, and happiness would follow like day follows night.

The leader of this commission, Nobel Prize winner Simon Kuznets, had no such illusion. He understood full well that other measurements were needed to assess our progress. "The welfare of a nation," he said, "can scarcely be inferred from a measurement of national income." He was echoing the voice of Thomas Jefferson, who, in developing the constitutional Bill of Rights, replaced the right to "property" with a right to the "pursuit of happiness."

But since happiness is hard to measure, we use GDP. Unfortunately, not only is there little correlation between happiness and a nation's total throughput of goods and services, there may be an inverse relationship. By creating policies that favor the biggest producers of goods and services, we're exacerbating the Hourglass Effect, transferring more of the country's wealth and power to the top while squeezing the middle class down to the bottom. Today, GDP could be seen as a significant driver of *unhappiness.*

What if, instead of measuring income, we were to measure evolutionary progress? What if we could measure increasing fairness, freedom, peace, and creativity? Wouldn't these be more precise indicators of happiness than GDP? Better yet, why don't we try harder to measure happiness itself?

This is exactly what the people of Bhutan have been doing since 1972. Gross National Happiness, as they call it, has set off a global effort to adapt the measurement for international use. Nicolas Sarkozy established a commission to study it in 2008, led by Nobel Prize winner Joseph Stiglitz. American economist Jeffrey D. Sachs and British prime minister David Cameron are both strong proponents. So are epidemiologist Michael Pennock from Canada, who helped Bhutan design its original GNH instrument, and Dr. Susan Andrews, who spearheaded a series of formative events in Brazil.

In the United States, the Gallup-Healthways Well-Being Index has struck a chord with workers and economists. Every year since 2008, Gallup has phoned a minimum of one thousand adults at random to inquire about indicators such as eating habits, stress levels, wellness records, emotional states, and job satisfaction. They estimate that disengaged workers are costing the country a whopping $300 billion each year in productivity losses. They found that American workers are increasingly unhappy with their supervisors, apathetic about their companies, and disengaged from their work. As you might imagine, job satisfaction is a leading indicator of job performance. Unhappy workers are unproductive workers.

In *The Progress Principle*, authors Teresa Amabile and Steven Kramer report that their study of 64,000 specific workday events, drawn from electronic diaries of 238 professionals across seven companies, brought them to a surprisingly pointed conclusion: "Of all the events that engage people at work, the single most important—by far—is simply making progress at meaningful work." What makes people happiest, then, is not money, nor incentives, nor status, nor titles. It's getting where we want to go. As we begin to question the productivity goals of the Industrial Age, our desire to have more is giving way to our desire to be more.

There's a new world struggling to be born. It's a world of greater creativity, higher purpose, and deeper fulfillment.

So where does the Gallup-Healthways index say we should look for hints of 21st-century happiness? California District 14, otherwise known as Silicon Valley, a well-known bastion of workaholism. A not-uncommon workweek in District 14 is 80 hours, and it's mostly voluntary. There are no job descriptions that specify an 80-hour week, or even a 50-hour week. What causes people here to invest so much time in their jobs is "making progress at meaningful work," as Amabile and Kramer suggest.

But there's even more to it. Silicon Valley thrives on passion. People there have a vision of themselves toiling at "the burning point of history," as science historian James Burke described it in his BBC series *Connections*. They're out to change the world, and they have the freedom to contribute to the mission as they see fit. "Being the richest man in the cemetery doesn't matter to me," said Steve Jobs. "Going to bed at night saying we've done something wonderful…that's what matters to me."

In 1943 psychologist Abraham Maslow wrote a paper called "A Theory of Human Motivation." It was based on a pyramid called the *hierarchy of needs*. He theorized that human beings tend to work their way from physiological needs such as air, food, and water at the bottom of the pyramid, up to self-actualization such as spontaneity and creativity at the top of the pyramid. Self-actualization is a privilege that must be earned, according to this model, by working up from the bottom. The term self-actualization is related to what the Greeks called *eudaimonia*, the joyful fulfillment of one's potential, or the pursuit of higher-order goals.

When eudaimonia is blocked, either by companies or society, human creativity goes underground. That's what happened during the Industrial Age. The demands of the assembly line produced not only uniform products, but uniform people as well. There was virtually one kind of education, one sort of social behavior, one basic religion, one acceptable gender orientation, and one view of work. Those who didn't fit in were stamped "defective" and discarded. In the headlong pursuit of productivity, the Industrial Age managed to take most of the joy out of work, the humanity out of business, and the beauty out of everyday life. Yet it also built the *self-esteem* layer of the pyramid, to which we can now add the soul-enriching pinnacle of *self-actualization*.

There's a new world struggling to be born. It's a world of greater creativity, higher purpose, and deeper fulfillment. To bring it into being, we'll need a new set of abilities that goes beyond what suf-

The Industrial Age
brought us to the brink
of self-actualization.
Will the Robotic Age
bring us the rest
of the way?

SELF-ACTUALIZATION
CREATIVITY, AUTONOMY, GROWTH, AND FULFILLMENT

ESTEEM
ACHIEVEMENT, CONFIDENCE, STATURE, AND RESPECT

BELONGING AND LOVE
FAMILY, FRIENDSHIP, AFFECTION, AND SEXUAL INTIMACY

SAFETY
SECURITY, STABILITY, EMPLOYMENT, AND SHELTER

PHYSIOLOGICAL
HEALTH, WATER, WARMTH, FOOD, AND SLEEP

MASLOW'S HIERARCHY OF NEEDS

ficed in the 20th century—higher-order skills that our schools have yet to prioritize.

The workplace of the 21st century is a massive fulcrum for change. If we can transform the way we work, we can transform the way the world works. In the process, we're likely to find something more than money in our pay packages.

THE OBSOLETE INDUSTRIAL BRAIN. The operating metaphor of the 20th century was the factory, so it follows that the goal of education was to assemble graduates as efficiently as Ford assembled cars. We've been alarmingly successful at this. Education today is now a streamlined process based on maximum throughput (the highest number of graduates), extreme efficiency (the fewest number of instructors), and reliable metrics (easy-to-grade standardized tests).

Streamlined education produces the type of graduates who excel in measurable areas of intelligence such as memorization, math, logic, and language. Unfortunately, this comes at the expense of hard-to-measure areas such as creativity, interpersonal abilities, emotional maturity, and resilience, which have been de-prioritized in the interests of efficiency. As researchers are quick to point out, it's precisely these hard-to-measure areas of intelligence that make for great leaders and successful human beings. Therefore we shouldn't be surprised if we've created a society of oddly unimaginative and uncultured people. As educational activist Ken Robinson put it, "Complaining that graduates aren't creative is like saying, 'I bought a bus and it sank.'"

There's nothing inherently wrong with fact-based knowledge and rote skills. These are useful and necessary tools for success. But in an era of massive change and daunting challenges, we need more than rote skills. We need the ability to think and act in new ways to ensure our long-term survival.

Socrates once told a story about King Ammon of Egypt. Ammon had an argument with the god Theuth about the new invention of writing, saying it would destroy society. "If men learn this, it will implant forgetfulness in their souls; they will cease to exercise memory because they will rely on that which is written, calling things to remembrance no longer from within themselves, but by a means of external marks." This, he said, "will make them seem to know much, while for the most part they will know nothing."

King Ammon's fear was partially borne out. In the two-and-a-half millennia since Socrates walked the earth, the spread of literacy has clearly reduced our reliance on memory. To be fair, that was part of the deal. If you could easily pull a farmer's almanac down from your shelf, you didn't have to remember the exact rainfall probabilities for June. If you could walk to the public library, you could borrow a book on the Peloponnesian War rather than tracking down an expert who had memorized every battle. And, today, if you can access the Internet, you can look up the spelling of Peloponnesia, and find out a great deal more about it besides. (Did you know that Athens was ruled by thirty tyrants after losing to Sparta? That's a lot of tyrants!)

Whether or not Wikipedia will implant forgetfulness in our souls is hard to say. But one thing's for sure: The amount of knowledge we've accumulated since the invention of writing is too big to fit in a biological brain. We need Google and Wikipedia and other organizations to collect, store, and organize our knowledge, not only to access it, but just to make sense of it.

Psychologist Carl Jung proposed the *collective unconscious* as a way to understand our inherited, unconscious memory of human experience. Today the Internet seems to be creating a collective *conscious*, a shared memory that exists outside of our physical brains. It might be even argued that the collective conscious is a *fourth brain* that we're adding on top of the three brains we already have.

> **We need the ability to think and act in new ways to ensure our long-term survival.**

The three-brain model, or "triune brain," was popularized by neuroscientist Paul McLean in the early 1990s. He theorized that evolution equipped us with three brains, one grown over the other, which he labeled the reptilian brain, the limbic brain, and the neocortex. The reptilian brain, or "lizard brain," first appeared in fish about 500 million years ago, and

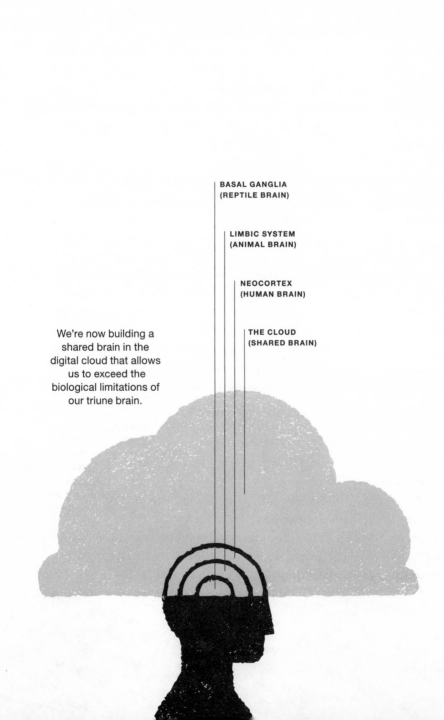

BASAL GANGLIA
(REPTILE BRAIN)

LIMBIC SYSTEM
(ANIMAL BRAIN)

NEOCORTEX
(HUMAN BRAIN)

THE CLOUD
(SHARED BRAIN)

We're now building a shared brain in the digital cloud that allows us to exceed the biological limitations of our triune brain.

reached its apex in reptiles about 150 milllion years ago. It works well at a simple level, but tends to be somewhat rigid and compulsive. Around the same time, on top of the reptilian brain evolved the limbic brain, or "dog brain." This is the seat of value judgments, mostly unconscious and emotional, that have a powerful say over how we behave. The third brain, which grew over the limbic brain, is the neocortex or "human brain." The neocortex showed up in primates two or three millions years ago, and gave us the flexible learning abilities that allowed the building of sophisticated technologies and complex cultures.

Yet we're restless. Evolution moves too slowly for us. So we're taking evolution into our own hands, so to speak, building ourselves a shared artificial brain. And just as our hands had been freed to make tools when we emerged from the trees, our minds are now being freed to think in more creative ways as we come out of the factory.

WANTED: METASKILLS. Today's robots are primitive. They can do certain kinds of repetitious work fairly well, but their brittle skills cause them to fail if changes are introduced to their routines. This is not unlike our own Industrial Age skills, which have been mostly job-specific and not easily transferable to other tasks.

When I worked the night shift at an aircraft factory, my job was to mold parts with a huge hydropress. But that skill was not transferable to a small drill press. So I had to learn to use the drill press the same way I learned the hydropress, by being shown each operation, one step at a time, by a senior person. If I'd had a general understanding of factory tools, plus a general understanding of how airplane parts were made, I could have mastered these skills rather quickly and gone on to invent shortcuts and improvements that might have become best practices for the factory.

This higher-level understanding is the realm of *metacognitive skills*, or *metaskills* for short. They act more like guiding principles than specific steps, so they can be transferred from one situation to another without losing their effectiveness. Metaskills determine the *how to*, not the *what to*. They form the basis of what Americans call know-how, and what the French call *savoir-faire*, "to know to do." They're adaptable, not brittle.

Skill-based knowledge, unlike fact-based knowledge, can only come from *doing*. Sure, you can read about the theory of a golf swing, but until you master it in practice, you won't have anything worth knowing. It's not just about the mechanics of the club head arcing through space, it's the feeling of the club in your hands, the way your body moves with the swing, and the state of your mind as you tell yourself where you want the ball to go. These things can't be understood from a manual. You have to experience them firsthand.

Skill-based knowledge, unlike fact-based knowledge, can only come from doing.

Metaskills are no different, just pitched at a higher level of knowing. For example, if you've mastered the metaskill of playing sports, your broad range of experience may reveal some patterns that you can then transfer to golf, making that particular game easier to learn.

But there's more. Metaskills have a superpower—they can be *reflexive*. Reflexivity allows you to apply a metaskill to itself, not just to other skills, thereby multiplying the effect. While the ability to learn is powerful, the ability to *learn how to learn* is unstoppable.

The problem today is that schools don't teach metaskills. They barely teach ordinary skills, since, by nature, skills are harder to measure than academic knowledge. It's easier to check the correctness of math answers, for example, than the quality of thought that went into them. It's as if we believe metaskills enter the body by osmosis. "You may never use calculus," the argument goes, "but the experience will teach you how to solve logical problems." If problem solving is important, why not teach it as a metasubject, and use calculus, statistics, philosophy, physics, debate, and other subjects as expressions of it?

Many of our policymakers believe if we just double down on testing standards and push harder on STEM subjects—science, technology, engineering, mathematics—we'll revive the economy and compete better with countries that are taking our jobs. This is not a strategic direction for any developed country. The world doesn't want human robots. It wants creative people with exceptional imagination and vision—and standardized testing won't get us there.

The Institute of the Future, on behalf of the Apollo Research Institute, took a long look at the workplace of tomorrow. They issued a document called "Future Work Skills 2020," which identified these six drivers of change:

1. *Extreme longevity.* Medical advances are steadily increasing the human lifespan, which will change the nature of work and learning. People will work longer and change jobs more often, requiring lifelong learning, unlearning, and relearning.

2. *The rise of smart machines and systems.* Automation is nudging human workers out of jobs that are based on rote, repetitive tasks.

3. *Computational world.* Massive increases in the number and variety of sensors and processors will turn the world into a programmable system. As the amount of data increases exponentially, many new roles will need computational thinking skills.

4. *New media ecology.* New communication tools are requiring media literacies beyond writing. Knowledge workers will be asked to design presentations, make models, and tell stories using video and interactivity.

5. *Superstructed organizations.* Social technologies are driving new forms of production and value creation. Superstructing means working at the extreme opposites of scale, either at very large scales or at very small scales.

6. *Globally connected world.* Increased interconnectivity is putting diversity and adaptability at the center of organizational operations. People who can work in different cultures, and work virtually, will deliver extra value to companies.

These future scenarios will demand metaskills such as sense-making, determining the deeper meaning of what is being expressed; social intelligence, the ability to connect with others; adaptive thinking, the ability to imagine solutions beyond the rote; a design mindset, the ability to prototype innovative outcomes; and cognitive load management, the ability to filter out nonessential information and focus on the essential problem at hand.

In Florence during the Renaissance, the archetype of *l'uomo universale*, the universal man, was born. The "Renaissance Man" was a person well-versed in all branches of knowledge, and capable of innovation in most of them. The total body of knowledge in the 16th century was modest enough that one person could hope to get his arms around it.

There's a growing recognition that the great advances of the future will come not from a single man or woman, but from the concentrated effort of a group. The operating principle today is, "None of us are as smart as all of us." Yet to activate the creativity of a group—whether it's a team, a company, a community, or a nation—we'll need to bring our best selves to the party. We'll need to come with our skills, our metaskills, and our full humanity. In the postindustrial era, success will no longer hinge on promotion or job titles or advanced degrees. It will hinge on mastery.

As long as business innovation is in the hands of the few, wealth will be distributed unfairly. What metaskills do is democratize creativity, spreading the responsibility for change more evenly and building a stronger middle class—the best-known engine for economic growth.

CONGRATULATIONS, YOU'RE A DESIGNER. Given the seriousness of the problems we face today, we need all hands on deck. A few creative specialists stashed here and there in the back rooms of our organizations won't be enough to crack complex problems like environmental responsibility, sustainable energy, or food production for seven billion people. These are called "wicked problems." A wicked problem is any puzzle so persistent, pervasive, or slippery that it can seem insoluble. You can never really "solve" a wicked problem. You can only work through it.

"Working through problems" is a phrase you commonly hear in design circles, since most designers know that there is never a complete or final answer to anything. There are only provisional answers that lie somewhere on a scale from bad to good. Designers are therefore comfortable—or at least not too uncomfortable—with the task of bringing order to complexity and ambiguity.

They're accustomed to cutting cubes out of fog.

Design as a distinct profession emerged only in the 20th century. It came out of the divide-and-conquer approach to production, in which one broke a complex process into its constituent parts so that each part could be studied and streamlined. Before that, designing was part of a general activity that included problem solving, form giving, and execution. When it finally became a discipline in its own right, with its own professional organizations and special history, design became more detached from the industrial world that spawned it.

In my last book, *The Designful Company*, I explained how organizations can transform themselves in order to harness innovation as a competitive advantage. The secret is simple: If you want to innovate, you have to design. Design and design thinking—as opposed to business thinking—is the core process that must be mastered to build a culture of nonstop innovation.

The problem with traditional business thinking is that it has only two steps—*knowing* and *doing*. You "know" something, either from past experience or business theory, then you do something. You put your knowledge directly into practice. Yet if you limit yourself to what you already know, your maneuver will necessarily be timid or imitative. Traditional business thinking has no way of de-risking bold ideas, so it simply avoids them. This is not a recipe for innovation but for sameness.

Design thinking fixes this deficiency. It inserts a middle step between *knowing* and *doing* called *making*. Making is the process of imagining and prototyping solutions that weren't on the table before. While this concept is easy to grasp, it's difficult to practice. Why? Because new solutions, by definition, cannot be drawn directly from an organization's repertoire of past responses. Neither can they be found in case studies or business books. They're *new*. And since true innovation is not a best practice, it sets off alarm bells in the boardroom: "If no one has done this before," the executive asks, "why should *we* take a chance? Why not just wait until someone else tries it, then jump on board if it works?" Of course you can, if your goal is to follow. But if your goal is to lead,

KNOW   DO

TRADITIONAL BUSINESS THINKING

KNOW   MAKE   DO

DESIGN THINKING

you have to embrace design. That's why innovation is so hard, and why it confers such a powerful advantage on those who master it.

Designing is not the exclusive territory of designers. If it were, the amount of innovation in the world would be a mere fraction of what it is today. A designer is simply someone who doesn't take yes for an answer—a person who searches for better and better solutions to *what could be*, when others are satisfied with *what is*.

According to Nobel Prize winner Herbert Simon, a pioneer in artificial intelligence, "A designer is anyone who works to change an existing situation into a preferred one." Using this definition, any one can be a designer. Even *you*. And while you may not have the aesthetic sensitivity of a trained professional, you're nevertheless following the same thought process that guides the work of automotive designer Chris Bangle or international architect Rem Koolhaas.

Design is not limited to the styling of cars or the planning of buildings. It can determine the success of any man-made object, process, or experience. It can be used to improve decision-making, corporate strategy, or government policy. It can shape the letterforms on this page so they say more than the words by themselves. Or it can show us how to recombine DNA to make living systems.

"Designers are in the miracle business," says Dr. Carl Hodges, founder of the Seawater Foundation. He's not intimidated by *what is*. He's an innovative scientist who's using the rise in sea level caused by global warming to turn coastal deserts into agricultural Edens.

The greening of deserts happens to be a good metaphor for the experience of furniture-maker Steelcase. Said President James Hackett, "Design can bring back value where it has been sucked completely dry by commoditization."

And the former CEO of Procter & Gamble, A.G. Lafley, underwent a religious conversion to design as he injected new life into his portfolio of brands. "I'm not doing this because I'm a frustrated liberal arts major," he said. "Good design is serious business."

THE FUTURE IN YOUR HANDS. As Watson's performance on *Jeopardy!* suggests, the competition between people and machines is heating up. The Robot Curve will continue to take jobs away, and we'll continue to search for higher ground where our contributions will have uniqueness and value. Our machines are forcing us to confront who we are.

Homo sapiens is Latin for knowing man. Are we the species that succeeds by knowing? If our machines end up knowing more than we do—*then* what? Will we be the slaves of "our new computer overlords"?

The fact is, our technology is so interesting that we often forget to credit the special gift that made it possible. It wasn't just knowing that brought us to this stage of our evolution—it was *making*. Our ability to make and use tools, starting with simple hammers and axes, and moving to spears, brushes, needles, grinding stones, and horticultural tools, came from a two-way conversation between our brains and our hands. Our hands—with their powerful grip, articulate fingers, and opposable thumbs—gave us the evolutionary advantage that created our superior intellect. In other words, our hands made our brains as much as our brains controlled our hands.

A turning point in human evolution may have come with the invention of language some 50,000 years ago. Language unleashed a torrent of creativity, including the invention of new tools, music, art, and mythmaking, plus enough survival and navigational skills to migrate thousands of miles from Africa to Europe and Australia. Without language, it seems, our culture would have been constrained to very slow progress indeed.

When a baby reaches toward her mother and utters her first word, we usually take this as evidence of language. It's not. The baby has no idea what "mama" means. Her actual "first word" is her outstretched hand. "Mama" is simply the attention getter for the real message, which is something like "Mama, come here," or "Mama, pick me up," or "Mama, give me that." Over time, she learns that different words stand for different things, and her language skills take off. But notice that the gesture—the outstretched hand and extended fingers—precedes the words for it.

All languages use similar structural elements, even those that developed in cultural isolation. How can this be? Are language skills hereditary, or even instinctual? No. It's more likely that they're simply patterned on the universal human experience of manipulating physical objects—in other words, moving things around with our hands. Neurologist Frank R. Wilson has written that "evolution has created in the human brain an organ powerfully disposed to generate rules that treat nouns as if they were stones and verbs as if they were levers or pulleys." While not all languages use nouns and verbs in exactly the same way, they all have rules that treat words as building materials—to be selected, shaped, and placed into meaningful structures.

When we talk about thinking, we often use words that are metaphors for the hand. We *hold onto* a thought or *handle* a problem. We *cling* to beliefs or attempt to *manipulate* people. We *reach* for a word or *grasp* a situation. We experience things *firsthand* and *touch* upon subjects. We *feel* our way forward and *point* to a solution. Our numbering system began with our fingers, so now we *digitize* information. There's a reason we talk with our hands—we think with our hands. The evolution of our hands pushed our brains forward, and our brains pushed back.

Over the two millennia since Plato, and especially during the last 500 years after the Renaissance, academic education in the West has been successful in separating the hand from the brain. We've decided that making things is less valuable than knowing things, and therefore making has a less exalted place in the classroom. This is not only wrong, but it denies the very evolutionary advantage that makes us human. And now, with the advent of ubiquitous information, our knowing muscles seem overdeveloped while our making muscles seem atrophied.

Biology would suggest reversing course. According to Wilson, "The most effective techniques for cultivating intelligence aim at uniting—not divorcing—mind and body." If our goal is to reshape the world, we'll need to cultivate a new set of talents in which making is rejoined with knowing.

These are the five talents—the metaskills—that I believe will serve us best in an age of nonstop innovation:

Feeling, including intuition, empathy, and social intelligence.

Seeing, or the ability to think whole thoughts, also known as systems thinking.

Dreaming, the metaskill of applied imagination.

Making, or mastering the design process, including skills for devising prototypes.

Learning, the autodidactic ability to learn new skills at will. Learning is the opposable thumb of the five talents, since it can be used in combination with the other four.

The bright thread that weaves through all five metaskills is aesthetics, a set of sensory-based principles that can stitch together the new and the beautiful. After all, would you really want to live in a world of robots, extended lifespans, body implants, space travel, and virtual reality if it weren't also filled with delight? The primary art form of our time is technology. To stay human—and become even *more* human—we need to imbue our inventions with the soul-stirring attributes of aesthetics. It's both our legacy and our destiny.

Across the walls and ceiling of Pech Merle, in the flicker of candlelight, the fluidly stylized drawings of horses, mammoths, and reindeer seem to thunder as they fly overhead. Go ahead. Place your hand over the stenciled hand of the ancient cave painter. Even after 25,000 years of continuous human evolution, it will still fit.

EMPATHY
AND
INTUITION

SYSTEMS
THINKING

APPLIED
IMAGINATION

DESIGN
AND
TESTING

AUTO-
DIDACTICS

FEELING

SEEING

DREAMING

MAKING

LEARNING

THE FIVE METASKILLS

FEELING

1

BRAIN SURGERY, SELF-TAUGHT. One advantage of computers is that they never get emotional. They're not misled by their dreams or desires. They're not seduced by the lazy answer or the simplistic story. They're not subject to mood swings, and they're not swayed by irrelevant data. In short, they don't suffer from the cognitive biases that make humans so irrational. Computers simply follow the instructions they've been given—quickly and accurately. That's their charm.

Yet here's a question no one ever asks: If the ability to make fast, accurate calculations is so valuable, why hasn't evolution equipped us to think like computers? Isn't four million years enough time to endow our brains with at least the computing power of, say, a cheap calculator? Or is computerlike processing a biological impossibility?

Apparently it's a distinct possibility, given the amazing feats of mathematical savants like Daniel Tammet. Tammet can do cube roots quicker than a computer and recite pi out to 22,514 decimal places. He can multiply any number by any number, and learn languages as easily as others learn capital cities. He can read two books simultaneously, one with each eye, and recall the details of all 7,600 books he's read so far. As far as Tammet is concerned, there is no calculating needed. He simply "sees" all this information in a flash, as others would see a photograph. Numbers, for example, look like shapes, colors, sounds, and gestures. The number two is a motion and number five is a clap of thunder.

Daniel is a high-functioning autistic, and, along with ten percent of autistic people, is a savant. Other savants have mastered a wide range of challenges, from memorizing every line of *Grove's Dictionary of Music*—all nine volumes of it—to accurately measuring long distances without any instruments. How many people could draw a precise map of the London skyline after viewing it briefly from a helicopter? Or play Tchaikovsky's *Piano Concerto Number One* the first time they heard it—without a single piano lesson? These are the kinds of feats we expect from computers, but we're amazed to see them performed by humans.

Allan Snyder, professor at the Centre for the Mind at The University of Sydney, believes we could all do these kinds of things with a little more insight into brain mechanics. "Savants usually have had some kind of brain damage." However, he says, "I think it's possible for a perfectly normal person to have access to these abilities." Yet do we really want them? If the human brain is fully capable of machinelike computation, and if nature has supplied us with a steady stream of savants, why hasn't natural selection figured out how to work the "savant gene" into the general population?

We have to consider the possibility that computerlike thinking is not central to our success on Earth; that there may be another set of abilities more important to our continued survival than calculation and memorization; and that what makes us truly human isn't so much our rational brain as our emotional brain. This hypothesis would seem to contradict 2,000 years of Western orthodoxy, but the more we use modern neuroscience as a lens, the more likely it appears. René Descartes famously wrote: *Cogito ergo sum,* or "I think, therefore I am." Yet Aristotle may have been closer to the mark some 1500 years earlier when he wrote: *Sentio ergo sum,* or "I *feel,* therefore I am." Our emotions are what tell us that we're more than machines.

During the Industrial Age our feelings were unceremoniously kicked to the curb. There was no place in the factory for emotions, since emotions were believed to cloud one's judgment and slow one's efficiency. Even today, if you inject your feelings into a business conversation, you can almost watch your credibility leaving the room. This is too bad, since we now know that our emotions are far smarter than our rational brain for handling complex tasks.

> We have to consider that another set of abilities may be more important to survival than calculation and memorization.

Until recently some people thought that emotion was simply a vestige of our primitive past, a residual flaw that needed correcting with rational thinking. Sigmund Freud likened the ego and the id—the emotional brain and the rational brain—to a horse and rider. "The horse provides the locomotive energy, and the rider has the prerogative of determining the goal and of guiding the movements of his powerful mount towards it." Freud often advised his patients to "hold their horses" rather than "give free rein" to their emotions.

Scientists have long speculated on why a particular area of the brain known as the orbitofrontal cortex (OFC) is larger in humans than in other primates. Freud might have guessed that its purpose was to protect us from the animal instincts of our emotions. Thanks to recent advances in neuroscience, however, we can see that the purpose of the OFC is actually the opposite—its job is to *connect* us with our emotions. It turns out that the more evolved a species is, the more emotional it is.

Why would emotion be so important? Because it allows us to "feel" our way through situations that are too complex to think through. Our feelings are central to our learning, our intuition, and our empathy. They allow us to make sense of rich data sets that our rational brains are not equipped to comprehend. Emotion is not a substitute for reason, but a partner to it. If our rational brains were deprived of emotion, even the most banal decisions would become impossible.

Emotion was less than welcome on the assembly lines of the Industrial Age. But in the creative labs of the Robotic Age it's essential. Feeling is a prerequisite for the process of innovation. It feeds learning, fuels intuition, fosters empathy, and powers creativity.

Let's take these abilities one at a time.

I'll define *learning* as the process of acquiring new knowledge, skills, or habits. Later in the book I'll elevate it to the status of a metaskill, but here I'm talking about it as a physical process of the emotional brain. Whenever we get a jolt of joy, fear, happiness, or sadness, our brain rewires itself, building neurological pathways that connect the emotion back to the sensory signal. In other words, we're learning how to make predictions about ourselves and the world.

The reason emotions are so smart is that they've evolved to turn mistakes into learning opportunities. Errors create emotional events that the brain can easily remember. This insight is key to understanding innovation. Innovation requires working through a series of prototypes, or predictions, to find out which ones work and which ones don't.

The brain operates in a similar fashion, testing predictions against reality while our dopamine cells keep score. Before our predictions can be right, they first have to be wrong. A wrong prediction then becomes a "wake-up call" that our dopamine cells convert into a powerful emotion, which then lets our anterior cingulate cortex take note of what we've just experienced. Put another way, failure triggers an emotion that we remember as knowledge.

Emotional learning leads directly to intuition, the ability to "think without thinking," to arrive at a solution or conclusion without the use of logic. Once you've taken the time to train your dopamine neurons, you don't have to make as many conscious decisions—you simply recognize the pattern and act. You switch to autopilot and let your subconscious do the driving. This is particularly useful when you're faced with difficult decisions, complex information, or situations where you need to act quickly. Easy problems are best suited to the conscious brain. Complex problems need the superior processing power of the emotional brain.

Intuition is a result of deep experience in a particular activity, profession, or domain. We're not born with it. We have to earn it. There's a chicken-and-egg problem with intuition: It takes many hours of trial and error before we can trust it, yet if we don't trust it we'll never develop it. The Industrial Age has been particularly hard on intuition, rewarding people who stick to the script over those who "waste time" guessing at the answers. Now that intuition is rising to the top of the talent wishlist, we're at a loss to find people who have it.

Intuition isn't just for artists, scientists, or other professionals in so-called creative fields. It's for anyone who has to make decisions or find solutions when there's not enough information or time to be painstakingly thorough. It's for the doctor whose patient presents a commonly found set of symptoms, and still something doesn't "feel" quite right. Or the accountant who scans a balance sheet and without focusing on it finds an anomaly that seems to jump off the page. Or the mother who doesn't hear any sounds coming from her child's room and realizes that something is wrong. In other words, it's for everyone who lives in the modern world. It's the eyes in the back of your head, the extra sense that defies rational explanation.

These are the nonlogical processes that help us to "know," not through reasoning, but through judgment, decision, or action. Learning expert Donald Schön called this process "reflection in action," because this type of knowledge doesn't come from books but from the conversational back and forth of doing. Think of the painter who puts a brushstroke onto a canvas, then reacts to that brushstroke with another, then another, and so on, never knowing exactly where the painting will go, but always comparing its trajectory to the original vision in the process.

> Emotions allow us to "feel" our way through situations that are too complex to think through.

While we learn best by doing, we also learn by watching. What help make this possible at the brain level are "mirror neurons," a small cluster of cells in a part of the brain associated with muscular control. When neurophysiologist Giacomo Rizzolatti was studying the frontal and parietal cortex of the macaque monkey, he and his team noticed that the neurons needed for a given task would automatically fire in the brain of one monkey as it observed another monkey performing the same task. This gave rise to speculation about a "monkey see, monkey do" gene in humans. Whenever we see someone else smile, our mirror neurons light up as if we ourselves were smiling. Whenever we watch someone else swing a golf club, they light up as if we ourselves were swinging the golf club.

Mirror neurons, said Rizzolatti, "allow us to grasp the minds of others, not through conceptual reasoning, but through direct simulation; by feeling, not by thinking." Tellingly, this area of the brain seems to be compromised in people with autism. Intuition is closed off to autistics, leaving them to think their way through every experience and every situation using reason alone.

The behavior-mirroring part of the brain may be largely responsible for our ability to interpret the thoughts and feelings of others. We call this ability *empathy*. In a world with seven billion people, empathy has become a valuable commodity. It lets us work together to achieve results we couldn't achieve separately. It facilitates business by helping us understand the needs and desires of customers. And it allows us to live together in relative peace, based

Mirror neurons allow us to empathize with others by internally "mirroring" their movements, expressions, and emotions.

on mutual respect for one another. When empathy breaks down, actual war becomes possible as we redefine our enemies as less human than ourselves.

This brings us to *morality*, another specialty of the emotional brain. Here I'd like to create a slight separation between morality and ethics: morality is a natural instinct for "doing unto others" as reflected in the universal laws of both religious belief and secular philosophy; ethics, however, is more nuanced, requiring the fine-tuning that only conscious thinking can deliver. I'll return to this subject later in the book.

The ancient laws of morality were already in effect before the Ten Commandments was ever carved in stone. They were written into the genetic code of the primate brain. What the religions of the world did was to translate these natural laws into spoken language. Our ancestors may not have agreed on the ethics of eating someone else's dinner, but they most certainly knew you didn't push your best friend from the top of a tree.

Science writer Jonah Lehrer pointed out that psychopaths aren't the ones who can't manage to behave rationally. They're the ones who can *only* behave rationally. Their emotional brains have been damaged. When we act in a moral manner—when we recoil from violence, treat others fairly, and help strangers in need—we're making decisions that take other people into account. We're thinking about their feelings, sympathizing with their states of mind. This is what psychopaths can't do.

Without basic morality we could never have reached a population of seven billion people. If we should put aside our basic morality in the coming years, it's doubtful that we could continue evolving as a species. Feeling, our oldest metaskill, is likely to be an important ally, as we begin to invent artificial life and to augment our natural gifts with manmade ones.

WHEN THE RIGHT BRAIN GOES WRONG. Now that I've just spent several pages extolling the virtues of feeling, let me give equal time to the drawbacks of relying on feeling alone. None of these should be surprising to you, since they're same cautions that have kept our emotions in the back seat during the Industrial Age.

Here's a research question taken from Daniel Kahneman's book, *Thinking, Fast and Slow,* revealing the limitations of intuition:

> *Linda is single, outspoken, and very bright. As a student she was deeply concerned with issues of discrimination and social justice. Which is more probable? 1) Linda is a bank teller. Or 2) Linda is a bank teller and is active in the feminist movement.*

Number two, you say? If so, your intuition is working perfectly. But your conclusion is perfectly wrong. There's no way that number two could be more probable, because it's more limiting. If Linda happens to be active in the feminist movement, she fits description number one as well as number two. But if Linda is not active in the feminist movement, she's eliminated from number two. Don't feel bad if you blew it. A full 85% of Stanford business students, steeped in probabilities, were tricked by this question.

This is merely one variety of *cognitive bias,* a large category of logical pitfalls that play havoc with our intuition. Other traps include *negativity bias,* in which bad is perceived to be stronger than good; *perceptual defense,* which causes us to ignore inconvenient facts; *hindsight bias,* the illusion that we "knew it all along"; the *gambler's fallacy,* or believing in "streaks" or in "being due" when no such possibilities exist; the *anchoring effect,* causing us to weigh a single piece of evidence far too heavily; *belief bias,* in which we evaluate an argument based on the believability of its conclusion; and the *availability heuristic,* which causes us to estimate the likelihood of something according to what is more available in memory, favoring events that are vivid or emotionally charged.

These are all examples of how the human mind tries to make sense out of just about anything. Our brains are meaning-making machines, according to anthropologist Carolyn M. Bloomer, author of *Principles of Visual Perception.* She proves it by asking her students to clip cartoons out of magazines. She then has them separate the captions from the pictures, making one pile of captions and one of pictures. When the students connect the captions and pictures randomly, they're surprised to find that at least half of them are still funny. She says, "Creating meaning is an automatic process."

This automatic quality of the emotional brain is both a boon and a bother. On one hand we depend on it for turning experiences into learning, and learning into mastery. By repeating a task over and over, we're able to delegate our practiced skills to our subconscious minds so we can move on to a next-level task. A common example of this is how we manage to drive to work while thinking about what to say at the morning meeting. When we get to work we can barely remember our commute.

On the other hand, our emotional brains can trip us up when we need to learn something new. If our dopamine neurons have been well trained in an old task, they can have trouble performing a competing task.

The Stroop Test is a good demonstration of this principle. If you're asked to identify a series of words for colors, such as red, blue, green, brown, and purple, you'll have no problem reading back the words. But if the words are printed in colors other than what the words say, and you're asked to identify only the colors, you'll find it almost impossible to read them back. Your dopamine cells have been trained to recognize words more easily than colors, and only a superhuman effort by your pre-frontal cortex can contradict the training of your emotional brain.

The prefrontal cortex gives us executive control over our emotional brains. As in Freud's metaphor of the horse and rider, it allows us to "override" our instincts and behave more rationally. It can also help us behave more *irrationally* in certain sitations, such as when we're trying to exercise our imagination or think in new ways. Executive control gives us the profound aptitude of *metacognition*, the ability to think about our own thinking.

> If our dopamine neurons have been well trained in an old task, they can have trouble performing a competing task.

Yet executive control is subject to yet another bias: the illusion that we know more than we do. The workings of the human brain are best approached with a great deal of curiosity, humility, and appreciation of mystery. For there is no greater mystery than how we make sense of the world.

When mislabeled colors are flashed on a screen, people can't resist naming the colors incorrectly.

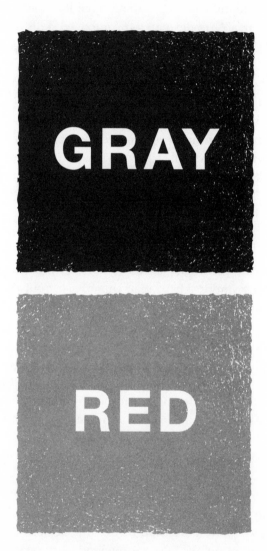

THE STROOP TEST

THE MAGICAL MIND. Consciousness, intellect, and the mind are overlapping ideas that are hotly contested among—well—brainy people. But since the requirements of the Robotic Age include a passing acquaintance with the process we call thinking, I'd like to introduce you to three people who can shed light on the subject.

The first is Mihaly Csikszentmihalyi, a psychology professor whose Hungarian name is more fun to pronounce than it seems (ME-high CHEEK-sent-me-HIGH-ee). He's a founder of positive psychology and author of a series of books on *flow*, a mental state that describes what it's like to be fully engaged in creative work.

The second is Tor Nørretranders, Denmark's leading science writer, whose book *The User Illusion* goes far to explain consciousness in terms of information theory.

And the third is Nicholas Humphrey, an English psychologist who has written a number of books on the evolution of the human mind. His most recent, *Soul Dust*, contains a delightful theory on the evolutionary advantages of consciousness.

Let's start with a few rudimentary definitions of the words above so we can be on the same page. When you engage in thinking, or cognition, you're using your *mind* to bring order out of chaos. Your mind is not your brain or some physical thing, but an emergent property that arises from the interaction your brain and body with your environment. You experience your conscious mind as a combination of emotion, perception, imagination, memory, and cognition.

Your mind is part of your *intellect*. Intellect is a conscious ability to understand things, or to reach conclusions about what is true or real in the world. Western philosophy has tended to separate intellect from behavior, as if your mind and body were two separate entities. But in reality your intellect is a seamless integration of your conscious mind, your physical body, and your environment. Psychologist Howard Gardner defines it as "a biopsychological potential to process information," a way to solve problems or create products in a cultural setting. Creativity, the subject of this book, is a special quality of your intellect.

Where the real mystery is, however, is *consciousness*. Generally speaking, consciousness is the subjective experience of being awake and aware. But the function of consciousness, according to Csikszentmihalyi, is to represent information about what is happening inside and outside our bodies in such a way that we can evaluate it and act on it. The information-processing ability of the intellect would be useless without some way of representing the world to ourselves. So we have consciousness to serve as a clearinghouse for our sensations, perceptions, feelings, and ideas, establishing priorities among these inputs.

Without consciousness we would still "know" what was going on, but we'd have to react to it in a reflexive, instinctive way. Consciousness lets us judge what our senses are telling us and respond accordingly. We can also invent information that didn't exist before. "It is because we have consciousness that we can daydream, make up lies, and write beautiful poems and scientific theories," says Csikszentmihalyi. While automatic emotions take care of the immediate variables, our conscious mind can do more—it can expand the list of possibilities.

As amazing as consciousness is, it's capable of much less than we imagine. We're constantly fooled into believing that rational thought is our most powerful way of knowing. Our rational brain often behaves like a bully, trash-talking our emotional brain and autonomic nervous system simply because it can. The fact is, most of the brain is engaged in unglamorous but crucial work like bodily metabolism, glandular functions, muscle control, and the sensations we get from touch, taste, smell, sight, hearing, and motion. Conscious thought takes up a tiny percentage of this total effort.

Nørretranders looks at consciousness from the point of view of information. Drawing from work done by Manfred Zimmermann at Heidelberg University, he highlights a remarkable fact that has been known for half a century, yet remains relatively obscure. Namely, that although our senses receive eleven million bits of information per second, our conscious minds normally process *sixteen* bits per second. The eye sends at least ten million bits per second to the brain. The ear, a hundred thousand. The nose, another hundred thousand, and the taste buds about a thousand bits.

Can you imagine trying to read a computer screen with only a few pixels lighted up at a time? The only way you could do it is by moving the lighted area around the screen pixel by pixel, picking up little pieces of information one by one and putting them together into some semblance of a whole. This is the plight of consciousness.

It should be no surprise, then, that accident rates shot up when drivers began sending texts from their cars. Even race drivers have trouble with digital distractions. Their cars now have up to 26 electronic buttons to divert their eyes from the road. Said race driver Vitaly Petrov, "Playing with all the steering-wheel dials at 300 kilometers per hour will be, I guess, like answering three Blackberry messages while making fried eggs and doing your shoelaces at the same time. We'll see how it goes." In the US Air Force, test pilots have a warning about this: "Wheels up, IQ down."

According to psychologists, we can only hold a maximum of four "items"—thoughts or sensations—in our conscious mind at the same time. If you're like me, and your wife complains that you don't always listen, you now have a good excuse: To fully understand what another person is saying, you have to process forty bits of information per second, and nature has given us a normal speed of sixteen.

Luckily, we have a powerful mechanism to turn this severely constrained bandwidth to our advantage. It's called *attention*. By tuning out most of the information we receive, we can focus on what's immediately useful. This is particularly important for anyone learning a skill or practicing a craft. Csikszentmihalyi uses the example of a musician who structures her attention so as to focus on nuances of sound that other people may not hear, or a stock speculator who can sense tiny changes in the market. A good clinical diagnostician has an uncanny eye for symptoms, because he has trained his attention to process information others would miss.

> To fully understand what another person is saying, we have to process forty bits of information per second, and nature has given us a normal speed of sixteen.

Csikszentmihalyi says that paying attention can involve extra processing work beyond the usual baseline effort, but focusing attention is relatively easy for people who have learned to control their consciousness. They simply shut off all mental processes except for the relevant ones. "Attention shapes the self," he says, "and in turn is shaped by it." Thanks to the limitations of consciousness, we *are* what we attend to.

But what exactly *is* consciousness? Although we can understand its functional properties, including perception, information processing, attention focusing, and so forth, it's more difficult to understand its qualitative properties, or *qualia*, such as the redness of red or the painfulness of pain. This is known as the "hard problem of consciousness," a phrase introduced by Australian philosopher David Chalmers. How can mere physical matter, such as three pounds of flesh inside a human skull, give rise to nonphysical qualia? Is it possible to understand consciousness when our only lens is consciousness itself? Is it like standing between two mirrors that reflect infinite copies of "me" while revealing no new information? And if even if we can understand it, what's the evolutionary purpose of consciousness?

These are questions that Nicholas Humphrey handles nicely in his book *Soul Dust*. His answers run parallel to those of Nørretranders and Csikszentmihalyi, and if all three are right, the consequences for creativity are enormous.

Humphrey is persuaded that there's nothing that conscious experience actually *is*, apart from what we *think* it is. In other words, our mental representation of reality *is* our consciousness, and our consciousness is merely a mental representation. The objects we perceive "out there" are based on real things, but our experience of them is an illusion we create in our minds so we can make sense of them. This is not unlike Plato's cave, a parable in which a group of prisoners must construct reality from the shadows on the wall, since they're restrained from turning around to see the source of the shadows.

René Descartes proposed a similar model of consciousness many centuries after Plato, known as the Cartesian Theatre. He believed the brain replicates the outside world as a kind of picture, which is displayed for the edification of the mind.

Humphrey believes Descartes got it slightly wrong. Replication, he says, is not what theaters are about. Theaters are places where events are staged to *comment* on the world, not *replicate* it. They exist to educate, persuade, and entertain. Our consciousness, then, is a self-created entertainment for the mind, a magic show that dramatically changes our outlook on life.

This ability, he says, has conferred an evolutionary advantage on the human race. It spells the difference between truly wanting to exist and merely having some sort of life instinct. "When you want something," he says, "you tend to engage in rational actions—flexible, intelligent behavior—to achieve it." Our ancestors might have engaged in activities that weren't rewarding in themselves, but were calculated to deliver this goal. The added *joie de vivre*, the enchantment in living, would have given them an extra boost in terms of natural selection. It would have increased the investment they were willing to make in their survival.

> Our consciousness is a self-created entertainment for the mind, a magic show that dramatically changes our outlook on life.

And how far back did this ability go? Humphrey makes a guess that this enhanced level of consciousness evolved during the Upper Paleolithic revolution—the same period in which we began painting in caves. While anthropologists view the paintings, carvings, tools, and weapons of early humans as functional, it's now clear that part of their function was to delight the senses.

Forever afterwards we've longed to share our conscious experiences—our personal versions of the magic show—with our fellow human beings. Yet conscious experiences are by nature private. No one else can really feel what we feel or see what we see. We can't simply unveil our experiences or hand them over to be experienced in the same way.

All we can do is master various forms of *art* that approximate our experiences, or else place other people in similar situations—smelling the same rose or looking up at the same night sky—and hope that somehow their experience of transcendence will be similar to ours.

"Imagine an ocean of islands," says Humphrey, "each with its own internal world of shared ideas, dreams, and desires, able to communicate to its neighbors only by smoke signals." This is the predicament of being human, and it's why we aspire not only to be scientists but artists.

LEONARDO'S ASSISTANT. Does the flap of a butterfly's wings in Brazil set off a tornado in Texas? This was the title of a paper about predictability given by Edward Lorenz in 1972. Ever since that moment the scientific community has buzzed with talk of the "butterfly effect." The flapping wings are a symbol for how a small change in the initial condition of a system can trigger a chain of events that could never have been predicted. Had the butterfly not flapped its wings in Brazil, the outcome might have been vastly different.

One such effect that we struggle with today is the bifurcation of art and science. Up until the Renaissance, art and science were two sides of the same coin. The arts were toughened up by the rigor and rationality of science, and science was set free by the intuition and imagination of the arts. Today they work in separate buildings and are mutually impoverished by the separation.

It's quite possible that the flapping wings in this situation were a series of unfortunate events that happened in the 16th century. Leonardo da Vinci, the great genius of art and science, was the personification of Renaissance creativity. He was also a homosexual, a vegetarian, and an anticlerical—at a time when the Catholic Church had spread its sinewy tentacles throughout Europe and looked askance at such proclivities.

No surprise that Leonardo was a bit secretive. He kept his ideas hidden in a series of notebooks, eventually totaling as many as 100,000 drawings and 13,000 pages of mirror writing (all the better to discourage prying eyes). He never shared these with his contemporaries, fearing, among other things, that his livelihood might be compromised. He intended to sort his notebooks into themes and chapters and have them published upon his death. Unfortunately, he died in 1519 before he could accomplish this task.

Leonardo's assistant and occasional lover, erstwhile Francesco

Melzi, ended up with the bulk of his estate, which included the full set of notebooks. Francesco, then only 27, did little with the materials except keep them safe in his studio, occasionally displaying the drawings as souvenirs from his 12-year apprenticeship.

Upon Francesco's death in 1570 his son Orazio (who was by this time sick of hearing about the great man) unceremoniously dumped the notebooks into chests in the attic. Whenever curiosity seekers turned up at the villa, Orazio let them walk out with whatever they wanted. Any materials that were left were eventually scattered across Europe, their significance underestimated and their author forgotten. For more than 200 years the increasingly disparate worlds of science and art were deprived of the unifying example of Leonardo's notebooks. Eventually, the materials that survived—only about half of the total œuvre—began to see the light of day, made available to scholars through museums, libraries, and private collections.

One of the best known notebooks is the Codex Leicester. It contains theories and observations about astronomy, geology, and hydraulics. Leonardo explains that the pale glow in the dark part of the crescent moon is due to sunlight reflecting off the earth, presaging Johannes Kepler's discovery by a hundred years. He shows why fossils from the seabed can be found high up in mountains, advancing the concept of plate tectonics centuries before it became accepted theory. He tackles the mechanics of water with detailed drawings of how rivers flow around rocks and other obstacles, adding recommendations on how to build bridges and deal with erosion.

> For more than 200 years the increasingly disparate worlds of science and art were deprived of the unifying examples of Leonardo's notebooks.

If only Francesco had followed through on Leonardo's wishes. If only he had published the notebooks as Leonardo intended, and revealed his secrets to the nascent field of scientific inquiry. If only he had, the world of today might be a better place. Instead, the flap of a butterfly's wings in Lombardy caused a fracture between Western art and science, with science going the way of Galileo, Newton, and Einstein, and art following the path of Michelangelo, Rembrandt, and Picasso. In Peter Watson's 822-page "complete compendium," called *Ideas: A History of Thought and Invention, from Fire to Freud*, Leonardo's name does not even appear.

So now we place science and art in separate categories. We want science to explain the *truth* of things, and art to express the *experience* of things. Put another way, science carefully excludes feelings, while art draws them out. In the long, painful divorce between science and art, science came out on top. Art—and the human feeling it expresses—has been *persona non grata* in the halls of power. The exile of emotion, says Ken Robinson, is apparent in everyday language. "Arguments can be easily dismissed as only 'value judgments', or 'merely subjective'. It's hard to imagine any argument being dismissed as 'merely objective.'"

We seem to have forgotten that truth is only a construct, a provisional model of reality that allows us to build our world. What we call truth is not objective at all, but a subjective measure of how useful a given piece of information will be for a given time.

Factual knowledge was actually an invention of the 16th-century European legal system, which allowed lawyers to use *facts*, or shared observations, as concrete evidence. Science then grew out of this system. Scholars began linking one fact with another to create a web of knowledge that other scholars could agree on and contribute to. Yet during the ascendance of Newtonian science after the Renaissance, something more happened. Educated people began believing that science was the only source of truth.

Leonardo, for all his belief in evidence, did not exclude art from science. Instead, his deep appreciation of nature and beauty became the gateway into science. *Sperienza*—or experience—was the starting point for Leonardo's knowledge. In making drawings of the objects and movements of nature, he was able to experience them as heightened reality, to own them in ways that merely looking doesn't allow.

If you've ever taken a drawing class, you've experienced the powerful feeling of "knowing" a subject well enough to describe it on paper. There's something special that happens between the hand and the brain in drawing—and between the body and the brain by moving through space—that creates meaning.

Neurologist and author Oliver Sacks agrees that we're suffering from this split between science and life—between the apparent poverty of scientific formulation and the richness of phenomenal experience. "The infant immediately starts exploring the world, looking, feeling, touching, smelling," he says. "Sensation alone is not enough; it must be combined with movement, with emotion, with action. Movement and sensation together become the antecedent of meaning."

What captivated Leonardo's interest was the dynamics of nature—the way water swirls or wind travels, the way sound moves through air, how organic forms unfold and grow. Beneath the mechanics of all his inventions lay a holistic and ecological view of life that we're only now beginning to appreciate. The equations of Newton and the geometry of Euclid are inadequate to describe the objects and actions that Leonardo explored. For these we'll need a new kind of qualitative mathematics that can reach beyond quantitative answers. Fritjof Capra, in his book *The Science of Leonardo*, notes that the mathematics of nonlinear dynamics, also known as complexity theory, may just be that tool.

Meanwhile, we have a chance to reunite science and art through the discipline of design. Modern science is already forging ahead with synthetic biology, nanotechnology, and artificial intelligence. Design and design thinking can add a human dimension to what might otherwise be little more than an exercise in manufacturing. They can bring beauty back after 500 years of diminishment, giving future generations much reason to be grateful.

> **Design and design thinking can bring beauty back after 500 years of diminishment.**

The last of Leonardo's notebooks to remain in private hands is the Codex Leicester, acquired by Bill Gates from the art collection of industrialist Armand Hammer. It had been named for the Earl of Leicester, who bought it in 1717, then renamed Codex Hammer in 1980. Gates changed the name back when he bought it at auction in 1994. Like several collectors before him, he cut the notebook into separate pages.

THE USES OF BEAUTY. As a rule, wealthy art collectors are a sorry lot. They long to possess beauty so badly that they end up possessing it just that way—badly. They tend to focus on secondary factors such as investment potential, artist celebrity, popularity of style, and pricing trends—everything but the art itself. They're like church members who make hefty donations so they can feel more spiritual. If you listen to exchanges between art collectors and art dealers, you're unlikely to hear any conversations about craft, meaning, or purpose. Instead, you'll hear endless gossip about who knows whom or what someone paid or who's showing where.

How do you possess beauty well? Like Leonardo, you possess it fully by earning it. You open your senses, give your whole body and mind to it, and trace the same path as the originator—if not literally, then through your physical understanding of it. In the same way that a sports fan gets more pleasure from watching a sport he or she has played, an appreciator of art gets more pleasure from art forms he or she has spent time creating. Music is more beautiful to a musician, math is more beautiful to a mathematician, and nature is more beautiful to a scientist.

Beauty certainly hasn't been the hallmark of the Industrial Age. If we talk about it at all today, it's mostly in the context of cosmetics, fashion, or female conformation (swimsuit issue, anyone?). There's very little talk about the beauty of an algorithm, the rapture of an architectural space, or the elegance of a phrase.

American philosopher William James once offered this thought experiment: "Conceive yourself, if possible, suddenly stripped of all the emotion of which your world now inspires you, and try to imagine it, as it exists, purely by itself, without your favorable or unfavorable, hopeful or apprehensive comment. It will be almost impossible for you to realize such a condition of negativity and deadness." Yet in James's time, industrial America was busy creating just that kind of world for factory workers. The ideal employee was one with no emotional response, an automaton who could be satisfied with the soul-deadening repetition of a command-and-control business structure. While the worst abuses of the assembly line are fading into memory—at least in the developed world—we're still struggling to escape their legacy. Billboards, strip malls, traffic jams, factory farms, landfills, and housing projects are either concepts or consequences of a mass-production mindset.

If that's ugliness, what's beauty? Can beauty be defined? Or is analysis impossible, like cutting a kitten in half to see why it's cute? Personally, I think we can define it without harming any animals. Let's try this: Beauty is a quality of wholeness or harmony that generates pleasure, meaning, or satisfaction. Using this definition, a traffic jam fails the beauty test, and so does a landfill. A landfill may generate meaning, but it doesn't communicate wholeness or harmony to very many people. At the other end of the spectrum, the movie *Casablanca* does embody wholeness and harmony, giving pleasure, meaning, and satisfaction to a broad audience.

While it's somewhat possible to define beauty, it can't be reduced to a pat formula for the simple reason that one of the components of beauty is *surprise.* In everything we experience as beautiful, there is a moment of surprise when we first encounter it. If there's no surprise, there's nothing new. Nothing new, no interest. No interest, no beauty.

While we can certainly encounter an object or have an experience that gives us mild satisfaction—say, a nicely sculpted vase or a well-crafted melody—true beauty has something more going for it: memorability. Memorability is almost always the result of sudden emotion—the jarring pop of disrupted expectations. The pleasure, meaning, or satisfaction that follows this pop can be experienced as a warm glow, a slowly spreading smile, or the hair standing up on our arms. Physiologically, it's a blast of serotonin to your central nervous system.

> Memorability is almost always the result of emotion—the jarring pop of disrupted expectations.

Beyond the emotional pop of surprise, beauty has two other components: *rightness* and *elegance.*

Rightness is a kind of "fitness for duty," a specific structure that allows the thing we're encountering to align with its purpose. If the purpose of a carafe is to pour liquid cleanly into a glass, then "rightness" may demand a certain shape of spout, a certain type and position of handle, and a certain proportion of interior space for the liquid. Charles Eames, the midcentury designer of innovative furniture, among other things, called this quality "way-it-should-be-ness." You might think after ten thousand years of making carafes we would have this down, but we don't. Many of the carafes, pitchers, and measuring cups on the market still pour badly, sloshing out their contents or dripping liquid down the sides.

Organizations can also suffer from a lack of rightness. Either they're missing a clear, compelling purpose, or they haven't aligned their activities with their purpose, and therefore lack focus. Like a poorly designed vessel, the results are inefficiency and wasted resources. The concept of beauty can be applied to businesses as easily as to objects, people, events, or experiences.

Elegance, the third component of beauty, has been subverted by the fashion industry to mean luxury or overdecoration. Yet it really means the opposite. It's the rejection of superfluous elements in favor of simplicity and efficiency. It's arriving at the minimum number of elements that allow the whole to achieve its purpose. An elegant dress, in this definition, would be the simplest dress that achieves the purpose of flattering one's figure, or bringing out one's personality, or signaling a certain position in a social setting. Any extra elements or unneeded decoration would be examples of *inelegance.*

Inelegance plus a lack of rightness, when taken to an extreme, is the essence of *kitsch*. Kitsch is delightful in its way, because it usually contains surprise. We're delighted to find a table lamp made from a stuffed iguana, or a reproduction of Michelangelo's *Pietá* that doubles as an alarm clock. But beauty it ain't. So most kitsch ends up in attics and landfills after the original surprise has faded. Rightness and elegance, by contrast, require a little work to appreciate. And they last much longer and tend to retain their value. The original *Pietá*, sans clock, is more likely to stand the test of time than the kitschy copy.

Anthropologist Carolyn Bloomer defines beauty in terms of *optimal closure.* Some objects or experiences can seem so perfect, she says, that they leave no room in the imagination for anything

SURPRISE

TINGLE
EXCITEMENT
EMOTIONAL POP
INTEREST
MEMORABILITY

RIGHTNESS

INTEGRITY
FITNESS FOR DUTY
RESONANCE
HONESTY
AUTHENTICITY
VIRTUE

ELEGANCE

SIMPLICITY
ORDER
EFFICIENCY
CRAFTSMANSHIP
RESTRAINT
NUANCE

better. "If we think of the human mind as a pattern-making, pattern-seeking system, then optimal closure is what satisfies this drive. Beauty can be experienced in almost any aspect of human life—a nail driven perfectly into wood, onions sautéed to perfection, dancing in perfect synchronization to music. Optimal closure gives an object or an activity its greatest power, for it admits of no extraneous perceptions."

The qualities of surprise, rightness, and elegance are not discrete but overlapping components of beauty that can't be easily separated. While they don't yield a formula, they can serve as a reality check. If all three aren't present, then the result is probably not very beautiful.

For example, the popular typeface I'm using here, called Lucida Calligraphy, delivers a bit of surprise by virtue of its special decorative flourishes. It may offer rightness, since it serves the purpose of creating a dignified voice for certain kinds of text. Yet it's not very elegant, because it "overdoes" its decorative qualities, thereby stealing some attention from the text. If I'd set this whole book in Lucida Calligraphy, by the last page you might feel as if you'd eaten too much dessert. Lucida Calligraphy masquerades as beauty, but is eventually revealed as mere sentimentality.

Another example is the software I used to write this book. Microsoft Word is the standard for word processing, but it falls short on all three counts. It doesn't offer surprise along any particular dimension. It also lacks rightness, since its features are not well aligned with its basic purpose of helping me convey my thoughts in text. And it's devoid of elegance, since there are far more features than I'll ever need, including overeager ones that try to "correct" my writing, requiring me to correct the corrections as I go.

Contrast this with the laptop I used to write the book, a Mac-Book Air from Apple. While it may not be for everyone, it's a good example of beauty. It offers surprise, because, among other things, it's lighter and thinner than previous alternatives. It exhibits rightness, since it clearly pays off on its primary goal of portability (I can toss it in my bag and work easily from anywhere). And it has elegance, keeping its extras to a minimum and its efficiency to a maximum. It also has an elegance of form, a simple yet nuanced physical design that makes it a pleasure to see and touch.

In the Industrial Age, beauty might have mattered less than it does today, since people were often thrilled just to have the basic item at a price they could afford. But now that customers have more choices, beauty has become the tiebreaker in many categories. BMW's Mini Cooper is not beautiful in the traditional automotive sense of *sleek* or *luxurious*, but it's beautiful in the surprise-rightness-elegance sense. It's surprisingly small in a market dominated by hulking SUVs; it has rightness, focusing its features and communications like a laser on providing a fun experience; and it accomplishes all this with an elegant, low-cost design. Mini spends about one percent on design, yet design accounts for 80 percent of purchase decisions, according to customers.

Kevin Kelly believes that beauty in the design of products and other things is not a passing fad but a long-term trend that's deeply rooted in evolution. "Most evolved things are beautiful, and the most beautiful are the most highly evolved." He says that it's not unusual for one pair of scissors to be highly evolved while another is not. "But in the highly evolved scissors, the accumulated knowledge won over thousands of years of cutting is captured in the forged and polished shape of the scissors halves. Tiny twists in the metal hold that knowledge. While our lay minds can't decode why, we interpret that fossilized learning as beauty."

The concept of beauty can be applied to businesses as easily as to objects, people, events, or experiences.

It's clear from an increasing body of research that design is a leading factor in the success of innovative products and companies. And Kelly is probably right that evolution will push us even further in the direction of beauty. Therefore we can guess that beautiful design will be a growth industry, conferring a competitive advantage on any company or individual who can get out in front of the evolutionary average. Still, to do this will require something not yet taught in school: a practical grasp of *aesthetics*.

AESTHETICS FOR DUMMIES. People use the word aesthetics to cover a wide range of concepts, many of them shallow, unhelpful, or wrong. Leonard Koren catalogs ten separate definitions in his little book, *Which "Aesthetics" Do You Mean?* Among them are "the superficial appearance of things," as in "Charlie doesn't give a damn about aesthetics—he just wants a car that runs"; "a style or sensibility," as in "Objects scavenged from the Manhattan sewers were used to create the edgy aesthetic of Bob's downtown loft"; and "a synomym for artistic," as in "Lorraine applied her aesthetic imagination to come up with tonight's dessert—lavender-infused grappa sponge cake with pan-seared guacamole frosting."

Many creative people would just as soon throw the whole notion out the window. They'll tell you that there are no universal rules for creating beauty, and that anyone who says there are can't be a real artist. There's some truth in this, because invention consists of generating new rules rather than following old ones. Maybe this is why painter Barnett Newman said, "Aesthetics is for the artist as ornithology is for the birds."

But aesthetics is not a set of rules or a book of laws. It contains a collection of principles—perceptual tools—that every artist and inventor uses, whether consciously or unconsciously. My personal belief is, after trying it both ways, that a deliberate use of aesthetic tools is more effective than relying on "natural genius" alone. Once you understand the basic principles, you can use them to get unstuck, address new problems, or cross over into other disciplines. With practice they become absorbed by your unconscious mind, at which point they become intuitive.

My own definition of aesthetics is this: the study of sensory and emotive values for the purpose of appreciating and creating beauty. Aesthetic principles, also called formal qualities, are the tools we use to give form to the objects of design. These include concepts such as shape, line, rhythm, contrast, texture, and so forth, which can be employed in endless combinations. There are no hard and fast rules for using aesthetic tools. They only need to make the object "more of what it wants to be" instead of merely more. Using aesthetic tools just to use them is aimless—like using kitchen tools just because you find them in the drawer.

Some philosophers believe that objects impart aesthetic value through their formal qualities alone. Others disagree, saying the value of the object comes from its reference to other things. This difference of opinion sets up a false dichotomy. Is beauty timeless or temporary? Universal or personal? Skin deep or down to the bone? The reason these questions plague us is that beauty can be any or all of these things, depending on the object itself (person, place, thing, experience, situation), the object's embodiment (its formal qualities), and "the eye of the beholder" (one's personal or cultural associations with it). Formal qualities and symbolic qualities are not necessarily opposites, but may simply exist on different planes.

Imagine beauty as a birthday cake. (It could be a bicycle, a ballroom, or a balalaika, but let's keep it simple.) In this example, the cake itself is the content, or the basic thing being experienced. We can appreciate content for its informational or functional value alone (as food), but there's no real beauty without the other two planes of experience. The content supplies the "quiddity," or "*is-ness*" of the object, yet by itself is rather neutral and emotionless.

Of course, the cake can't exist without a specific *form*—or a set of formal qualities—to embody its content. In this case the formal qualities include six layers of sour cream chocolate cake with semisweet dark chocolate filling, a cylindrical shape, rum-flavored cream cheese frosting dripping down the sides, lime green script on the top, and thirty pink candles spaced evenly around the circumference.

> There are no hard and fast rules for using aesthetic tools. They only need to make the object "more of what it wants to be" instead of merely more.

Formal qualities are always determined by the type of object they embody. They might include shape, sound, color, pattern, balance, sequencing, a way of operating, or anything else, depending on the category. The formal qualities of music, for example, include melody, harmony, and rhythm while the formal qualities of painting include line, pattern, color, and scale. The formal qualities of a business model include products, pricing, sales, and distribution. Of course, these are just a few of the elements needed to give form to these things.

Formal qualities by themselves are fairly abstract. But married to content, they bring the object to life, giving it properties that awaken strong feelings. When content and form are well matched, the combination can seem iconic, a marriage made in heaven. And in some artistic endeavors, such as modern music or abstract expressionism, the form comes very close to *being* the content. With the example of the chocolate cake, we could stop with content and form and still end up with a good aesthetic experience. But there's a third plane, the plane of personal associations.

Associations can include the memories, understandings, cultural norms, tribal allegiances, and personal aspirations we bring to our experiences. When we experience content and form through the lens of our associations, we create meaning. In fact, for most people, association is the most powerful determinant of beauty.

Beyond the sheer yumminess of the chocolate and rum-flavored cream cheese, the cake may remind you of happy birthdays from your childhood, giving you the warm glow that comes from feeling loved. Or it may impart a feeling of wistfulness, because it happens to be your birthday, and after thirty years of struggling you had hoped to achieve more with your life. These are the associations the cake is triggering—influencing the meanings you take from it and the reason it matters to you. For most people, it's this plane of experience that's easiest to appreciate and the most emotionally charged.

Does that mean we can dispense with formal beauty and just create things that people can connect with on a meaning level? Sure. We do it all the time. We produce cartloads of kitsch, floods of fashion, torrents of tribal identifiers such as logo products, lot-filling "luxury" homes, me-too tattoos, derivative genre music, and trendy personal electronics that help us fit into the groups of our choice. But the satisfaction we get from these objects is often shallow and fleeting, and eventually we wonder if there might be something more.

With a little effort and thoughtfulness, we can begin to appreciate beauty for its formal qualities, apart from its content and our personal associations with it. We can marvel at everyday things,

Objects and experiences can be appreciated on three levels, which explains why there's room for disagreement on matters of taste.

CONTENT
WHAT THE OBJECT IS ABOUT
(DEPENDS ON VIEWPOINT)

FORM
HOW THE OBJECT IS EMBODIED
(DEPENDS ON EDUCATION)

ASSOCIATIONS
WHY IT MATTERS TO THE BEHOLDER
(DEPENDS ON EXPERIENCE)

THREE LAYERS OF AESTHETICS

like the asymmetrical placement of an upper story window, or the roughness of chipped paint on a child's toy, or the sound of a delicate cymbal floating over a gruff bass line. We can take delight in the shape of certain phrases or the unresolved contrast of bitter and sweet or the negative space inside a lowercase *a*. We can find fascination in the symmetry of an equation, the poetry of battle, or the shrill cacophony of a grammar school playground.

When we experience content and form through the lens of our personal associations, we create meaning.

At this point the realm of aesthetics opens up to us. We're able to escape the narrow confines of personal meaning and embrace the beauty that's hidden everywhere. We move out of the house and into the world. We start to demand more from the things we buy, the people we take up with, the experiences we give ourselves. Using aesthetics, we learn to separate the authentic from the fake, the pure from the polluted, the courageous from the timid. In short, we develop *good taste*.

Good taste is the promise and the payoff of aesthetics. And like beauty, good taste can't be bought. It's not a manual you can memorize, or an attitude you can adopt. It's not a synonym for snobbishness, because snobbishness isn't, well, in good taste. Good taste has long been considered a quality that existed mostly in the eye of the beholder. The Romans had a saying for it: "*De gustibus non est disputandum*," or "About taste there's no argument." But this isn't completely true. While there's a wide range of what might be considered good taste, it doesn't stretch on forever. There's such a thing as bad taste, too, and most of us know it when we see it.

What the "birthday cake" model of aesthetics allows is the coexistence of personal associations (the eye of the beholder) with formal qualities (the eye of the educated beholder). The education of the eye and other senses is what separates those with good taste from those with ordinary or bad taste. This is not snobbishness. It's a recognition that you have to work to develop good taste, and it's mostly in the area of understanding formal principles.

The psychologist Howard Gardner writes about it in his book *Truth, Beauty, and Goodness Reframed*: "All young people will acquire and exhibit aesthetic preferences. But only those who are exposed to a range of works of art, who observe how these works of art are produced, who understand something about the artist behind the works, and who encounter thoughtful discussion of issues of craft and taste are likely to develop an aesthetic sense that goes beyond schlock or transcends what happens to be most popular among peers at the moment." In other words, good taste is *learned* through conscious effort.

If we were to plot aesthetic learning on a continuum, we could label the left side of the scale "meaningless messes," indicating ugly objects that exhibit no formal order and trigger no associations. We could label the right side of the scale "high aesthetics", indicating beautiful objects with perfect order and the ability to trigger truly meaningful associations.

Without an educated sense of aesthetics, your appreciation of beauty is likely to fall nearer the left side, toward objects that are high in associative meaning, but low in formal excellence. This favors "tribal aesthetics," or a preference for the symbols that identify people with a certain group. For example, the Harley-Davidson trademark does not contain truly beautiful formal qualities, but its associations make it beautiful to members of the Harley tribe. So beautiful, in fact, that some are happy to tattoo the trademark onto their living flesh.

Those with a greater degree of aesthetic education can more easily separate the formal elements from their personal associations, so that the formal elements can be appreciated—to some extent—on their own. A dramatic example of this is the ability of some graphic designers to appreciate the formal properties of the Nazi flag, with its bold shapes and strong colors, while still being horrified by its associations. Similarly, an aesthetically sophisticated person may love horses and high-tech puppetry, yet find the play *War Horse* lacking in character development. This is the practiced ability to separate the trick from the magic.

> The education of the eye and other senses is what separates those with good taste from those with ordinary or bad taste.

The tricks usually depend on the nature of the magic in question. Philosopher Susanne K. Langer made the interesting observation that every art form has its "primary illusion." For example, the

THE AESTHETICS TOOLBOX

AMBIGUITY

COMBINE INCOMPATIBLE
MEANINGS OR EXPERI-
ENCES TO TRIGGER
NEW MEANINGS
OR EXPERIENCES

BALANCE

ARRANGE ELEMENTS
INTO A PLEASING WHOLE
TO CREATE SATIS-
FACTION, EFFICIENCY,
OR FAIRNESS

COLOR

APPLY COLOR TO EVOKE
EMOTION, IDENTIFY
DIFFERENCES, OR
REPRESENT NATURE

CONFLICT

INTRODUCE DISSO-
NANCE, DISCORD, OR
ANOMALY TO CREATE
EMOTIONAL TENSION
OR PROVOKE INTEL-
LECTUAL INTEREST

CONTRAST

EMPHASIZE THE
DIFFERENCES BETWEEN
ELEMENTS TO CREATE
DRAMA, CLARIFY A POINT,
SHOW PROPORTION,
OR INDICATE HIERARCHY

DEPTH

MANIPULATE VIRTUAL
SPACE TO IMPART AN
EXPERIENCE OF DIMEN-
SION, COMPLEXITY, OR
LAYERED MEANING

FOCUS

DRAW ATTENTION TO
A SINGLE ELEMENT TO
MAKE A POINT, ORGANIZE
AN EFFORT, OR SEPARATE
A SUBJECT FROM ITS
BACKGROUND

GESTURE

USE A SPONTANEOUS
FLOURISH TO IMPART A
FEELING OF MOVEMENT
OR DESCRIBE A
PHYSICAL ACTIVITY

GROUPING

PLACE ELEMENTS
TOGETHER OR ARRANGE
THEM INTO A PAT-
TERN TO INDICATE
A RELATIONSHIP

HARMONY

ARRANGE THE ELEMENTS
OF A COMPOSITION SO
THAT THEY ARE COMPLE-
MENTARY RATHER THAN
CONFLICTING

JUXTAPOSITION

PLACE TWO OBJECTS
SIDE BY SIDE TO
SHOW DIFFERENCES,
SIMILARITIES, OR
RELATIONSHIPS

LINE

DRAW A BOUNDARY,
INDICATE A DIRECTION,
BUILD UP A PATTERN,
OR REPRESENT
CHANGES OVER TIME

PATTERN

ARRANGE A NUMBER
ELEMENTS INTO AN INTER-
ESTING OR PLEASING
OMBINATION THAT CON-
VEYS INFORMATION OR
TIMULATES THE SENSES

PERSPECTIVE

CREATE AN ILLUSION
OF PHYSICAL SPACE
OR DETERMINE THE
CLOSENESS OR DIS-
TANCE OF ELEMENTS

PROPORTION

SHOW THE RELATIVE
SIZES OR IMPORTANCE
OF ELEMENTS WITHIN
A COMPOSITION

RHYTHM

ARRANGE THE PACING
OF A SEQUENCE TO
IMPART EXPERIENCES
SUCH AS INTENSITY,
SPEED, CALMNESS, OR
AWKWARDNESS

SCALE

DETERMINE THE
SIZE OF AN ELEMENT
OR COLLECTION OF
ELEMENTS TO BEST
ACHIEVE ITS PURPOSE

SEQUENCE

PLACE ELEMENTS IN A
CHRONOLOGICAL ORDER
TO CONTROL HOW INFOR-
MATION IS REVEALED
OR EXPERIENCED

SHAPE

CREATE THE FORM
OR EXTENT OF AN
OBJECT BY DRAWING
ITS BOUNDARIES

SYMMETRY

USE A MIRROR-IMAGE
BALANCE TO MAKE AN
OBJECT OR COMPOSITION
TO CREATE STABILITY,
CALMNESS, OR DIGNITY

SYNCOPATION

USE AN IRREGULAR
OR UNPREDICTABLE
RHYTHM TO SUSTAIN
INTEREST OR STIMU-
LATE THE SENSES

TENSION

SET UP CONFLICT
BETWEEN TWO OR MORE
ELEMENTS TO CREATE
EMOTIONAL INTEREST

TEXTURE

EVOKE EMOTION OR
CREATE INTEREST BY
ADDING TACTILE QUALI-
TIES SUCH AS ROUGH-
NESS, SMOOTHNESS,
BUMPINESS, STICKINESS,
OR PATTERNING

VARIETY

INCLUDE A MIXTURE
OF ELEMENTS TO POPU-
LATE A SERIES, OFFER
CHOICES, OR STIMULATE
INTEREST

primary illusion of painting is *space*, including whether the painting looks flat or deep, naturalistic or abstract. The primary illusion of music is *time*, unfolding moment by moment in a rhythmic sequence of notes, melodies, and movements. The primary illusion of dance is *physical power*, the ability of the dancer to appear both lighter and stronger than he or she is. And the primary illusion of storytelling is *memory*, as if the past can be perfectly reproduced in the present.

Each of these art forms, and many others which are less obvious, achieve their illusions through the deft use of formal elements. These are the conceptual tools of the artist, many of which can be used across a variety of art forms and goals. Some of the more common ones are shown on the previous pages.

If these tools seem too abstract to you, it's probably because you haven't felt their weight in your hands, or applied them consciously to real tasks. With enough practice they begin to make sense and become powerful extensions of your creative skills. It's important to remember that in any artistic pursuit—whether painting, playing music, writing software, building a business, or constructing a scientific theory—aesthetic choices are never right or wrong, just better or worse. It doesn't pay to look for a correct answer to an aesthetic problem.

In *The Elements of Style*, E.B. White discusses the difficulty of dealing with aesthetics: "Who can confidently say what ignites a certain combination of words, causing them to explode in the mind? Who knows why certain notes in music are capable of stirring the listener deeply, though the same notes slightly rearranged are impotent? There is no satisfactory explanation of style—no inflexible rule by which the young writer may shape his course. He will often find himself steering by stars that are disturbingly in motion."

Yet the fact that aesthetics is approximate doesn't mean that artistic knowing is less important than scientific knowing. The insights and ideas discovered through art can be every bit as profound as those discovered through science. As Ken Robinson says,

"To assume that artistic judgments are simply personal opinion is as mistaken as assuming that all scientific opinion is undisputed fact. Meaning and interpretation are at the heart of all creative processes."

When ordinary people make aesthetics-based judgments, they tend to *satisfice*—they choose the good-enough answer over the best answer. Yet, if given the ability to see their alternatives side-by-side, they'll choose in favor of the one with the best aesthetic cues. They do exactly what designers, artists, scientists, and critics do—they decide through comparison. The process of *knowing by comparing* is called analogical intelligence. The difference is that, for professionals, the basis for comparison is locked into their intuition through experience. They don't need multiple choice to recognize quality.

Aesthetic choices are never right or wrong, just better or worse.

Lately it's been fashionable to suggest that aesthetic judgment comes preloaded into the human nervous system through genetics. Experiments have shown that newborn babies seem to prefer complex patterns over simple ones, and three-dimensional spheres over flat circles. After a few months, they begin to respond better to patterns that look like faces over patterns that are more random. Later, as adults, people seem to prefer faces that are regular rather than those that are asymmetrical or unusual. They also seem to prefer scenes of nature to abstract art. (My dentist would be happy to hear it.)

Yet this may be another example of science underreaching itself, bringing a complex phenomenon down to a level where it can be easily measured. What science should question instead is why so many adults can't see aesthetic differences and don't have an adequate framework for critiquing beauty.

My wife and I got hooked on a TV series called *House Hunters International*. Maybe you've seen it. In each half-hour program, would-be expats choose among three properties based on a wish list they've given to their agents (which is always bigger than their budget). The wishes themselves are always couched in terms of functional benefits—a certain number of bedrooms, access to the beach, proximity to town, or other concrete parameters. There are no parameters concerning the quality of the light, the authenticity of the materials, or the relationship of the house to its surroundings. More often than not, the highest praise during a walkthrough is "This a nice size room." The same sentence is uttered up to a dozen times in each show. (Check it out—it's a running joke in our household.)

Yet in the end, it's obvious that the buyers base their decisions mostly on their feelings. If all that mattered was the size of the rooms, they could just bring a measuring tape. What actually matters, beyond basics such as price, is the beauty that they believe will give meaning to their lives. It's just that they don't have the vocabulary to express it.

Question: If average people aren't conversant with beauty or the qualities that determine it, why should designers and other professionals bother with aesthetics?

Answer: Because average people *are* deeply affected by beauty, whether of not they're conscious of it. The average person would choose—and has chosen—Cirque du Soleil over Circus Vargas, Google over Lycos, and the iPhone over the BlackBerry. The average person wants, deserves, and will pay for, the most beauty he or she can afford.

IT'S NOT BUSINESS—IT'S PERSONAL. In the movie *You've Got Mail,* bookshop owner Kathleen Kelly complains about larger rivals who excuse cutthroat practices with the "godfather" mantra: It's not personal—it's business. "What is *that* supposed to mean?" she says. "I am so sick of that. Whatever else anything is, it ought to *begin* by being personal." At the end of the movie, the chain bookstore wipes out little shop around the corner.

Warm-touch transactions increasingly seem like a thing of the past, replaced by cold-touch transactions such as self-service online stores, self-service checkout in real stores, and the tedious automated voices of call centers. Technology companies have gone crazy with CRM—Customer Relationship Management software—spawning myriad variations such as VRM, PRM, EEM, and SFA (don't ask). Despite the technological focus on customers—or maybe because of it—market research has discovered the "80/80 rule": 80 percent of the economy consists of service, and 80 percent of customers report *bad* service. It seems that many businesses will do anything to avoid direct contact with customers.

The service problem is actually part of a bigger issue, which has to do with branding. As competition for customers increases, companies offer customers more choices. Customers, faced with a wider array of choices, have begun to make their purchase decisions more on emotional benefits—such as delight, trust, or tribal identity ("If I buy that product, what will that make me?"). The way a customer "feels" about a product or company is, by definition, its brand. A brand is akin to a commercial reputation. And while it's built by the company, it's defined by the feelings of customers.

> A brand is akin to a commercial reputation. While it's built by the company, it's defined by the feelings of customers.

This transfer of power from companies to customers has had an enormous impact on the value structure of the S&P 500 and other companies. Over the last thirty years, brand values have shot up from five percent of market capitalization to over thirty percent. That means that more than one-third of a company's worth now comes from intangible assets. Some companies, such as Coca-Cola and Apple, figure their brands account for two-thirds or more of their market caps.

This would seem to put the rise of branding and the rise of technology on a collision course. Customers demand the warm touch of service in return for their loyalty, while companies require the cold touch of technology to make them more competitive. What's the solution: reduce technology, or give up brand share? Neither. The solution is to use empathy—the ability to recognize how other people feel—to design technologies, processes, and interactions that increase delight, engender trust, and reinforce tribal identity. In other words, place brand first and revenues second. Brand momentum is the leading indicator of sustained profitability.

Take Zappos, for example. The online shoe retailer has managed to combine technology and humanity to build the world's largest online shoe store. You'd think that offering to pay shipping on all returned products, plus their replacements, would kill profitability, as people sent back every pair of shoes that didn't fit or flatter. Yet somehow the company worked around these costs. They started with the premise that customers and employees should be treated well, then worked back from there to build the rest of the business model. They built a thriving brand around customer emotions.

Starbucks impressed the world by building a huge business on expensive coffee drinks. But coffee drinks are not really what they sell. What they sell is an aesthetic experience that combines surprise (a fresh idea about the meaning of coffee), with the emotional warmth of community (a "third place" to hang out with friends), tribal identity (the feeling of belonging to European-style culture), and company sincerity (the demonstrated belief in a mission). However, as Starbucks has grown, growth itself has become its *raison d'être*, and customers have begun to doubt its sincerity. This is what founder Howard Schultz had always worried about— the loss of the company's "soul." Its only long-term salvation will be to place empathy ahead of operations. We'll see how they do.

A stark contrast in empathy can be found in the stories of two low-cost airlines, Southwest and Ryanair. Both airlines have adopted a "point-to-point" strategy of selling one-way rather than round-trip tickets, often routing planes through secondary airports. And they both have the goal of pushing prices so low that it's often cheaper to fly than to drive. But how they go about achieving this goal shows a shocking difference in their regard for customer delight.

Europe-based Ryanair has defined its competitive advantage solely in terms of low price (or at least the illusion of low price). Every decision the company makes is aimed at reducing costs while keeping as much of the profit as possible. The prices of their flights are low—sometimes as low as one penny for a return ticket—but there are hidden costs, including fairly high emotional costs.

The price of a ticket doesn't cover taxes, administration fee, or baggage fees. Any bags larger than a gym tote must be checked, and will cost you up to 150 euros. Your first bag is limited to 20 kilos, and your second bag to 15. If you go over these limits, you can still check your bags, but only for an additional fee of 20 euros per kilo. Of course, you're bound to go over these limits. And when you do (your bags will be weighed at the airport) you'll have to get out of one line and wait in another to pay your penalty fee. If you try to regain your old place in line, you'll suffer the wrath of other passengers as well as the Ryanair check-in agent who sent you away.

Additional fees may apply. Let's say, for example, in your rush to get to the airport, you've forgotten to print your boarding pass, thereby depriving Ryanair of a few pennies of profit. That'll be 40 euros, please. Forty euros, really? A Ryanair representative was asked if this penalty seemed a bit harsh. "They'll only forget to do it once," he said. When you add up these extra fees, you may find that your one-penny flight now costs at least 100 euros, a 10,000-fold increase. Suddenly you're not feeling very good about Ryanair. And your experience is just beginning.

Once on the plane, you may feel a bit cramped. The seats are closer together than the usual "pitch" of other airline seating, and they don't recline, so your knees are pushing into the hard plastic back of the seat in front of you. Maybe it simply *feels* more cramped, because the tops of all the seat backs are shiny yellow plastic, creating a visual foreshortening as if the seatbacks were a garish deck of cards standing on edge. You might begin to worry that, in an emergency, your chances of reaching an exit would be slim. In any case, the plastic safety card is right in front of you, glued to the back of the seat (to save on cleaning and replacement costs).

After your ordeal in the airport, you're no doubt looking forward to closing your eyes for a few blissful moments during takeoff. This is not to be. Ryanair regards you as a captive audience for an aggressive menu of overpriced food, drink, and duty-free trinkets. So an announcer keeps up a steady monolog over the PA system, putting special emphasis on raffle tickets that you can purchase in order to win—guess what—more trips on Ryanair! The staccato blare of special deals in the blue-and-yellow plastic cabin is the perfect complement to the company website, which features the same garish colors along with flashing euro symbols and bikini-clad spokesgirls.

And never content to rest on its laurels, the airline has been busy inventing new ways to cut costs (and improve profit margins). President Michael O'Leary has suggested getting rid of two toilets to make room for six more seats; redesigning the planes so passengers can fly standing up; charging extra for overweight passengers; and asking passengers to carry their checked-in bags to the plane themselves. "Just kidding," he said. But he *would* like to charge admission for the toilets. It's part of Ryanair's commitment to low, low prices.

On the other side of the Atlantic, Southwest has been equally committed to low prices. When the airline began operations, passengers were surprised to be herded onto the planes like cattle instead of getting seat assignments. You could hear the sarcastic sounds of "moooo" as people crowded into the jetway. Yet the employees, especially the flight attendants, were able to defuse the situation with large dollops of humor. Their in-flight announcements were so funny, in fact, that passengers began recording them for friends. Eventually the company solved the cattle problem by designing a first-come-first-serve system for boarding lines at the gate.

In 2008, when airlines in the United States and elsewhere began to feel the pinch of rising operational costs, most followed the lead of Ryanair and began charging extra for luggage. Southwest's chief executive, Gary Kelly, refused. He took the opportunity to increase the difference between his airline and the others, effectively lumping them into a single category called "pickpockets," while claiming for Southwest the category of "good Samaritan." It was a brilliant PR move, which the company underscored with a "Bags Fly Free" ad campaign.

Why does one low-cost carrier lavish love on customers, while another antagonizes them? The difference, of course, is *empathy*. Without a developed sense of empathy for customers you're more likely to misjudge the prevailing mood of the market. You're prone to mistake money for meaning and low prices for loyalty. While Ryanair may survive its lack of feeling for a short time, its brand is unlikely to make a full contribution to the bottom line, and its customers will almost certainly jump ship the minute a real competitor comes along.

Elsewhere in Europe, a coffee brand has outmaneuvered Starbucks by bringing the *barista* experience home. Swiss food giant Nestlé has tapped into a different kind of emotion with its sleek Nespresso coffee-brewing system. The idea is simple: a home appliance that brews espresso from single-serving "pods" of ground coffee. Nestlé uses a razor-and-blades pricing strategy, in which most of the profit comes from continuous purchases of the pods rather than the machines themselves. The pods are only available to "members" of the Nespresso Club through its website or its 200 boutiques.

A few years ago my wife and I inherited a Nespresso machine as part of a house purchase in France. It sat in the kitchen unused for months. When we finally fired it up, we were pleased to find the coffee *pas mal*, and quickly drank our way through the capsules.

Weeks later, as we walked along a street in Bordeaux, we came to a store that was buzzing with excitement. "Nespresso," said the sign. As a line of customers waited to get in, others were walking out with bags full of coffee. In the "showroom," the architecture, surface materials, lighting, product displays, and packaging had more in common with Tiffany's than Starbucks. Multihued coffee capsules glowed like jewels against dark wood paneling. Catalogs with the production values of coffee table books were positioned in soft pools of light. Clearly, this was a company that had a vision for its brand.

> Without empathy, companies are prone to mistake money for meaning and low prices for loyalty.

Even so, why would people pay Nestlé up to three times what it would normally cost to brew a cup of coffee at home? Why wouldn't they simply buy one of the competing offerings from Sara Lee, Kraft, or Mars? The secret, once again, is empathy. The Nespresso designers were able to "feel" what it might be like join an exclusive Nespresso tribe. Instead of putting costs first, they put customer delight first, then engineered the pricing model to fit customer expectations. Everything about the Nespresso business model makes customers feel coddled, cared for, and special. True, the capsules are costly. But customers are buying much more than coffee. They're buying something that can't be measured, counted, or even described.

Thanks to a well-crafted experience and a slew of patents to keep competitors out, the Nespresso brand has logged sales increases of 30% per year over a ten-year period. Those patents, however, are expiring, and customers are free to buy cut-rate capsules from a number of other sources. Will some of them defect? Sure, because money matters. But the most valuable segment of customers, the Nespresso loyalists, will continue to support the company because of the emotional benefits that come with membership in the original tribe. Its less innovative competitors will have to settle for the dregs.

In *The Myths of Innovation*, author Scott Berkun has correctly noted that innovative ideas are rarely rejected on their technical specs. Instead, they're rejected because of how they make people feel. "If you forget people's concerns and feelings when you present an innovation, or neglect to understand their perspectives in your design, you're setting yourself up to fail." This applies equally to coffee brands, airlines, and online shoe stores. It also applies to residential architecture.

One of the last century's leading architects, Le Corbusier, made a colossal error of judgment when he set out to design a new approach to public housing. Instead of using his emotional brain to focus on the feelings of inhabitants, he used his rational brain to focus on the possibilities of the buildings. He envisioned people as interchangeable parts in a system, inputs to a "machine for living." Informed by a rigid Modernist ideology, the theories were bracing but the results appalling: geometric clusters of identical stacked cells, devoid of emotional benefits such as individuality, historical reference, or a connection to nature. Most of these projects ended up as "dirty towers on windswept lots," as critic Tom Lacayo put it, "the kinds of places we have been critiquing in recent years with dynamite."

Contrast this with the Katrina Cottages designed by Marianne Cusato. In response to the emergency housing needs of Hurricane Katrina victims, she developed plans for small traditional-style houses that can be built quickly for the cost of an emergency trailer. The 300-square-foot interiors feel surprisingly spacious (*this* is a nice size room), thanks to their nine-foot ceilings and thoughtful floor plans. Their front porches encourage interaction with neighbors, and the original structures can be expanded when the owners' insurance money comes in. There's no emotional sacrifice to be made with these houses, since they tap into deep associations with family, community, and tradition. And on a strictly formal level, their proportions are sensible and satisfying. As a result, some people who could afford custom architecture are using the Katrina plans to build their vacation homes and guest houses.

The success of the Katrina Cottages has led Cusato to design a 1700-square-foot version, called a New Economy Home, in the same traditional style. She sees it as an antidote to the "McMansion," the feature-laden but inauthentic architecture of the 1990s that exudes all the charm of a checklist. "Let's see. Extra-tall portico, check. Multilevel roofline, check. Round-top windows, check. Marble foyer, check. Fully wired media room, check. Spacious exercise room, check. Large master bedroom with enormous bath, check. French country kitchen with granite counters, walk-in pantry, professional-grade appliances. Check, check, check."

Yet when all the boxes are checked, one feature is still missing: the feeling of being part of a community. Cusato hopes to remedy this situation by promoting an alternative vision for living, one that gets people out of the house and into the neighborhood. Would you really need your own cinema, exercise room, lavish kitchen, and large yard if you had theaters, gyms, restaurants, and parks all within walking distance? Would you really need the "look of wealth" if your house had architectural integrity and fit nicely into the neighborhood? "The checklist is only necessary in the void of design," says architect Cusato.

> The metaskill of feeling is becoming more vital as we move into the Robotic Age.

Naturally, there will always be home buyers who measure taste by the square foot, and developers and architects willing to cater to them. Knowing what buyers want does take a certain level of empathy, but it's a fairly narrow definition of the concept. What a buyer wants may not be what the community wants, or even what the buyer needs.

Empathy, like morality and responsibility, spirals outward as it grows. It starts with caring for oneself, expands to include one's family, then friends, then community, then region, then nation, then the world and all of nature. The highest level of empathy takes all these circles into consideration. The metaskill of feeling, the ability to draw on human emotion for intuition, aesthetics, and empathy, is a talent that's becoming more and more vital as we move into the Robotic Age. It's the ability to connect deeply with people through vicarious imagination, or "putting yourself in another person's shoes."

Daniel Goleman, author of *Emotional Intelligence*, says that technical skills are merely an entry-level requirement for most jobs. What lifts some people to the status of stars are their social skills. A UC Berkeley study followed a group of PhD students in science and technology over a 40-year period. It turned out that EI abilities "were four times more important than IQ in determining professional success and prestige by the end of their careers." People with EI often exhibit highly developed interpersonal skills such as team building, leadership, conflict resolution, selling, communication, and negotiation. You can be as brilliant as you like, but if you can't connect with people, you'll be relegated to the sidelines.

We find ourselves caught in the upward sweep of technological progress, with all the complexity and novelty this entails. Yet the deep desires of human beings don't change much at all. We still want to laugh, to feel pleasure, to love and be loved, to express our thoughts, share our feelings, see and be seen, and finally make a small contribution to the arc of history. It's not business—it's personal. Those who understand this are the ones we reward with power, the ones we want as leaders.

I'm not saying there's no room for technology in the realm of personal interactions. It's just that our technology needs to come from a place of empathy and not from a place of fear, greed, or lazi-

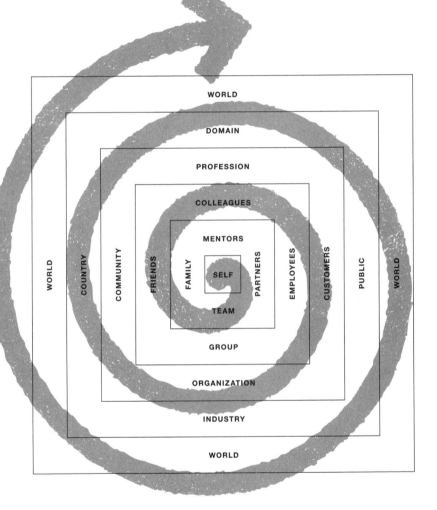

Empathy spirals outward from ourselves as our emotional maturity expands.

ness. It has to make personal interactions *more* personal, not less. CRM and VRM and PRM are early attempts at organizing business relationships, and will someday evolve into valuable tools for bringing customers and companies closer.

Today the big chain bookstores are either on the ropes or down for the count. Meanwhile, many of the little shops are still in the ring, bobbing and weaving with thoughtful product selections and strong customer ties. Customers do want the warm touch, and are willing to support businesses that give it to them. They're also willing to support businesses like Amazon and Zappos, whose online transactions, though mediated by technology, manage to be personal and empathetic.

ON WHAT DO YOU BIAS YOUR OPINION? I've just spent the last seven chapters persuading you that the emotional brain is the key to success in the Robotic Age. Now I'm about to tell you the opposite. Your emotions are just as likely to trap you, blind you, and turn you into a bigot. There's a popular homily, "Seeing is believing," which suggests we're more likely to put our trust in hard evidence than in hearsay or gut feeling. This is wishful thinking most of the time, because, thanks to the workings of the emotional brain, we're actually more likely to see what we believe than to believe what we see. Psychologists call this phenomenon *confirmation bias.*

Confirmation bias is a tendency to prefer evidence that fits what we already believe, blocking out any "inconvenient truths" with a mechanism known as *perceptual defense.* So our view of reality is not so much a product of what we *can* perceive, but of what we *do* perceive. Our perceptions are filtered through a mesh of beliefs, norms, values, and narratives that shape our mental models of the world. In a recent study of 8,000 respondents, people showed that they were twice as likely to seek information that confirms their beliefs than to consider evidence that contradicts them. In other words, it seems we'd rather lie to ourselves than change.

I decided to test this hypothesis on a cab driver on the way to a conference in Florida, where I was due to give a talk. "Hot today," I said. "You think this is what they mean by global warming?"

"I don't believe in global warming," he said.

"You're a global-warming denier?"

"I am," he said. "It's just a bunch of scientists protecting their grant money."

"I read that the number of scientists who go along with global warming is something like 90%. How many scientists do you think there are?"

"I don't know—maybe a million," he said.

"And you think almost a million scientists are getting grant money to study global warming?"

"Yep."

Undoubtedly, his beliefs fit a narrative borrowed from talk radio and conservative cable. But think about the number of assumptions that would have to be true to support the cab driver's view. First, the findings of many of the world's top scientists would have to be inferior to his personal intuition. Second, global governments and foundations would have to be supplying a half-million grants for global warming alone. Third, the scientists who received grant money would have to be corrupt or gullible. And fourth, the mainstream media would have to be involved in a massive cover-up. While one or two of these assumptions might be true, all four would take a miracle of cooperation.

Yet confirmation bias is not restricted to cab drivers and conspiracy theorists. Take a look at Research in Motion, the highly successful company that introduced the BlackBerry smartphone. The BlackBerry took off because it made communication between executives and managers easier and more mobile. As soon as the product gained wide acceptance in the marketplace, the company put its head down and started manufacturing BlackBerrys like there was no tomorrow.

When tomorrow did come in the form of the Apple iPhone, RIM denied any real threat. The mental model they held onto was that the BlackBerry was a serious corporate phone, and the iPhone was a trendy consumer device. They couldn't see that the same kind of design, marketing, and development network that appealed to consumers might appeal to

> Our perceptions are filtered through a mesh of beliefs, norms, values, and narratives that shape our mental models of the world.

business people as well. By the time they figured it out, they were so far behind the curve that Apple was able to steal their business in broad daylight. The company's two CEOS hired marketer Keith Pardy away from Nokia to turn the brand around. But they couldn't accept his assessment of the situation, so they blocked his moves at every juncture. He and two other marketing executives quit the company in frustration.

In the center of the Campo dei Fiori in Rome stands a statue of Giordano Bruno, a philosopher who was burned alive on that very spot in 1600. His crime? Claiming that the sun couldn't possibly be orbiting the earth, that it must be the other way around. This was heresy, according to the Roman Catholic Church, and when he wouldn't retract his claim they lit the fire.

Galileo Galilei also claimed the sun didn't orbit the earth, but he was careful not to insist on it, thus managing to avoid the stake. It took the Vatican 400 years to apologize for its minor astronomical error. Each year the Italian Association for Freethinking celebrates Bruno by inviting the mayor of Rome to say a few words in front of the statue. If you listened to one of these cautious speeches, you'd think Bruno died from a car accident rather than a church decree. The Vatican, after all, is right across the river from the Campo dei Fiori.

When we have a "religious belief" in something—a cause, a course of action, or even a brand—our decision-making process becomes that much easier. Our emotional brain is happy with this state of affairs, because it prefers to make decisions that *feel right*. They feel right because we've trained our brain through constant repetition, like training a dog to sit, come, or heel. The difficulty occurs when a situation calls for a trick we haven't learned, such as designing beautiful phones when we've only had practice designing expedient ones. Concerning the emotional brain, the lesson is clear: Be careful how you train your inner dog.

Confirmation bias is not always self-inflicted, since it's built into the fabric of culture. Anthropologist Bloomer describes culture as a seamless web of beliefs, all working together so they seem natural, universal, even unquestionable. "Culture is the most prominent nongenetic influence on human perception," she says. It gives us acceptable ways to attribute meaning to experience.

Culture produces stories that bind people together, allowing them to function as a team, a family, a group, a company, a community, or a nation. Stories are helpful when they make our lives easier, but harmful when they keep us from the truth. Nearly a century ago, newspaper editor Walter Lippman used the word "stereotypes" to describe the easily digestible narratives used by media to make sense of events. "We define first," he said, "and then we see." Today we should have a similar distrust of sound bites, glib statements that have the ring of truth—"truthiness," to use comedian Stephen Colbert's word—but discourage deeper investigation.

Lawrence Lessig, author of *The Future of Ideas*, observes that a given culture is defined not by the ideas people argue about, but the ideas they take for granted. "The character of an era hangs upon what needs no defense," he says. "Power runs with ideas that only the crazy would draw into doubt." The "taken for granted" is the test of sanity, while "what everyone knows" is the line between us and them. Once we identify with a culture or an ideology, our rationality can easily become a liability, allowing us to justify almost any belief. When we argue from a strongly held belief, we tend to put our feelings first and reasons second, gathering our evidence like stones to throw at each other.

The artist Goya fretted that "the sleep of reason produces monsters," meaning that unchecked emotions can lead to nightmare behaviors. Yet the sleep of *emotion* also produces monsters. Without emotion, we would have no access to the part of our brain that gave rise to the Golden Rule or that lets us make difficult decisions quickly. We think of sociopaths as people who can't control their emotions, but it's actually the opposite. Sociopaths are people with damaged emotional brains. Every decision they make is coldly rational, designed to serve themselves without regard for others. Obviously, we need both reason and emotion to navigate the world. They're like two sides of a pair of pliers that let us grasp ideas and

> Stories are helpful when they make our lives easier, but harmful when they keep us from the truth.

create knowledge.

In his book, *The Big Questions*, economics professor Steven Landsburg talks about an impromptu survey he conducted in the lunch room of his department at the University of Rochester. He asked a group of six PhDs to explain how water gets from a water heater to a shower. Six out of six believed that a pump was responsible for the feat. "No plumber shares this misconception," says Landsburg. "On the other hand, the world teems with plumbers who think protectionism will make us prosperous. When it's important to get things right, we try to replace our beliefs with actual knowledge."

To replace beliefs with knowledge is not an easy task. Emotion by itself won't get you there, and neither will simple reasoning. The only path to profound knowledge, the kind of knowledge you'll need to make a difference in the Robotic Age, is proficiency with *systems thinking*. Systems thinking, along with its more technical cousin, cybernetics, is not well understood by most people, but its principles are lurking in the language of Western culture, and are right up front in the philosophies of Eastern culture. In the simplest sense, systems thinking is the ability to contemplate the whole, not just the parts. It's the metaskill I call *seeing*. Seeing let's you hold your beliefs lightly as you seek deeper truths about the world and how it works.

For PhDs: The heater keeps the water hot and under constant pressure all the way to the tap. Turning the tap releases the pressure so the hot water flows from the showerhead.

SEEING

2

THE TYRANNY OF OR. Most people can't draw what they see. When they use a pencil to transfer an object or a scene onto a sheet of paper, they tend to draw not what they *see* but what they *know*. Or at least what they *think* they know. So a sketch of a face ends up looking like a Cubist sculpture, and a drawing of a street scene looks like primitive folk art.

Optical, or naturalistic, perspective doesn't come naturally. It requires a trick of the mind, in which you use your executive brain to override your beliefs. Instead of looking at a subject as a three-dimensional person, place, or thing, you mentally flatten it out to two dimensions, focusing only on the relative distances and relationships among lines, edges, angles, and shapes.

"Oh, I *see*," your eye says. "In flattened space, the distance between that corner and that line is about half the distance between that edge and that point"—even though your knowledge of the three-dimensional world tells you something quite different. By constantly measuring the relative distances between points in two-dimensional space as you go, you can bring the drawing into some semblance of visual realism. The trick lies in overriding your beliefs, biases, and mental models—temporarily—through rigorous, rational discipline.

However, the human mind doesn't like discipline. Discipline is hard work, exacting a cost in time, energy, and ego while we're learning. It's much easier to make our decisions quickly, go with the flow, and not expose ourselves to failure. In the West especially, we prefer decisions to be multiple choice rather than open and ambiguous. And when they *are* open and ambiguous, we try to shrink them down to a size we can deal with. The mind likes simple choices, and it loves a choice between opposites. "Either/or" propositions are so prevalent we hardly question them.

But we should.

Our preference for simplistic either/or propositions—good or bad, right or wrong, conservative or liberal, friend or foe, us or them—blinds us to the deeper questions we need to address if we're to survive beyond the 21st century. In many developed countries, including the United States, either/or is baked into the political voting system through a simple choice between opposing parties. It's a direct extension of popular sports, in which two opponents battle for supremacy, and fans choose sides based on beliefs, feelings, and allegiances. In the two-party system of government, winning becomes a substitute for progress.

Sociobiologist Rebecca Costa observes that, from a historical perspective, civilizations based on opposition eventually face gridlock, and finally collapse. Her book, *The Watchman's Rattle: Thinking Our Way Out of Extinction*, presents the Roman, Mayan, and Khmer empires as vivid examples of our biological tendency to prefer simplistic solutions. "When we are presented with only two choices, we often choose the less objectionable option, which in effect becomes decision by default." She explains that choosing between two extreme options doesn't work for highly complex problems such as global recession, poverty, war, failing education, or the depletion of natural resources, since it forces the brain into choosing *which* instead of *what*.

With complex problems, either/or propositions tend to be *false dichotomies*. A false dichotomy is a logical fallacy in which a situation seems to have only two alternatives, when in reality others are possible. Some everyday examples:

> *If you're not with us, you're against us.*
> *If you favor charter schools, you're against public schools.*
> *If you're for gun control, you're against personal freedom.*
> *If you're a capitalist, you don't care about the environment.*
> *If you support abortion rights, you must be anti-life.*
> *If you want universal health care, you want socialism.*
> *If an idea is new, it must be risky.*

Those of us who accept false dichotomies can easily be manipulated by unscrupulous leaders in government, business, religion, and other institutions. All we need is a simple choice between two unequal alternatives, one obviously good and the other obviously bad, and *boom!*—decision made. Our beliefs have been confirmed, and no further reflection is necessary. Meanwhile, society heads

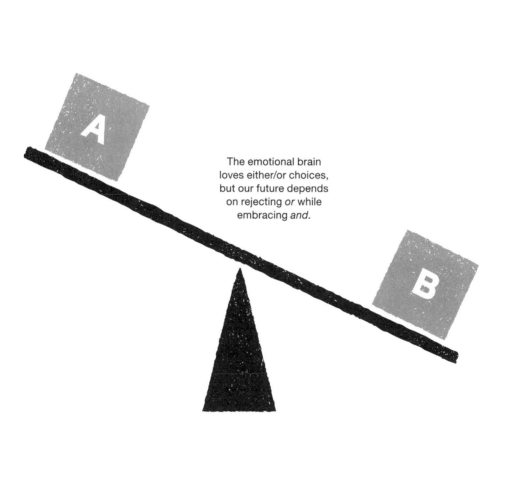

The emotional brain loves either/or choices, but our future depends on rejecting *or* while embracing *and*.

toward gridlock as both sides of the dichotomy dig in their heels.

When two sides attack a problem, the problem is no longer the problem. The problem is the sides. As long as there are two opposing sides, there's no possibility of progress, only compromise. Politics, goes the conventional wisdom, is the "art of compromise."

Choosing between opposites doesn't work for complex problems, since it forces the brain to choose *which* instead of *what*.

Unfortunately, this is true. With dichotomous decisions, there are only three possible outcomes: win-lose, lose-win, or compromise. None of these is optimal, and all can lead to gridlock.

The solution? Reject the tyranny of *or* and embrace the genius of *and*. Leave the sides behind. Look for a third narrative based on common ground instead of compromise.

Roger Martin, author of *The Opposable Mind*, calls this process "integrative thinking." Integrative thinkers don't break a problem into separate pieces and work on them one by one. Instead, they see the entire architecture of the problem—how the various parts fit together, and how one decision affects another. By resolving the tensions, or oppositions, that launched the problem to begin with, they can craft a holistic solution. Often this means rejecting the urge for certainty and grappling with the messiness of paradox.

Physicist Niels Bohr was fascinated by the discovery that electrons could be in one place, then appear in another place, with no apparent movement in between. How wonderful, he said, that scientists had met with a paradox, since now they could make real progress. Paradox, ambiguity, and conflict can be the triggers for innovation and discovery, providing we don't settle for the quick compromise or remain boxed in by our beliefs.

"Beliefs aren't nurture," says Costa. "They're nature." They're a basic human need. Yet we need to be aware that throughout history, whenever knowledge has been difficult to acquire, or when ambiguity has overwhelmed our biological ability to deal with it, we've "run home to mama." We've defaulted to the emotional comfort of belief rather than using our rational brains to see the problems in their full, awesome complexity. If we hope to escape the fate of previous civilizations such as the Romans, Mayans, and Khmer, we'll need to look for bigger answers.

THINKING WHOLE THOUGHTS. Drawing a picture in a visually realistic way is not really a drawing problem. It's a seeing problem. Until we can clearly see what's in front of us, free of misleading beliefs and partial knowledge, our picture will necessarily be distorted or fragmented. Painter Robert Irwin said, "Seeing is forgetting the name of the thing seen." As soon as we label something, we put it in a box and move it to another part of our brain. We stop seeing it as it really is.

Seeing and thinking are related concepts. We claim to *see* what people mean; we *look* for answers; we *envision* a solution; we follow a *line* of thought; we *draw* conclusions; and with any luck we *connect the dots*. In trying to make these connections, we're searching for patterns that show us how objects and events are linked, or need to be linked, in order to make sense. We're looking for the emergence of a complete picture.

Leonardo da Vinci epitomized this relationship between seeing and thinking, as amply illustrated in his notes. His scientific insights came straight from his passion for drawing; he drew things to understand them. He was fascinated by the repeating patterns of nature, intensely curious about the fundamental experience of being human in the natural world. He made hundreds of drawings of the human eye, of whirlpools in streams, of sound moving through the air, of the similarities and differences among people, plants, and animals. He was trying to *see* how things are connected, and the way nature continually transforms itself. He was searching for a unified vision of the world.

We might well call Leonardo the father of holistic invention. His approach to art and science, and to feeling and thinking, was both simultaneous and seamless. The ideal of the Renaissance Man doesn't suggest that we learn everything about everything, but that we see the world as an interconnected system of systems, instead of separate parts.

On a good day, this is exactly what designers do. They observe a situation—a product, service, experience, process, a communication, or business model—then devise new components, new relationships, new interactions that reshape the situation into something better. Their metaskill of visualization—of seeing how to see—makes this transformation possible.

Since the peephole of consciousness is so small, most people find it easier to focus on a single tree than a whole forest. But if our goal is to reshape a situation, we need to see the trees, the forest, and the relationships among them. We've been playing checkers when we really need to play three-dimensional chess. As design thinker John Thackara says, we need to employ *macroscopes* as well as microscopes. We need to understand how the parts interact if we want to improve the larger situation. The whole is not the sum of the parts, and merely improving the parts can court unwelcome surprises.

As a young designer, I used to wonder about the common remark, "I'm no artist—I can't even draw a straight line." A straight line had always seemed to me evidence of *non*creativity, the refuge of the logical, the prosaic, the *un*artistic. Why would anyone think drawing a straight line was an important skill? We have T-squares for that! Someone finally took me aside and said, "It's just an expression." Oh.

Yet straight-line thinking has co-opted Western thought to the point that we have trouble understanding cause and effect. We forget that the world isn't linear. It's full of arcs and loops and spirals. It often seems more like a Rube Goldberg contraption than Newtonian equation. We can pull a lever here and get an unintended consequence over there.

For example, today the developed world is fighting recession. Should we balance the books with a massive austerity program? Or grease the wheels with a series of stimulus packages? Both "solutions" might seem logical, but either one could bring the roof down on our heads. Complex problems are embedded in complex systems, making them impossible to solve using linear thinking. We send aid to foreign countries to fight poverty, only to find we're feeding corruption instead. We formulate new drugs for viruses, only to find that the viruses mutate into stronger ones. We develop pollution-free nuclear energy, only to end up with a nuclear waste problem that could haunt us for ten thousand years.

With complex problems, things are not always what they seem. Trying to turn a nonlinear world into a linear world for our emotional comfort is usually a bad idea, because linear planning only works with problems that can't resist our plans. People, viruses, and atomic particles don't conform to linearity—they have a way of fighting back. They seem to mock our naïve attempts to analyze them. As science-fiction writer Poul Anderson once said, "I have yet to see any problem, however complicated, which, when looked at in the right way, did not become still more complicated."

The Industrial Revolution has been a triumph in reductionist thinking. By focusing on narrow problems, we've learned how to move large weights over long distances, increase our production of food, eradicate a whole raft of diseases, transport people through the air, communicate instantly around the world, and perform any number of miraculous feats. Yet to the extent we've been thinking in fragments instead of whole thoughts, our solutions have only created bigger problems that are now beyond our comprehension. We now have to grapple with pollution, obesity, overpopulation, terrorism, climate change, and recession, to name just of few of our ailments.

> We forget that the world isn't linear. It's full of arcs and loops and spirals. Linear planning only works with problems that can't resist our plans.

The only way to address these so-called *wicked problems*—slippery conundrums that disappear around the corner when you try to follow them—is to heed the advice of philosopher Ludwig Wittgenstein. "Don't get involved in partial problems," he said. "Always take flight to where there is a free view over the whole single great problem, even if this view is not a clear one." In other words, think in whole thoughts instead of fragments. Step back from the drawing board and notice the relationships among the lines, the edges, the angles, and the shapes. Check them against reality, one by one and all together.

This mode of seeing is variously known as systems thinking, adaptive thinking, cybernetics, and holistic thinking. Wicked problems don't easily yield to hard analysis, linear logic, or propositional knowledge. They're more likely to give up their secrets to observation, intuition, and imagination. Like an artist composing a canvas, a systems thinker squints at a problem to see the complete picture instead of the components.

HOW SYSTEMS WORK. A system is a set of interconnected elements organized to achieve a purpose. For example, the plumbing in your house is a system organized to deliver clean water and flush waste water away. A business is a system organized to turn materials and labor into profit-making products and services. A government is a system that's organized to protect and promote the welfare of its citizens. When you think about it, even a product like a movie is a system, designed to create a theatrical experience for an audience.

A system can contain many subsystems, and it can also be part of a larger system. How you define the system depends on where you draw its boundary. And where you draw its boundary depends on what you want to understand or manipulate. If you're the director of a movie, for example, you'll want to draw a boundary around the whole project so that you can manage the relationships among the story elements, the locations, the sets, the performances, the technical production, the schedule, the costs, and so on. You might also draw boundaries around subsystems like individual scenes, stunts, and camera moves, so you can control the various relationships within each of those, as well as their relationships to the whole.

The structure of a system includes three types of components: *elements, interconnections,* and a *purpose.* It also includes a unique set of *rules*—an internal logic—that allows the system to achieve its purpose. The system itself, along with its rules, determines its behavior. That's why organizations don't change just because people change. The system itself determines, to a large extent, how the people inside it behave. It's useless to blame the collapse of the banking industry on individual executives or specific events. The very structure of the banking system is to blame, since it's tilted in favor of corrupt actors and selfish behaviors. Therefore we might think about redesigning the system so corruption is not so easy or profitable. Or we might make improvements to the larger system in which it operates, say capitalism itself. We might even question the cultural norms and beliefs that gave rise to 20th-century capitalism in the first place.

To improve a complex system, you first have to understand it— at least a little. I say "a little" because complex systems are always part mechanics, part mystery. Take the example of a company. Like all systems, a company has inflows and outflows, plus feedback systems for monitoring their movements. A CEO might have a good grasp of the system's *elements* (its divisions, product lines, departments, competencies, key people), its *interconnections* (communications, distribution channels, partnerships, customer relationships), and its *purpose* (mission, vision, goals). She might also understand the system's operational *rules* (processes, methodologies, cultural norms). But it's still difficult for any one person to know how the company is actually doing in real time. So she uses the system's *feedback mechanisms* (revenues, earnings, customer research) to get a read on the situation.

But there's a catch.

The feedback mechanisms in most systems are subject to something called *latency*, a delay between cause and effect, or between cause and feedback, in which crucial information arrives too late to act upon. While the revenue reports are up to date in a traditional sense, they only show the results of last quarter's efforts or last year's strategy. They're lagging indicators, not leading indicators, of the company's actual progress. By the time she gets the numbers, the situation is a *fait accompli*. Any straightforward response based on the late information is likely to be inadequate, ineffective, or wrong.

> Complex systems are always part mechanics, part mystery.

How can she work around this problem? By looking at the company as a system instead of individual parts or separate events. She can anticipate the eventual feedback by finding out which indicators are worth watching.

For example, she might watch levels of brand loyalty as an indicator of future profit margins. Or products in the pipeline as an indicator of higher revenues. Or trends in the marketplace as an indicator of increasing demand. Of course, leading indicators can be tricky, since they're only predictions. But if she keeps at it, continuously comparing predictions with outcomes, she can start to gain confidence in the indicators that matter. This is known as "getting a feel" for the business.

In systems theory, any change that reinforces an original change is called *reinforcing* or *positive* feedback. Any change that dampens the original change is called *balancing* or *negative* feedback.

For example, if a company's product starts to take off, other customers may notice and jump on the bandwagon. This is an example of *reinforcing* feedback. If the product keeps selling, it may eventually lose steam as it runs out of customers, meets with increasing competition, falls behind in its technology, or simply becomes unfashionable. These are examples of *balancing* feedback. By keeping an eye on these two feedback loops, the CEO can get ahead of the curve and make decisions that mitigate or reverse the situation.

But let's get back to the problem of latency. Every change to a system takes a little time to show up. This is best illustrated by the classic story of the "unfamiliar shower." Imagine you're staying at the house of some friends, and you go to use their shower for the first time. It's a chilly morning. You turn on the taps, step in, and suddenly jump back. Whoa! The water comes out like stabbing needles of ice! So you gingerly reach in again and turn the hot up and the cold down. No change. Okay, one more adjustment and—ahhh—the water warms up enough to stand under the shower head. Then, just as suddenly, the reverse occurs. The water turns violently hot and this time you jump all the way out. "Yowww!" you scream, waking up the house.

What just happened? In systems-thinking terms, the delay between cause and effect—between adjusting the taps and achieving the right temperature—deprived you of the information you needed to make appropriate changes to the hot and cold water. After a few times using the shower (assuming you were allowed to stay), you learned to wait for the feedback before fiddling with the taps. And you later learned where the taps should end up to achieve the right temperature.

THE LATENCY TRAP

1 YOU SEE A PROBLEM

2 INTRODUCE A CHANGE

3 NOTHING HAPPENS

4 INCREASE THE CHANGE

5 PROBLEM GETS WORSE

Whenever you're
surprised by a system,
you'll often discover
a feedback delay.

Here are some other examples of system delays:

The state government raises taxes on business. The immediate result is more revenue for public works, but over time businesses pull out and fewer move in, thereby lowering the revenue available for public works.

A mother is concerned that her children may be exposed to danger if they're allowed to roam the neighborhood freely, so she keeps them close and controls their interactions with friends. At first this keeps them safe, but as they grow older they suffer from impaired judgment in their interactions with the broader world.

A company is hit by an industry downturn and its profits begin to sag. It reacts quickly by laying off a number of highly paid senior employees. While this solves the immediate problem, the talent-starved company falls behind its competitors just as the economy picks up.

A student feels that his education is taking too long, so he drops out of college and joins the workplace. He makes good money while his college friends struggle to pay their bills. Over time, his lack of formal education puts a cap on his income while his friends continue up the ladder.

A salesman meets his quota by pressuring customers to buy products that aren't quite right for their needs. The next time he tries to make a sale, he finds them less agreeable.

A bigger child learns that she can bully the other children in school. At first this feels empowering, but over time she finds she's excluded from friendships with other children she admires.

Our emotional brains are hardwired to overvalue the short term and undervalue the long term.

The common thread in all these stories is that an immediate solution caused an eventual problem. None of the protagonists could see around the corner because they were thinking in short, straight lines.

Our emotional brains are hardwired to overvalue the short term and undervalue the long term. When there's no short-term threat, there's no change to our body chemistry to trigger fight or flight. If you pulled back your bedsheet one night and found a big, black spider, your brain would light up like a Christmas tree. But if you were told that the world's population will be decimated by rising ocean waters before the year 2030, your brain would barely react. We're genetically attuned to nearby dangers and unimpressed by distant dangers, even when we know that the distant ones are far more dangerous. For example, I know I should earthquake-proof my house in fault-riddled California, but today I have to oil the squeaky hinge on my bedroom door. It's driving me crazy.

Latency is the mother of all systems traps. It plays to our natural weaknesses, since our emotional brain is so much more developed than our newer rational brain. It takes much more effort to think our way through problems than to merely react to them. We have to exert ourselves to override our automatic responses when we realize they're not optimal.

In this way, systems thinking isn't only about seeing the big picture. It's about seeing the long picture. It's more like a movie than a snapshot. My wife can predict the ending of a movie with uncanny accuracy after viewing the first few minutes. How? Through a rich understanding of plot patterns and symbolism, acquired over years of watching films and reading fiction, that lets her imagine the best resolution. In other words, she understands the *system* of storytelling.

But there's more to systems than watching for patterns, loops, and latency. You also have to keep an eye on archetypes.

GRANDMA WAS RIGHT. The first rule of systems is that they create their own behavior. During the protests of the late 1960s, students around the world took to the streets and raised their voices against the "system." The overall system, they said, not individual people, was to blame for the broken culture. Civil rights, women's rights, war, overpopulation, and the environment were seen as tangled strands in a single hairball. While this instinct was correct, hairballs don't untangle easily. If you pull a strand on one side, you may find that another strand gets tighter on the other side. The only solution is to undo the knots one by one. And, of course, it helps to know what kind of knot you're dealing with. Is it a simple overhand knot, or a real granny knot?

A complex system, by virtue of its structure, behaves exactly as it should, but its behavior still mystifies us. "What goes around comes around," was a favorite phrase of the '60s, but we still haven't learned that life moves in circles, with confusing delays between cause and effect. We keep expecting the world to be linear and predictable.

Systems create archetypes. These are behavioral patterns that commonly crop up in systems, and therefore can be understood and managed—provided we have mental models to give us a framework. While the archetypes may seem counterintuitive, they're counterintuitive in ways that we've expressed in our culture for centuries.

When you need help with a granny knot, who better to ask than Granny? Let's examine nine of the most common archetypes and the ways we characterize them everyday language.

1. *Information delay,* or as Grandma would put it, "closing the barn door after the horses are gone." This is the most basic systems trap, the problem of late-arriving feedback (as illustrated by the unfamiliar shower). In this archetype, a person or group is pursuing a long-term goal, and they make decisions according to the information that returns from the last decision they made. If they don't take the information delay into account, every new decision will be wrong.

For example, a consulting firm finds that, after a protracted economic slump, the number of its client engagements finally starts to increase. Yet based on its most recent experience, it holds off on hiring staff until it can confirm that the uptick will continue. The number of engagements grows to the point where the firm can only accept a fraction of the work it's being offered. So it begins an aggressive hiring program and leases additional office space, which it then builds out with expensive furniture, equipment, and interior design. As soon as the new space is ready, the flow of client work drops off a cliff, and the new space remains empty while the firm focuses on cutting staff.

> If decision makers don't take information delay into account, every new decision will be wrong.

The problem is latency. If the firm had had advance information about the upturn, it could have begun the hiring process earlier and taken advantage of growing volume of work. And if it had had advance knowledge of the downturn, it could have held off on additional office space and gotten by with contractors instead of full-time employees. Advance knowledge, of course, is in short supply. No one can predict the future, at least not with any accuracy. But a basic understanding of systems would have taught the firm to look for pertinent signs. Maybe business trends in this firm's industry show up in another industry first. Maybe downturns can be seen first in weaker firms, the "canaries in the coal mine." Without using these kinds of signals, the firm's moves will always be too late, causing it to lose money on both the upturns and the downturns.

Rick Perry, a Republican candidate in the 2012 U.S. presidential primary, was asked by a reporter what he might do about climate change. His answer was the political equivalent of comfort food: "The science of global warming is not yet settled, so we shouldn't risk our economy by addressing it." Of course, by the time the science is settled, the time for action will have passed and the economy will be the least of our problems. Granny would have reminded Rick that "a stitch in time saves nine."

2. *Addiction*, or "when the cure is worse than the disease." Whenever we use a short-term fix for a long-term problem, we're in danger of addiction, because we begin to depend on the temporary fix instead of solving the root problem. Let's say you experience a sleepless night, so you stop at Starbucks for a grande latte on the way to work. This helps in the short term, but by the afternoon you're even more tired, so you toss down a venti latte in lieu of lunch. At night you're wired from the caffeine, so you calm your nerves with a couple of glasses of wine and wander off to bed. You go to sleep right away, but by three in the morning you're tossing and turning. You struggle up the next morning and repeat the whole process, hooked on a downward cycle of quick fixes while the root problem grows worse.

Where's the feedback delay in this system? It's between drinking the coffee or wine and seeing the results. A jolt of caffeine works quite well in the first two hours, but later makes us feel more tired. If coffee led immediately to tiredness, none of us would think twice about rejecting it. Instead, we tell ourselves that now is more important than later, turning the "solution" into an additional problem. What systems thinking does is help us see the whole problem by thinking through—in Grandma's terms—"how one thing leads to another."

The cure for addiction requires making changes to the false solution—in this case, the cycle of caffeine and alcohol. If the long-term problem is insomnia, then the long-term solution is to address the root cause of insomnia. It may be anxiety, stress, sleep apnea, or alcoholism (especially if it's more than two glasses of wine), each of which dictates its own solution. One thing the medical profession knows—and everyday experience confirms—is that the caffeine-alcohol cycle only compounds the problem.

3. *Eroding goals*, or "lowering the bar." We've seen this phenomenon in school, where a teacher gives up measuring students against a broader standard and begins "grading on the curve." The students, instead of competing as a team against the outside world, are now pitted against each other. This solution creates two new problems: The first is that learning becomes stressful instead of joyful, and the second is that the students lose confidence in their ability to succeed in the real world.

The feedback delay in this archetype, between the lowered goals and the resulting lack of mastery, can take years to notice. It becomes very easy to settle for lowered expectations rather than struggle against a higher standard.

Take the example of software development. The design of software is often a complex and lengthy undertaking, requiring the interaction of many people and many parts. While the working time can easily stretch out, the deadlines are usually less flexible. The quick fix, then, is to meet the deadlines by lowering the quality, while vowing, of course, to clean up the design on the next version. Over time the company creates a culture of "good enough" instead of a culture of excellence, leaving the door open to competition.

One antidote to this archetype is not to lower the goals but to raise the performance. If there's a performance gap in the classroom, the solution might be to go more slowly, work with students one-on-one, get parents engaged, or institute new rules for classroom behavior. If the software team is performing poorly, the solution may be to clarify the goals, rebalance the workload, collaborate in a different way, or look for better models. The long-term fix could also be a new policy of realistic deadlines, which could be addressed by placing the problem in a larger frame.

Another antidote is to reward people who embrace rising goals. Instead of punishing those who don't meet the standards, encourage those who surpass them. Let the high achievers serve as inspiration for everyone else, and mine their successes for best practices. In this way, the archetype of eroding goals is flipped to the positive.

4. *Escalation*, or "an eye for an eye, plus interest." While an eye for an eye may seem like justice, it usually comes with a side of revenge or dominance. "If you execute one of *our* soldiers, we'll execute two of *yours*," says General One. "Oh, really?" says the General Two. "If you execute *two* of our soldiers, we'll execute *ten* of yours." And so on. It's easy to see how this becomes a trap for both sides. But it takes an understanding of systems to escape it.

The US and the USSR lived through forty years of escalation, caught in a mindless competition to build the largest arsenal of nuclear weapons. Meanwhile, a whole generation learned that life could end any moment in a fiery mushroom cloud, and that planning for the future was futile. The best one could hope for was to live for the moment—a recipe for suboptimization if there ever was one. The situation came close to solving itself in a fireball of mutual destruction during the Cuban missile crisis. Luckily—or unluckily—the USSR finally ran out of money and could no longer fund its side of the game. The US didn't "win" the Cold War, it simply outlasted it, and is less robust for having engaged in it.

This dangerous game is not confined to the past. We're still playing it today against factions in the Middle East. Beginning with the Bush administration and continuing more aggressively with the Obama administration, the CIA has been sending drones over borders to kill perceived enemies, reportedly killing 2,000 militants and an unknown number of civilians. "Is this the world we want to live in?" asks Micah Zenko, a member of the Council on Foreign Relations. "Because we're creating it."

The best way to exit an escalation trap is to find a way for both sides to win. It's not about compromise so much as common ground. By using empathy to understand the needs of the other side, you can design a third solution that changes the original positions for mutual benefit. It helps enormously when both sides see the picture as a system, but even one side can release the trap by unilaterally disengaging.

> **The best way to exit an escalation trap is to find a way for both sides to win.**

There's another kind of escalation—reverse escalation—that can happen with price wars. It's a race to the bottom in which companies leapfrog each other down the slope to lower and lower prices. Of course, this is a game many can play, so each company lowers its prices to match. They soon compete away their profits, thus hampering their ability to invest in innovation or serve their customers at the former level of quality. As customer loyalty erodes, the companies get stuck in the low-price trap until one or more go out of business. Customers win in the short term, but in the long term they suffer from fewer options in the marketplace.

The way out of a price war is not to engage in the first place. It's one thing to build a business on low prices, and quite another to sacrifice your profit margins to keep up with the Joneses. As Grandma would say, "Just because your friends jump off the Empire State Building doesn't mean you should do it." A better answer is to invest the potential loss of profits into a new product, an improved service, or a change in strategy to reposition the brand. In the short term there might be some pain, but in the long term you'll have something to show for it.

5. *The tragedy of the commons,* or "don't be selfish—take turns!" This trap is related to the escalation trap, except that it takes place in a fragile commons. A commons can be any shared resource that

becomes endangered by overuse. A highway is a commons that can accommodate only so many cars before it becomes gridlocked. A park is a commons that can become trampled by too many picnickers. A company home page is a commons that becomes less effective with every inessential item that's added to it. A fishing area is a commons that benefits no one after it's fished out.

This archetype is named for a 1968 article by ecologist Garrett Hardin. In it he told the story of a village with a publicly owned pasture on which herdsmen were encouraged to graze their animals. Since the privilege was free and the pasture was large, each herdsman in the village began to think, What harm could there be in adding more animals to the pasture? After all, Farmer Jones is doing it, isn't he? But every herdsman had the same idea, and before long the pasture was ruined by overgrazing, thereby wrecking it for everyone. "Ruin is the destination toward which all men rush," said Hardin, "each pursuing his own best interest in a society that believes in the freedom of the commons." Irresponsible freedom always leads to less freedom.

The main problem, once again, is feedback that never arrives. If no one can see that the resource is being ruined, there's no reason to limit their use of it. But like the straw that finally breaks the camel's back, the resource looks perfectly healthy until one day it tips into the danger zone. By then it's too late to turn around.

Author Donella Meadows, in her excellent primer, *Thinking in Systems*, suggests three ways out of this trap. The first is to educate and persuade participants to be temperate, appealing to their human decency. The second is to privatize the commons so that each person reaps the consequences of his or her own actions. And the third is to regulate the commons by agreeing on certain rules, then enforcing them.

The American highway system is a frustrating experience for many drivers, not because of the quality or capacity of the roads, but because of the mental models people use for driving them. The reigning model is that, on a four-lane highway, there's a slow lane and a fast lane in each direction. These are subject to a speed limit that's sporadically enforced. The result is that each driver is free

The slow-lane-fast-lane image of driving causes traffic flow to clot. The driving-lane-passing-lane image keeps it moving.

AMERICAN DRIVING

EUROPEAN DRIVING

to decide what constitutes slow and fast. One driver may want to exceed the speed limit to shave some time off his trip, and therefore chooses the fast lane. Another driver feels that since she's adhering to the speed limit, she should be able to use the fast lane, too. Yet another driver feels that the speed limit is too fast for safety, but still wants to go faster than the trucks in the slow lane, so he moves to the fast lane and simply drives slowly. The result is "clotting," in which vehicles in the fast and slow lanes often go the same speed side by side, thus blocking all the vehicles behind.

European drivers avoid this problem by using a different mental model. Instead of a slow lane and a fast lane, they conceive of them as a driving lane and a passing lane. They stay in the driving lane until they need to pass, then move into the passing lane, then immediately back into the driving lane, leaving the passing lane open for others. Everyone can go the speed they want without slowing the flow of traffic. The result is very high throughput with very little frustration. While European highways certainly have speed limits, there's little need for police enforcement since accidents are rare. If we Americans want more freedom on the road, we could do worse than learn from the European system.

6. *Rule beating*, or "obeying the letter of the law, but not the spirit." If there's one quick way to subvert a system, this is it. The rules that govern a system are rarely perfect, since it's difficult to predict its behavior until it has some operating history. Even then, some problems won't show up right away (due to latency), and others may be too difficult to address without making the rules ornate.

In 2005 the United Nations began issuing carbon credits to companies that make a coolant for air-conditioning that's known to be harmful to the ozone layer. The companies receive 11,000 credits for destroying one ton of HFC-23, an even more harmful gas that's left over from the manufacturing process. They can then sell those credits on the open market, adding revenues that fall straight to the bottom line. The goal of the program is simple: to discourage companies from dumping HFC-23 into the atmosphere. What could go wrong?

Well, 19 international companies, which account for more than 40 percent of the United Nation's credits, have begun to *increase* their manufacturing of the harmful coolant. Why? To get the credits from destroying the waste gas. The more coolant they make, the more credits they get for destroying the waste. Not only that, but the higher manufacturing volume lowers the price of the unfriendly coolant so that friendlier alternatives can't get traction in the marketplace. The companies win while the planet loses.

Some everyday examples: A driver slows down in the presence of a patrol car, and then breaks the speed limit to make up for lost time. A salesman meets his sales quota by keeping the remaining supply of products hidden from the other salespeople. A politician says he didn't have sex with an intern—technically speaking. A moviegoer sidles up to an old acquaintance to get a better position in the line. A wealthy American investor keeps a large part of her fortune in the Cayman Islands to avoid US taxes.

These are snapshots of rule beating, often excused by the rule beater with the old saw: "Well, everyone does it." The problem is that everyone *does* do it, so the effect is multiplied by the number of people in the system. When the system becomes damaged enough to cause concern, the finger of blame is often pointed at the moral character of the participants. But the problem can be partially solved by redesigning the rules so that participants find more advantage in following them than in breaking them.

For example, maybe the computerized speed traps that result in hefty traffic fines could be altered to reward safe driving as well, tracking cars in order to bestow "responsibility points" on their owners. The points could then be used to lower their insurance premiums. Or maybe the largest taxpayers could be awarded "status," not unlike frequent flyer programs, that confers symbolic benefits such as special parking privileges or invitations to White House events. In designing rules for systems, it pays to reward the behavior you want. As Grandma always said, "You'll catch more flies with honey than vinegar."

> **Rule-beating can be tamed by redesigning the rules so participants find more advantage in following them than in breaking them.**

7. *Limits to growth,* or "what goes up must come down." Every form of growth eventually encounters limits. A wildfire that runs out of trees to burn, a city that runs out of buildable land, a virus that runs out of victims, and a business that runs out of customers are all examples of bumping up against limits. When the growing entity hits the wall, it often reverses itself and contracts as quickly as it had expanded.

When a growth line is heading straight up, it's difficult to imagine that it will ever stop. The leaders of a rapidly expanding business will feel little incentive to change the formula. The phrase, "If it ain't broke, don't fix it," will often be heard. As success feeds upon success, the growth line soars and the company keeps it accelerating by hiring more staff, opening new offices, launching subbrands, and layering complexity upon complexity. The faster the company grows, the faster it hurtles toward its unseen limits. When it finally hits them, the very inputs that kept it accelerating now turn against it, weighing it down with costly complexity that accelerates its fall back to Earth.

The latency in this archetype is the lag between fanning the flames and burning down the forest. The company should have known the party would soon be over, but they couldn't see it. They're shocked and confused by their new situation. They blame the market, the economy, their competitors, their customers, and even each other. But they failed to see that the system held the seeds of their demise. If they had channeled Grandma, they would have remembered that "all good things must come to an end."

Even so, the end can often be staved off with the application of courage and vision. IBM and Kodak saw what would happen if they continued down their respective paths. In 1990, IBM knew that the market for large computers would eventually desert them, while Kodak could see that digital cameras would soon replace film cameras. IBM radically transformed itself from a seller of "big iron" into a consulting company that also sold computer systems. Kodak, on the other hand, tried to preserve its profitable film business too long, starving their digital investments in the process. There's still meaning in the Kodak brand, but little momentum in the business.

Entropy causes fast-moving things to slow down, and order to collapse into chaos. There's a price to pay for maintaining any kind of difference or individuality. When you see the limits approaching, getting around them is theoretically straightforward: If it ain't broke, *fix* it. What's not so straightforward is convincing others to follow. After all, things are still pretty good, aren't they?

8. *Success to the successful,* or why "the rich get richer and the poor get poorer." In Grandma's day there was a popular song that struck a chord across the country:

> *You load sixteen tons, and what do you get?*
> *Another day older and deeper in debt.*
> *Saint Peter, don't you call me 'cause I can't go—*
> *I owe my soul to the company store.*

The song was sung to chain-gang rhythm by Tennessee Ernie Ford. And what it captured was the harsh reality of Industrial Age mining towns, in which workers couldn't afford to leave and couldn't afford to stay. The main source of groceries and other goods was the company itself, and the mark-ups became usurious. This created a vicious cycle in which the workers increasingly owed the store more than they made, and therefore could never leave.

In ecology, the rich getting richer and the poor getting poorer is known as the Competitive Exclusion Principle. It says that two species can't continue to live in the same habitat and compete for the same resource. Eventually, one species will win a larger share of the resource, giving it an advantage in future competition, until it becomes impossible for the other species to compete. Finally, the winner takes all, and the habitat suffers from a lack of variety.

This is the situation the US finds itself in now. The moneyed have become increasingly powerful by virtue of their wealth, which has allowed them to rewrite the rules in their favor. As the rich have gotten richer, more of the middle class has joined the working class, and now the wealthiest are feeling the economic pinch of a consumer population that can no longer afford the products that their investments depend on.

The way out of the success trap is by leveling the playing field. In past situations like the current one, we've used techniques such as strengthening labor unions, passing antitrust laws, and levying estate taxes. Other possible techniques are closing income tax loopholes, launching social programs, and limiting the power of lobbyists. Perhaps the most sensible rule is simply to match the power of the public sector to the power of the private sector. When one half is able to dominate the other, the Exclusion Principle kicks in and the economy gets the bruises.

9. *The wrong goal*, or "be careful what you wish for." The behavior of a system is determined largely by its purpose. Since the purpose of Fannie Mae was to enable home ownership for as many Americans as possible, we shouldn't be surprised that it worked. Financial institutions were happy to embrace the purpose by cutting corners and lowering standards, secure in the knowledge that Fannie Mae would cover any losses. Somewhere along the line, the goal of the system changed from "responsible homeownership" to "increased homeownership." Systems have a way defaulting to the shallowest goal instead of the deeper goal we had in mind.

The well-intentioned goal of the No Child Left Behind Act was to improve the quality of US education by making sure students performed well on a standardized test. Sounds logical, right? But when the government made test scores a prerequisite for funding, the *de facto* goal became good test scores, not good education. Many schools immediately diverted their attention from teaching to testing. Others ignored subjects not on the test. Still others focused on the midlevel students who were most likely to make a difference, giving less help to struggling students who were likely to fail, or gifted students who were likely to pass on their own. Funding was the all-glittering prize. In the process, the best teachers lost interest in teaching, since there was little room left in the system for individuality.

> The way out of the success-to-the-successful trap is by leveling the playing field.

The way to avoid the wrong-goal trap is to separate *effort* from *outcome*. Any system directed toward effort is likely to produce effort. Any system directed toward outcome is likely to produce an outcome. So the measurements, indicators, and other feedback loops must be focused on the ultimate goal of the system, or risk the surprise of unintended consequences.

There are other archetypes as well, but you can see that the common threads are feedback loops and feedback delays, behaviors that make the world more complex and unpredictable than we'd like. As Grandma reminds us, "One thing leads to another." And another, and another, and another, until the result looks nothing like the intention. This could be extremely dangerous as our systems scale up in size and complexity in the Robotic Age.

Systems thinking is the counterweight to intuition, the metaskill that makes the best use of our rational brain. Donella Meadows sums it up like this: "Obvious. Yet subversive. An old way of seeing. Yet somehow new. Comforting, in that the solutions are in our hands. Disturbing, because we must do things, or at least see things and think about things, in a different way."

THE PRIMACY OF PURPOSE. The thing that exerts the most influence over a system is what's often the least obvious—its purpose. The purpose of a system is its overriding goal, the reason it exists. For example, the purpose of a thermostat is to keep the temperature at a predetermined level. The purpose of a blood cell is to carry oxygen throughout the body. The purpose of a leaf is to turn sunlight into energy. The purpose of a bicycle is to turn walking into riding.

These are relatively simple systems. As simple systems become more complex, they show signs of self-organizing. They begin to diversify, structure themselves, and adapt to external changes in order to maintain their existence and improve their chances for success. Think of plants, animals, companies, governments, societies, and ecosystems, all of which have the ability to respond to external changes on the fly. In a complex adaptive system, the purpose not only sets its direction, but suggests rules for behavior, produces feedback about performance, and addresses problems as they come up.

Social systems are particularly complex, since—let's face it—

they're full of people. Anyone serving on a committee can attest to the difficulty of working within a social system. Each member has a different personality, a different set of experiences, a different skillset, a different world view, a different relationship with each of the other members, and a different mood—depending on the time of day, what he or she had for breakfast, and an infinite number of other factors. Now scale the committee to the size of a company, community, or nation. The only hope of getting this many people to work together is a strong organizing purpose.

The organizing purpose of a company can be defined as the reason it exists beyond making money. Beyond making money? Isn't a company in business to make money? Yes, but if profits are primary, it may have trouble keeping customers, attracting talent, and building a culture that can sustain the business. Management expert Peter Drucker famously said that the only realistic definition of a business purpose was to create a customer. This may have been news to traditional business leaders a few decades ago, but even this is too narrow when measured against a backdrop of systems.

Let's look at some corporate purpose statements to see what kind of systems behavior they're likely to produce.

The stated purpose of Apple is "to make a contribution to the world by making tools for the mind that advance humankind."

The purpose of security-software maker Symantec is "to create confidence in a connected world."

The purpose of Patagonia, a maker of outdoor clothing, is "to inspire and implement solutions to an environment in crisis."

Now contrast these three statements with the following three.

The purpose of Chevron is "to achieve superior financial results for our stockholders, the owners of our business."

The purpose of Office Depot is "to be the most successful office products company in the world."

The purpose of Ametek is "to achieve enhanced, long-term shareholder value by building a strong operating company serving diversified markets to earn a superior return on assets and to generate growth in cash flow."

Which of these companies would you rather work for? Which

is most likely to turn you into a passionate customer? Which ones would people miss if they went out of business? And, finally, what do their purpose statements predict about their behavior? "Systems, like the three wishes in a fairy tale," says Meadows, "have a terrible tendency to produce exactly and only what you ask them to produce."

If a company's purpose is to achieve superior financial results, the company is likely to achieve superior financial results. In the process, it may also mistreat its employees, damage the environment, or bend the rules, which, over time, will undermine the very financial results it was seeking. If a company's purpose is to inspire solutions to the environmental crisis, it's likely to inspire solutions to the environmental crisis. And it's also likely to achieve decent financial results in the process, because it knows without sustained profits it can't carry out its higher purpose.

A company's purpose, norms, and shared meaning are the "self" that it organizes around, and which serves as a compass for all of its plans. This is the first step in building a durable brand. A participant in one of my brand strategy workshops summed it up nicely: "You can put your hat on first or you can put your boots on first. But before that, you have to decide you're a cowboy."

The *what* of purpose drives the *how* of behavior. Akio Toyoda explained that Toyota's recall crisis only happened because a few executives forgot their commitment to quality. "Some people just got too big-headed and focused too excessively on profit," he said. Maybe, but Toyota's purpose is "to sustain profitable growth by providing the best customer experience and dealer support." Were the executives simply sacrificing the *how* to get the *what*? A better purpose statement for Toyota might be "to bring the highest quality cars to the most people at the lowest price." Now there's a statement that leaves no ambiguity, and fits Toyota to a *T.*

A society, too, can have a purpose, although we may express it more as a vision. Comedian Eddie Izzard said that the American Dream is to work hard and buy a home, while the European Dream is to hardly work and own a motor scooter. Both of these seem like improvements on what's actually used to measure success—gross

In a healthy
organization,
goals support
the mission and
vision while the
mission and
vision support
the purpose.

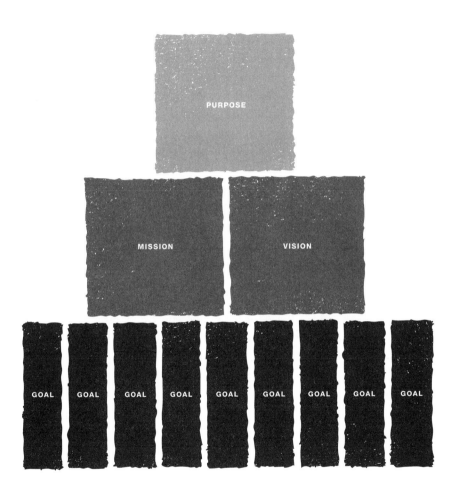

PURPOSE

MISSION

VISION

GOAL GOAL GOAL GOAL GOAL GOAL GOAL GOAL GOAL

THE STRATEGIC PYRAMID

national product. GNP is merely a record of consumption, bearing little resemblance to what gives a purpose to a society. In the United States, for example, our shared purpose is to thrive by virtue of a responsible commitment to freedom and happiness. Our purpose is not to continually increase consumption.

Robert F. Kennedy, during his 1968 election bid, clarified the difference with considerable eloquence: "The gross national product does not allow for the health of our children, the quality of their education or the joy of their play. It does not include the beauty of our poetry or the strength of our marriages, the intelligence of our public debate or the integrity of our public officials. It measures neither our wit nor our courage, neither our wisdom nor our learning, neither our compassion nor our devotion to our country; it measures everything, in short, except that which makes life worthwhile." By focusing on consumption rather than happiness, we're actually damaging both, because a happy society is a more productive one.

And what about you? Is there value in choosing a personal purpose? According to psychological research (and ordinary experience), having a sense of purpose is a powerful driver of happiness. A new field called *positive psychology* is exploding right now, based on evidence that people who live their lives with purpose are more likely to enjoy longevity, have better health, and stay free of dementia. In one seven-year study, people who reported a lesser sense of purpose were twice as likely to develop Alzheimer's disease than those who reported a greater sense of purpose.

The more consciously you define your personal purpose in life, the greater your chances of success and happiness. The Industrial Age discouraged the idea of individual purpose among workers, since it needed identical parts to plug into the big machine of business. The Robotic Age, on the other hand, rewards individual purpose, since it needs the creativity of flesh-and-blood humans who know who they are and think for themselves.

SIN EXPLAINED. One of the great gifts of religion has been the codification of good and bad into a system of rules that can easily be remembered, applied, and passed down from one generation to the next. The Ten Commandments are a good example of codification. In fact, the rules of all the world's religions are fairly similar, deriving from one master principle that says we should treat others the way we ourselves would like to be treated. When we break any of these rules, the infraction is called a sin.

But what exactly makes a sin a sin? Can we better understand the nature of sin by looking through the lens of systems? Yes, we can, and it could lead to our salvation. While the concept of commandments was practical in a simpler age, in today's era of financial derivatives, artificial intelligence, social networking, and genetic engineering, we need to think on our feet. We need to see the connections between actions and outcomes while taking latency into account. There are very few traditional sins that aren't also bad behaviors from a systems point of view. But there are many more bad behaviors that can't easily be codified into commandments. Systems thinking lets us dispense with a legalistic view of ethics and see with our own eyes how good and bad operate in the real world.

For example, "Thou shalt not kill" is a good rule of thumb, but it doesn't always hold true in actual practice. Depending on the culture and the situation, humans have known to kill convicted murderers, intruders, protesters, spies, unwanted fetuses, unfaithful women, and political enemies, all despite the fifth commandment.

Eisenhower warned against the military-industrial complex, but what about the military-religious complex? It's on full display in cathedrals such as Westminster Abbey in London, where the bloodiest warriors are enshrined alongside saints and clerics, often with more fanfare. Apparently, we take "Thou shalt not kill" and other commandments more as suggestions than as rules. Like Groucho Marx said, "These are my principles. If you don't like them, I have others."

> Systems thinking lets us see with our own eyes how good and bad operate in the real world.

The problem with commandments is that they're blunt instruments. They discourage reflection and encourage rule-beating. The Bible, like the Qur'an, is full of contradictory statements that can be used to support either helpful or harmful behaviors, though its spirit is clearly aimed towards truth, beauty, and goodness. If we're to make any progress in this direction, we need to stop using religious texts as rulebooks, and start thinking through the real consequences of our actions over time.

Truth is neither relative nor absolute. Philosophers of the Enlightenment believed everything could be known, and all truth is fixed. Postmodernists asserted that nothing could be known apart from its context, therefore all truth is relative. But systems thinkers are more likely to see truth simply as an evolutionary process of inquiry—dynamic, continuous, and communal—in which our notions of what is true and good become stronger and more widely accepted as we go.

In their parablelike book, *The Gardens of Democracy*, authors Eric Liu and Nick Hanauer call for a "new Enlightenment." They reject such dichotomies as modernism vs. postmodernism, liberalism vs. conservativism, and small government vs. big government. Instead they draw a distinction between self-interest and selfishness. They take the view that true self-interest is mutual interest. In a social system, there's no long-term winning unless everyone wins, and when some of us lose, we all lose. "It makes sense to be self-interested in the long run," they say. "It does not make sense to be reflexively selfish in every transaction."

We can easily tell ourselves that bad is actually good if we consider only the near and the now. For example, it felt really good

We can easily tell ourselves that bad is actually good if we consider only the *near* and the *now*.

to shove my friend under a bus yesterday when I was angry with him. It feels bad today, because I realize I'll miss him, and my actions will send waves of sadness and loss through the community for years to come. My bad behavior was initially good behavior—but only for me and only for the moment. This is the subtext of novelist P.D. James's mysteries. Instead of presenting murder as merely a puzzle to be solved, she goes further and reveals the crime's devastating effects on everyone connected with it.

A working definition of sin, therefore, is any act that values *selfish, short-term good* over *unselfish, long-term good*. From a systems viewpoint, evil is merely good that hasn't been thought through.

Why look at it this way? Because it makes human behavior more comprehensible, and it gives us a framework for assessing new or complex situations for which there are no commandments. Scientists have talked about a "dangerous flaw built into the brain" that causes a preference for instant gratification. Our feelings are thrilled by the prospect of quick rewards, but we're shortsighted when it comes to consequences.

To combat this tendency, we can ask ourselves two questions: 1) How will my action affect others? And 2) what will happen over time? When you play these out in your head, you may discover that what seemed like a good idea at first is not in anyone's long-term interest, including your own. Your ability to think whole thoughts—to see how one thing leads to another over time—is a crucial skill in the Robotic Age, given technology's scope for producing large-scale unintended consequences.

There's a persistent myth in the United States that citizens should be free to do whatever they want, provided they don't harm anyone else. On the surface, this seems like a logical extension of the Golden Rule: I'll give you your freedom if you give me mine. After Obama was elected president on a platform of change, a widely distributed bumper sticker appeared: "I'll keep my freedom, my guns, and my money—you can keep the change!" The underlying sentiment here is that our freedoms are under attack, including our inalienable rights to free speech, gun ownership, privacy, and so on. Unfortunately, there were no bumper stickers clamoring for inalienable *responsibilities*.

Ethics filter:
1) How will my action affect others?
2) What will happen over time?

In a systems view of democracy, responsibility and freedom are two sides of the same coin. "Freedom isn't free," say Liu and Hanauer. "It costs a little freedom." Generally speaking, the further your personal responsibility stretches—out from yourself and into the future—the more freedom you should be accorded. The more parsimonious you are with responsibility, the less freedom you should get. History shows that

High-level principles
can help us make
ethical decisions in a
fast-changing world.

1 START FROM CURIOSITY, NOT BELIEF	**6** GROW YOUR RESPONSIBILITY OUTWARD FROM YOURSELF
2 DISCOVER AND REFINE YOUR PERSONAL TRUTH	**7** INCREASE THE NUMBER OF CHOICES FOR EVERYONE
3 RESPECT THE PERSONAL TRUTHS OF OTHERS	**8** ENJOY AND CREATE BEAUTY IN ALL THINGS
4 PREFER BEING HELPFUL TO BEING RIGHT	**9** SERVE THE NEEDS OF NATURE
5 FAVOR LONG-TERM GOOD OVER SHORT-TERM GOOD	**10** EMBRACE LEARNING AND CHANGE

THE META COMMANDMENTS

giving broad freedoms to irresponsible people is a recipe for mayhem. This is especially true for rights that call for a high degree of responsibility, such as gun ownership. It's also true for business ownership. Milton Friedman believed that the only responsibility of business is to increase profits without engaging in deception or fraud. Really? What about bullying, pollution, or depleting natural resources? A behavior can be legal and still be irresponsible.

Economist Steven Landsburg, in *The Big Questions*, shares his own rule for good behavior: "Don't leave the world worse off than you found it." Unfortunately, simply living in the 21st century means you're doing damage to the planet. If you drive a car, buy groceries, use a computer, wear manufactured clothing, have children, own a home, fly to meetings, or read a newspaper, you're doing damage to the planet. While this may be the hand we were dealt by the Industrial Age, standing pat doesn't count as responsibility. "Don't tread on me" was a reasonable reaction to British rule during the War of Independence. But wrapping ourselves in the same flag, after dominating and polluting the planet for the last fifty years, is the behavior of a petulant child.

The answer is to move to a new model that asks for responsibility in fair proportion to freedom. Even children (except the petulant kind) appreciate the values of sharing and fairness. They seem to understand intuitively that you create the society you want by how you behave. A few years ago, educational leader Stephanie Pace Marshall was working with a group of students from a new middle school, and together they defined a set of rules for "belonging together." They came up with three: 1) Take care of yourself; 2) take care of each other; and 3) take care of this place. In fourteen simple words, they captured the credo of responsible autonomy.

Responsible autonomy means more than staying out of trouble. It means generating lasting goodness. Apalled by the atrocities of World War II, German sociologist Dr. Robert S. Hartman set about creating a new "science of value," which he hoped would organize goodness as efficiently as the Nazis had organized evil. He called his science *axiology*. Its goal was to study the values of ethics and aesthetics—ethics being the study of *right* and *good*, and aesthetics being the study of *beauty* and *harmony*—so they had a fighting chance against more fleeting values such as GDP and trade deficits. While axiology hasn't caught on as a mainstream science, it might be worth a second look.

We live in an "exaggerated present," says Donella Meadows. In other words, we pay too much attention to the now, and too little to the before and the after, giving us a warped view of what's important. Our preoccupation with measurement has taught us *how* to count, but not *what* to count, as if someone had changed the price tags while we weren't looking. Plus and minus, it seems, have become the new right and wrong.

The world is now too complex to be guided by ten simplistic commandments. We would need a thousand commandments to address all the decisions we face in modern life. "Thou shalt not create derivatives" might make sense in some situations but not in others, and also might spawn dozens of exceptions as we learn more about their effects in the real world. What we need instead are principles, meta-level guidelines that put the onus for specific actions where it belongs in the first instance—on the individual. By separating ethics from legality, we can start to see the bigger picture. We can embrace the kind of responsibility that increases autonomy, expands our choices, and creates lasting value.

"Living successfully in a world of systems requires more of us than our ability to calculate," says Meadows. "It requires our full humanity—our rationality, our ability to sort out truth from falsehood, our intuition, our compassion, our vision, and our morality."

THE PROBLEM WITH SOLUTIONS. A small country wants affordable energy for its growing population. Since it has an abiding concern for the quality of the environment and the health of its people, it comes to believe that the answer lies not in dirty coal power but in clean, renewable nuclear energy. It receives a great deal of encouragement, expertise, and financial help from a larger nation to make this initiative possible. Soon, fresh new power plants spring up around the countryside, and the environment improves. Yet the energy generated by the plants turns out to be anything but clean.

Live radioactive waste must be buried for up to ten thousand years before it's safe, and additional nuclear material must be contained in cooling pools where it's vulnerable to accidents. Eventually, a freak wave destroys a number of power plants, contaminating the environment and damaging the very health the country was trying to protect.

A young woman dreams of becoming a lawyer so she can devote herself to social issues. Wanting the best possible education, she enrolls in a well-respected college. She's not eligible for scholarships and takes out $150,000 in loans to cover the cost of tuition, books, housing, food, and transportation for six years of schooling. She graduates at the top of her class. However, due to a difficult job market, she's unable to find a position that pays enough to cover her loan payments. She goes to work for a firm that defends socially irresponsible companies from class-action suits, thereby betraying her own dreams.

A new CEO is hired to turn around a public company with eroding profit margins. He goes to work trimming any costs that are not likely to lead to immediate revenues. He offers "early out" retirement packages to highly paid managers and lays off a large percentage of employees who aren't involved in sales. He then divides the company into separate businesses, giving each manager the autonomy to run his or her business in a manner that increases revenues. Profits improve. He soon forges a strong bond with analysts, who begin to trust his quarterly earnings guidance. After a few years of steady financial gains, however, the company finds that its brand is no longer coherent, and the products in its pipeline are less than exciting. Earnings decline. Shareholders become nervous, so the directors find a way to remove him. The new CEO inherits a company that's worse off than before, and he's unable to fix the deepening systemic problems.

These are all true stories of how solutions can turn into problems. With complex systems such as companies, governments, and markets, the answers aren't always obvious. The difficulty is that they can *seem* obvious. Even when decision makers find the right levers, they often pull them in the wrong direction. A driver whose car skids on an icy road is more likely to turn the wheel the wrong way than the right way, simply because the right way is counter-intuitive. A CEO whose company suffers from sagging profits is likely to focus on costcutting instead of innovation, simply because the rewards are more direct and immediate.

There's a Sufi parable that goes like this: You think that because you understand *one* that you also understand *two*, since one and one make two; but you forget that you must also understand *and*. When we encounter a system that's complex enough to create multiple interactions, we need to beware of traps. Truly complex systems are not only riddled with traps, but can also be reactive, meaning that they fight back when we try to fix them. Thus was born the concept of wicked problems. The Israeli-Palestinian conflict is a wicked problem, as is the global economic crisis. Every solution seems to make the problem worse.

With complex systems the answers aren't always obvious—the difficulty is that they can *seem* obvious.

If we see that pulling a lever a short distance gives us a desirable response, we might think that pulling it twice as far will produce double the response. It certainly might, but if the system is complex enough, it might produce a much smaller response, or the response times ten, or an opposite response. For example, redesigning a supermarket package with a little more yellow might boost sales, but doubling the amount of yellow could kill sales. Nonlinear problems like packaging graphics can utterly confound the relationship between cause and effect.

When complex systems meet simple measurement, the results can be perverse. In the 1930s we began measuring our welfare by the goods and services we produce each year. It wasn't long before productivity became the Holy Grail for the entire society, replacing the previous goal of happiness with one that's more easily measured. This is the cultural equivalent of the drunk who forgets his car keys in the bar, but searches for them under the street lamp because the light is better.

Economist Victor Lebow introduced the term "conspicuous consumption" in the 1950s, complaining that we'd already begun to ritualize the purchase of goods in search of spiritual satisfaction.

"We need things consumed, burned up, replaced, and discarded at an ever-accelerating rate." The result has not been happiness, nor spirituality, nor economic health, but a national shopping jones that's turning our birthright into a landfill. Too harsh? We'll see.

Narrow measurement has also dogged educational reform, often producing exactly the opposite effect that we wanted. When we measured our progress in dollars spent per student, we got an increase in dollars spent per student. When we measured performance on standardized tests, we got improved performance on standardized tests. Meanwhile, the quality of education continued to sink. Football coach Vince Lombardi famously said, "If winning isn't everything, why do they keep score?" It's axiomatic in sports, education, business, and government that whatever gets measured gets better. So the lesson is this: Be careful what you measure; the scoreboard can easily become the game.

Is there a way to ensure that our proposed solutions are actually solutions? Probably not. But when you understand that complex systems don't behave in linear ways, you can often rule out linear solutions and measurements that produce nasty surprises. There's no such thing as a foolproof system. Anyone who says otherwise is underestimating the ingenuity of fools. All you can do is adopt a humble attitude and look at the challenge from a number of perspectives. Here are some questions to ask before tinkering with a system:

What will happen if I do nothing?
What might be improved?
What might be diminished?
What will be replaced?
Will it expand future options?
What are the ethical considerations?
Will it simplify or complicate the system?
Are my basic assumptions correct?
What has to be true to make this possible?
Are events likely to unfold this way?
If so, will the system really react this way?

What are the factors behind the events?
What are the long-term costs and benefits?

We shouldn't become too discouraged if at first we don't succeed. It took nature 13 billion years to create the systems around us, and they still don't always work perfectly.

THE ART IS IN THE FRAMING. The art of designing solutions starts with the frame. Where you draw the boundaries of an investigation will determine, in large part, what your conclusions will be and what kind of process you'll use to get there.

For example, if you decide to publish a business book, you could frame the principal problem like this: "How can I write a 60,000-word volume on my subject?" The solution would then become mostly one of quantity, and the process would be all about generating enough material to fill 300 pages.

Or you could frame it like this: "Where can I find a company who'll distribute my ideas to the world?" The solution then would be landing a publisher, and the process would include sending a manuscript to a large number of publishing houses or agents until it finds a home.

Or you could frame the problem more broadly: "How can I contribute to the understanding of my audience using self-paced content?" The solution here might be a 300-page book—but it also might be a 100-page book, or a series of books. It might be an e-book, an audio book, an app, a video, a self-paced online course, or some combination of vehicles. It might include more than words, such as illustrations, animation, video, navigational devices, or social connectivity. The process would be whatever steps were necessary to achieve the solution.

One way to conceive a frame is in two dimensions, one for scope and one for novelty. A solution can be big or small, and it can be conventional or unconventional. This model will produce four basic combinations: small and conventional, large and conventional, small and unconventional, and large and unconventional. Each of these subframes will produce a different solution.

Let's say, for example, we think clean drinking water will soon be in short supply, and we'd like to solve the problem before it becomes a global disaster. We could start by framing it four simple ways: 1) How can we create an affordable product that will purify water at the household level? (Small and conventional); 2) How can we build large water purification plants that can serve millions of households through existing plumbing systems? (Large and conventional); 3) How can we "manufacture" drinking water at the local level? (Small and unconventional); 4) How can we "manufacture" drinking water on a global scale? (Large and unconventional).

The small-conventional solution might be something like the filtration products Brita already sells, but for less money or with smarter materials.

The large-conventional solution might be similar to our existing water plants, but with better purification systems or better distribution methods.

The small-unconventional solution might be something not yet invented, such as a household appliance that combines hydrogen and oxygen or a low-cost version of the Whisson Windmill, a device that uses wind power to collect water from the atmosphere.

And the large-unconventional solution, to imagine one example, might be to use rising sea levels to flood coastal deserts, turning them into marshlands that remove salt and produce clean water, as the Seawater Foundation proposes. The type of frame you choose determines the type of solution you get.

In 2005, MIT professor Nicholas Negroponte had a world-changing idea. He and product designer Yves Behar would design a computer so simple, so durable, and so portable that children in underdeveloped countries could have access to the same educational resources as children in advanced countries. They called their initiative One Laptop Per Child. They succeeded admirably within their frame, but eventually learned that they had drawn it too small. They had neglected to solve the problems outside the problem, such as how to build a barrier to competition, how to navigate government bureaucracies, and how to change entrenched views about education. It was one of the most heartrending belly-flops of the digital age, due to the wrong choice of frame.

Of course, there are other possible dimensions to framing besides size and novelty. But what any kind of framing does is to protect us from accepting extreme opposites as the only alternatives. Whenever we become overwhelmed by complex problems, we're susceptible to false dichotomies. Should the Internet be free, or should we let large media companies control what we can see? Should I go into debt to get a college degree, or should I resign myself to a lower income? Should our company invest in innovation, or should we make our shareholders happy? These are examples of options that make our decisions easy by reducing the question to *which* instead of *what*. In the face of complexity, our default mode is multiple choice—we prefer shopping to creating. We've been trained by Industrial Age marketers to believe anything good is already on the shelf.

> We've been trained by Industrial Age marketers to believe anything good is already on the shelf.

When Einstein was asked which part of the Theory of Relativity gave him the most fits, he said: "Figuring out how to think about the problem." In another interview he said that if he knew a fiery comet was certain to destroy the earth in an hour, and it was his job to head it off, he would spend the first fifty-five minutes defining the problem and the last five minutes solving it. John Dewey had famously said that "a problem well defined is half solved." Einstein apparently believed it was more than 90% solved.

But what would Einstein's fifty-five minutes look like in everyday circumstances? Are there any universal techniques for drawing the edges of a problem? Luckily, there are. Here's a short course in the art of framing.

1. *View the problem from multiple angles.* Like it or not, we all get stuck in our own belief systems. The easiest way to get free is to look at the problem from three positions: our own viewpoint (known as *first position*), other people's viewpoints (known as *second position*), and the viewpoint from a higher-order system (known as a *metaposition*).

Seeing a problem from your own viewpoint comes naturally, of course. Putting yourself in the shoes of other people is more difficult. And getting outside the system to view it objectively takes a conscious effort. The outside viewpoint, or *metaposition*, is more attainable when you climb up to a higher level and look down on the problem. For example, if your personal view of your company's reorganization is that your job may be in danger, seeing it from a strategic viewpoint might reveal how it might unleash some opportunity for you as it makes the company stronger.

Leonardo believed that unless you could see a problem from at least three vantage points, you'd have trouble understanding it. When he designed the world's first bicycle, he looked at the problem first from his own point of view, from the rider's point of view, from the investors' point of view, and from the point of view of the communities where the bicycles might be used.

2. *Develop a problem statement.* Scott Adams, the creator of the "Dilbert" comic strip, is not only a witty observer but an insightful thinker. In a *Wall Street Journal* editorial he described the current budget deficit in a way that could be a model for all problem statements.

Problem statement: The US is broke. The hole is too big to plug with cost cutting or economic growth alone. Rich people have money. No one else does. Rich people have enough clout to block higher taxes on themselves, and they will.

Likely outcome: Your next home will be the box that your laser printer came in.

The beauty of this problem statement lies in its brevity and simplicity (no extra charge for the wit). If you think this kind of concision is easy, just try it!

> The outside viewpoint, or metaposition, is more attainable when you climb up to a higher level and look down on the problem.

3. *List the knowns and unknowns.* What are the known parameters of the problem? Can you visualize and name the parts? What are the relationships among the parts? What is the nature of the problem? Is it a simple problem? A complex problem? A structural problem? A communication problem? A political problem? What remedies have been attempted in the past, and why have they failed? Why bother solving the problem in the first place?

Of course, the knowns of a problem are one thing, and the unknowns are another. The danger with unknowns is the human tendency to replace them with assumptions. It's important to question whether the knowns are really knowns and not beliefs in disguise. Usually the best way to deal with unknowns is to let them remain a mystery while you forge ahead. They may reveal themselves as you test your hypotheses.

4. *Change the frame.* What happens when you make the frame bigger or smaller? Or even swap it for another one? For example, the movie industry now believes its biggest challenge is to stop piracy. But what if the problem were reframed?

Original problem statement: Viewers are accessing copyrighted content without paying for it, resulting in millions in lost revenue.

Likely outcome: If piracy isn't stopped, there will be little incentive to make movies.

Solution: Enact tougher laws against piracy.

So far, piracy laws haven't moved the needle, so it's unclear whether harsher ones will make a difference. They may simply drive piracy underground, or even cause a backlash among viewers. What if the problem were reframed?

New problem statement: Viewers have unprecedented free access to copyrighted material through the Internet, and there's little chance of stemming the tide.

Likely outcome: Unless the movie industry changes its models, it will miss out on the exciting possibilities created by advances in technology.

When the problem is stated this way, it looks more like an opportunity than a threat. Systems thinker Gene Bellinger says, "It's hard to make water flow uphill." Maybe the solution is to increase the flow of free content, and use it to create deeper relationships with viewers so that movies become a bigger part of their lives. Or maybe access could be restricted to new content only, using the old content as advertising for the new. Or maybe free downloads can produce valuable information about audiences, thereby adding value to future marketing efforts. Then again, maybe the

> Models are always wrong in that they don't serve as detailed illustrations. That's also why they're right.

movie industry can simply reduce its lobbying efforts, save a little money, and let time take care of the problem. It all starts with how you frame the problem.

5. *Make a simple model.* Constructing a model is a practical way of visualizing the key elements of a problem. Statistician George Box once said, "Essentially, all models are wrong, but some are useful." Models are always wrong in that they don't serve as detailed illustrations of the problem. This is also why they're right. The simpler you can make a model, the easier it is to understand the problem.

In *The Gardens of Democracy*, the authors simplify the problem of political gridlock by dividing the prevailing attitudes toward government into three main categories. Liberals, they say, believe in *big what* and *big how.* They believe the government should not only determine the direction of the country, but also supply the plan and the capital for getting there. Conservatives, however, believe in *small what* and *small how,* meaning that the public sector shouldn't determine the direction of the country or supply the wherewithal to get there. Libertarians are more extreme than conservatives. They want a government of *no what, no how.* The government in this model is *laissez faire,* doing the absolute minimum to determine the country's direction or to help it get there. Citizens in this model are on their own.

The authors then introduce a fourth model, *big what* and *small how.* In this model, the government has responsibility for setting the country's overall direction, but leaves the *how*—the tactical solutions—to individuals and the marketplace. The government's role is to name the game and level the playing field, while each citizen plays the game as he or she sees fit.

Obviously, these models are simplified to the extreme. Yet that's precisely why they work. By stripping away the details it's possible to glimpse a solution. After that, the necessary details can be added back in.

As practitioners in the creative and scientific fields master their professions, the art of *framing* problems eventually leads to the art of *finding* problems. Experience teaches which problems are worth solving, and which, if solved, would produce little significant effect. It also teaches which problems are most likely to be personally satisfying. Professionals know that even the toughest mysteries will give up their secrets under the pressure of unrelenting passion.

But where do you find problems that are both worthy and inspiring? While they could arrive from the blue, you can also hunt them down using questions like these:

> *What's the either/or that's obscuring opportunities for innovation?*
> *Where are the usual methods no longer achieving the predicted results?*
> *What's the can't-do that you could turn into a can-do?*
> *Which problems are so big that they can no longer be seen?*
> *Which categories or sectors exhibit the most uneven rates of change?*
> *In which area is there a great deal of interest but very few solutions?*
> *Where can you find too little order or too much order?*
> *Which of your talents could be scaled up in some surprising way?*
> *To what new areas could your passion take you?*

Feeling and seeing are complementary skills that work best when they're balanced. If we rely too much on intuition and not enough on rational thinking, we're like likely to create self-indulgent solutions that don't map to the real world. If it's the other way around, we're likely to miss out on the flashes of insight that fuel innovation.

While many of us have a natural ability in feeling or seeing or both, these can also be developed, nurtured, or strengthened with practice. In my experience, people who claim that all talent is inborn—you either have it or you don't—are often masking insecurity. The "born geniuses" know the truth: In developing talent, hard work trumps genetics. This is even true for the next talent, the amazing metaskill of *dreaming*.

DREAMING

3

BRILLIANT BEYOND REASON. Imagination is one of the more mysterious capabilities of the human mind. How is it possible to conjure up images, feelings, or concepts that we can't perceive through our senses? How can we arrive at perfectly workable solutions without the benefit of logical thought? Is imagination learnable, or is it only the preserve of eccentric artists and mad scientists?

The metaskill of imagination is conspicuously absent from the educational system. There are no classes called "Dreaming 101." Alexander Graham Bell, arguably one of our more prolific inventors, seemed to be unaware of the role of imagination in his own work. He laid down three rules for innovation: 1) Observe as many worthwhile facts as possible; 2) Remember what has been observed; 3) Compare the facts so as to come to conclusions.

Observe, remember, compare—then *presto!*—idea. Hello? Alex? Could there be anything missing between comparing and concluding? Like maybe an insight? No disrespect to the telephone, but since when does the comparison of facts produce innovation?

Let's say I compared a number of worthwhile facts about social media. I observed the ways people use Facebook, noted the increase in worldwide tweets, mapped the behavior of Pinterest users, and measured the market for advertising potential and investor interest. Then I compared these facts. While I might find them interesting, I would still need some insight, spark, or leap of imagination to out-innovate competitors who have access to the same facts. Bell's formula reminds me of the Monty Python skit in which a man is interviewed about how to make a million pounds. "First," he says, "get a million pounds."

When people talk about "dreaming up" an idea, they're not far from the truth. Imagination is closely linked to dream states. Neuroscientists Charles Limb and Allen Braun studied the brains of jazz musicians, revealing a "disassociated pattern of activity in the prefrontal cortex" when they played improvisational music. They found it was absent when they played memorized sequences. These disassociated patterns, they say, are similar to what happens in REM sleep. Dreaming is marked by a sense of unfocused attention, unplanned or irrational associations, and an apparent loss of control. When students exhibit this behavior in the classroom, teachers call it attention-deficit/hyperactivity disorder. When musicians exhibit it, we call it genius.

Dreams don't simply visit us. We actively *create* them while we're unconscious, not unlike the way we create our perceptions while we're awake. What makes dreams so fascinating is the absence of logical narrative. The word for dreaming in French is *rêver*—to rave, to slip into madness. Even though the scenes we create in our dreams may seem random or fantastical, their emotional trajectory often makes complete sense. Our emotions are fully engaged while our reasoning is disconnected.

What if we could harness this capability at will? Wouldn't this provide the mental leap needed to connect the facts to a new conclusion? As it happens, there's no other way to do it. Innovation needs a little controlled madness, like the controlled explosions of an internal combustion engine, to move it forward. Applied imagination is the ability to harness dreaming to a purpose. Innovators, then, are just practical dreamers.

The encouraging news from science is that people who have this talent are no smarter on average than other people. They've simply learned the "trick" of divergent thinking. Biographer Walter Isaacson described this quality in Steve Jobs: "Was he smart? No, not exceptionally. Instead, he was a genius. His imaginative leaps were instinctive, unexpected, and at times magical." Jobs had the ability to make connections that other people couldn't see, simply because they couldn't let go of what they already knew.

In order to innovate, you need to move from the known to the unknown. You need to hold your beliefs lightly, so that what you believe doesn't block your view of what you might find out. This is hard for most people. When asked to imagine a new tool for slicing bread, or a new format for a website, or a new melody for a song, they'll stare blankly as if to say, "How could there be such a thing?" They may recall many of the knives, or the home pages, or popular songs they've known, but nothing new will come to mind. At most they might try to combine the features of two or more existing examples to come up with a hybrid.

Originality is
the product of
imagination and
knowledge.

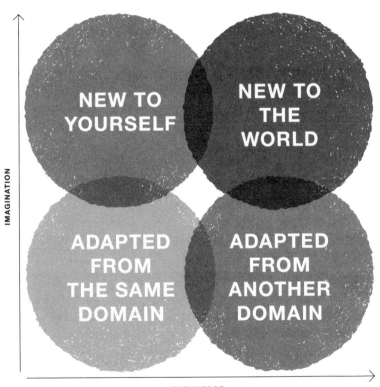

Why is this? What's stopping us from using our imagination? We can only guess that our world of ready-made everything has turned us into a population of idea shoppers. We expect to choose our solutions off the rack instead of building them from scratch. We mix them and mash them, never believing that real originality is within our power. And the companies that make our products are not much different. They shop for *best practices* to make their jobs easier, instead of imagining *new practices* that could set them apart or push them forward. Somewhere along the line we've lost our tolerance for trial and error, settling instead for the derivative, the dull, and the *dis*-integrated. We need to reverse this trend. If we don't, we'll end up low on the Robot Curve.

Originality doesn't come from factual knowledge, nor does it come from the suppression of factual knowledge. Instead, it comes from the exposure of factual knowledge to the animating force of imagination. Depending on the quality of knowledge and the level of imagination applied to it, an idea can fall into four categories: 1) an idea adapted from the same domain; 2) an idea adapted from a different domain; 3) an idea that is new to the innovator; 4) an idea that is new to the world. These are listed in ascending order, with "new to the world" being the rarest and most valuable. The path of learning starts with the more modest forms of originality and leads to larger ones over time.

Imagination is a renewable resource. It doesn't get depleted by use, but instead grows stronger with practice. When you learn the trick of dreaming, of disassociating your thoughts from the linear and the logical, you can become a wellspring of originality and brilliance. A client once asked architect Mark Kirkhart how he was able to produce so many fresh concepts for a single building. He said: "I have ideas I haven't even had yet."

Originality comes from exposing factual knowledge to the animating force of imagination.

Like all types of magic, dreaming is the result of practice. There are no shortcuts, only diversions and mental traps. In the following chapters I'll let you in on the hidden discipline that allows innovators to produce their acrobatic leaps of imagination.

THE ANSWER-SHAPED HOLE. The number-one hazard for innovators is getting stuck in the tar pits of knowledge. Knowledge has a powerful influence over creativity. While it can free us to imagine new-to-the-world ideas, it can also trap us into believing opportunities are smaller than they are. When we're stumped by a problem, or when we feel hurried to solve it, our brains can easily default to off-the-shelf solutions based on "what everyone knows." The problem-solving mind is a sucker for a pretty fact. But what we know today may not be what we need to know tomorrow, since every challenge brings with it new requirements for understanding.

Arthur Conan Doyle, in the voice of Sherlock Holmes, expressed something similar when he said, "It is a capital mistake to theorize before one has data. Insensibly, one begins to twist facts to suit theories, instead of theories to suit facts." To avoid jumping to conclusions, we need to hold off solving a problem until we can perceive the general shape of its solution. There are three steps in generating the answer to a problem: 1) discover *what is*; 2) imagine *what could be*; and 3) describe the attributes of success. Let's take them one by one.

What is. This is the body of known facts about a problem. Why is it a problem? What is its history? What is the conventional thinking about it? How have similar problems been solved in the past? In other domains? Other cultures? And what are the practical constraints of the problem?

Constraints are the limitations imposed by the subject matter, or by the context, of a problem. They might have to do with budgets, time, manpower, physics, habits, conventions, or human fears. They squeeze the problem down to a size you can focus on. They force you to writhe uncomfortably in its grip while you struggle to break free. Without constraints, solutions tend towards the ungainly, the unfocused, and the unimaginative. Unbounded challenges are anathema to innovators, draining their energy without delivering insight. Bounded challenges provide not only a starting place but a booster shot of adrenaline.

Louis Pasteur, in a famous 1854 lecture at the University of Lille, said: "*Dans les champs de l'observation, le hasard ne favorise que les esprit préparés.*" In the field of observation, chance favors only the prepared mind. Pasteur's statement is often used to support the idea that hard work trumps talent, but it also suggests that the better you understand the facts and constraints, the better your chances of solving the problem.

What could be. Facts and constraints are necessary but insufficient. To envision what's possible, you also need imagination. If innovation is determined by what's "useful, novel, and nonobvious," as the US patent system puts it, then you need ways to get beyond the obvious. One such way is by asking deeper questions.

For example, let's say you run a marketing department in a large company. The director of marketing, or perhaps the CEO, asks you to address declining revenues by improving the company's advertising. You could figure out how the existing campaign might be improved with stronger headlines, better product photography, or more precise targeting. Or you could go a little deeper and think about the strategy of the campaign, questioning the underlying concept. You could go deeper still and ask whether advertising is the best place to address the revenue decline. Maybe the real problem lies in product positioning, requiring a shift in brand strategy to outmaneuver the competition. Then again, you might wonder if positioning can save a product line that's become commoditized over time. Or maybe the problem is the company itself, increasingly hampered by an outdated business model or an uninspired workforce. As the questions go deeper, the answers get bigger.

When Thomas Edison imagined the light bulb, he didn't frame the question as, How can we create an alternative source of light? Instead he framed it as, How can we make electricity so cheap that "only the rich will burn candles"? While you can easily overreach the possibilities by thinking too big, it's much easier to tame a wild idea than reanimate a dead one. The best problem solvers are "high yearners," people who reach for the stars and land on the moon.

The attributes of success. The shape of the missing answer is formed at the intersection of *affordances* and *desiderata*. Affordances are the counterpoint to constraints. They consist of creative possibilities that are native to the subject, the method, the tools, or the challenge. For example, a movie about the early days of movies contains the possibility of being a silent film (*The Artist*). A car designed for the poor population of India contains the possibility of being extremely minimal (Tata Motors). A company with a breadth of experience but a commoditized product line has the possibility becoming a consulting firm (IBM).

Desiderata are secondary objectives that support a goal or a solution. I once hired a pair of young architects to help me build out a new office space. My company was a startup, so the budget for design and construction was modest. Yet I needed to leave my clients with a memorable experience, and also create a convivial and productive environment for my employees. The desiderata included the budget (small), the hoped-for look (stunning), the number of workspaces (15), the type of workstation privacy (semi-open), and the need for electrical outlets where there were none.

The architects came back with a plan to spend my entire budget on a single element: a large, curving wall of translucent, corrugated plastic that contained interior uplighting and electrical outlets to feed the entire workspace. Inside the wall was a huge logo looming softly over the reception area. In a single move, this simple but inspired solution established the identity for the new firm, separated the client spaces from the working spaces, supplied electricity to the workstations, and created a buzzworthy experience for visitors. When I asked the two how they were able to conceive such a surprising solution, they grinned at each other and replied in unison: "Talent."

The principle of desiderata can be applied to any number of problems. It's really as simple as compiling a wish list. Ask yourself this question and fill in the blank: Wouldn't it be great if _____? When you finish your list, call out the wishes that would create the most compelling outcome. These will form a sort of matrix, a convergence of vectors that define the shape of the answer. When the answer appears, it'll pop into place like the final piece of a jigsaw puzzle.

THERE BE DRAGONS! The frame of a problem is not a comfortable place. It's filled with tension, confusion, danger, and doubt. It's a veritable dragon pit of unresolved conflict. On one side you've got the reality of *what is,* or *what is common,* and on the other side you've got a vision for *what could be,* or *what could be different.* In between lies a battle. For this reason most people are eager to get in, make a decision, and get out. But creative people know they have to stay in the dragon pit because that's where the ideas are.

The uncomfortable tension between *what is* and *what could be* creates a mental spark gap—a space between two poles that can only be bridged by a leap of imagination. If you close the gap too quickly by making the easy decision, there's no spark. If you keep it open longer, ideas and insights will start to appear in rapid succession.

Pretend you're a commercial farmer growing tomatoes for a living. On one side you feel competitive pressure to use more pesticides and chemical fertilizers to increase yields and control costs. On the other side you face mounting criticism from environmental groups and customers who are calling for organic farming methods. The quickest fix is to decide one way or the other—either go large and commercial or small and organic. However, neither is a very good solution. The demand for low prices will continue, and the desire for organic produce will keep growing. By staying in the pit it's possible to imagine a third alternative that exists outside this simple dichotomy.

How, you ask? By learning to embrace paradox. A *paradox* is a proposition that contains two contradictory thoughts while expressing a truth. For example, Thoreau's statement that "the swiftest traveler is he that goes afoot" would seem to be a contradiction. Everyone knows that walking is not the fastest mode of travel, but the paradox contains an idea: You might make more progress by keeping things simple. Or you might learn faster by doing things the hard way. By expressing a problem as a paradox, you force your mind to look for new answers.

Physicist Niels Bohr found that by holding two opposing thoughts in his mind at the same time he was able to move his

The frame
of a problem
forms the
dragon pit.

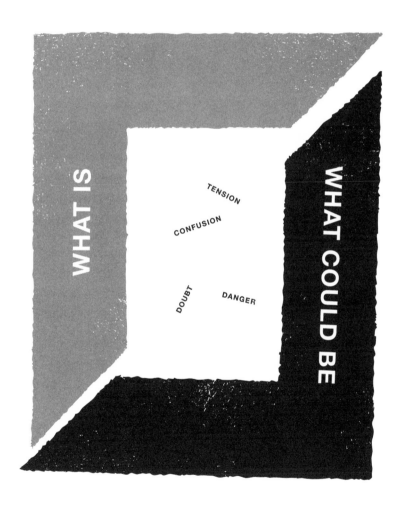

imagination to a higher level. In some cases, like the problem of understanding electrons, the paradox he met with was actually the answer. *Complementarity,* now a basic principle of quantum theory, proves that an electron can be both a wave and a particle at the same time, even though it can't be viewed both ways at once. While it confounds our sense of reality, it's true nevertheless.

The uncomfortable tension between what is and what could be creates a mental spark gap.

One of the qualities of a genius is a strong tolerance for ambiguity. This is often difficult, because the human brain seeks closure. We're uncomfortable with the feeling of cognitive dissonance, of not knowing the right answer. And a brain that doesn't like paradox is one that jumps to any conclusion, right or wrong, that can end the debate. The secret to getting the most out of your imagination is to keep the problem in a liquid state as long as possible.

The scientific tool of *hypothesis,* defined as a testable supposition, is less science than art. It's more akin to the maquette of the sculptor or the preliminary sketch of the painter than the provable truths we associate with the scientist. The painter has to be willing to draw badly or paint uncertainly while working through a new composition. "Art needs to incubate, to sprawl a little, to be ungainly and misshapen before it finally emerges as itself," says Julia Cameron, author of *The Artist's Way.* "The ego hates this fact. It wants instant gratification and the addictive hit of an acknowledged win." Creative thinking, whether in the service of art or science, requires that we postpone gratification while we try out different approaches.

New ideas can't be proved in advance. This comes close to being a tautology, as if saying, "New ideas are new." Yet the ways we're taught to use logic don't account for this simple fact. We're taught to reason using only deduction and induction, two methods handed down from the Greeks that make little use of imagination. *Deduction* is the logic of argument, drawing specific conclusions from general rules. *Induction* is the logic of educated guesses, drawing general conclusions from specific observations. While both of these are helpful in judging a hypothesis, neither is suitable for creating a hypothesis. For this we need a third kind of thinking called *abduction*, the nonlogic of *what could be*.

If architect Frank Gehry had used logical reasoning as a starting place for his projects, he never could have invented the swooping, shimmering forms of Bilbao's Guggenheim Museum. He would have designed a very nice building that the city could be proud of, but that few tourists would consider a destination. To escape the trap of logic, he started by drawing shapes that made use of his imagination, emotion, and gestural instincts. Undoubtedly, many of these were "ungainly and misshapen," but something mysterious and satisfying began to emerge, a highly sculptural edifice with the curving forms of a sailing ship. He called this stage "capturing the dream." It's not the result of logic but of nonlinear thinking, a conscious choice to avoid the deeply rutted road.

The search for innovation is progressive, starting with the most obvious ideas and moving further out with each attempt. First ideas are rarely the best ideas, and real innovators recognize this. They force themselves to climb onward and upward until they arrive in virgin territory. In some creative circles, this is known as "third-pasture thinking." When horses are let into a pasture, most will be content to eat the grass they find there, even though it's been trampled by previous herds. Some horses, however, will move up into a higher pasture where the grass is slightly fresher. One or two others will climb all the way to the third pasture, where the grass is pristine and new.

By expressing the problem as a paradox, you force your mind to look for new answers.

The New Yorker hosts a popular contest in which readers are invited to fill in the caption for a new cartoon. Tellingly, the editors found that about 20 percent of contestants would come up with the same funny line for the cartoon. Very few would make the leap to a surprising and concisely written caption that rose beyond the simply logical. Those 20 percent got stuck in the second pasture. They probably never realized there were fresher ideas further up the hill.

The proper approach to invention is not logic but wonderment. Creative thinking begins with phrases like "I wonder," "I wish," and "what if." It sets out from a position of not knowing, then winds slowly and circuitously through the problem until it finds something unexpected and untried. It then takes that something—the so-called "germ of an idea"—and begins to poke and pull and twist it until it resembles something new. It only attains the status of knowledge when it's been tested in the real world. How does it get to the real world? Through the dogged persistence of a dragon slayer.

A MOST UNPLEASANT YOUNG MAN. Steve Jobs, a cofounder of Apple Computer, was only 30 when I interviewed him in 1985. Back then I was the part-time editor of a design journal, and the interview was to be the highlight of a two-issue cover story. I could hardly wait to meet the man behind the Macintosh.

Right from the start it didn't go well. We argued. I don't know how this happened, because my only task was to pose questions and record the answers on a pocket tape recorder. Maybe it was similar to what occurs when you place the negative poles of two magnets together: they repel each other. I still wince when I remember the interview.

> ME: What's this device here on the table?
> STEVE: It's new. It's called a LaserWriter. You can print whatever you see on the screen.
> ME: You're kidding—that's fantastic!
> STEVE: No big deal. We just buy these from another company.
> ME: I see it has an Apple trademark on it. And the trademark looks a little different. Is that new, too?
> STEVE: Yeah, we've updated our logo.
> ME: You mean the typographical part?
> STEVE: No, I mean the symbol part. *Logo* is Latin for *symbol.*
> ME: Actually, it's Greek for *word.* I thought maybe you changed the letterforms, too.
> STEVE: You're wrong. *Logo* means *symbol.*
> ME: Okay.
> STEVE: It's Latin, not Greek.
> ME: Okay.

STEVE: What I like about our logo is that it's completely unique.

ME: Hmm, I thought it might have been a witty homage to Apple Records.

STEVE: That's absurd.

ME: Well, it's not completely unique, because I designed a similar trademark about eight years ago—an apple with a bite taken out of it—for an educational company. (I happened to have a copy of the awards annual in which it appeared. I shared. There was a pause.)

STEVE: Ours is better.

ME: Can you tell me who designed it?

STEVE: I have no idea.

ME: Well, I guess we don't have to credit the designer.

STEVE: Any other questions?

ME: I guess not.

STEVE: Then I think we're done.

I drove home feeling sick. I had the man of the year all to myself, and the best I could do was spar with him.

My wife kindly offered to transcribe the tapes, which also contained interviews with several other Apple executives. When she got to the last interview, she threw her headphones to the floor. "Who is this guy?"

"I think you mean Steve Jobs."

"Well, he's extremely unpleasant."

Apple's board of directors agreed. Three weeks later they forced him to leave the company he founded. When he returned after nearly 12 years in exile, the company's value had shriveled to about $4 billion, a fraction of Hewlett-Packard's $62 billion valuation. Yet over the next 12 years under his strong-willed leadership, Apple's value rocketed to $184 billion, surpassing the worth of both Hewlett-Packard and Dell put together. By the time of his death in 2011, Apple had become the world's most valuable company.

What was it about Jobs that enabled this level of success? Was it his immaculate design sense? His visionary stewardship? His Buddhist leanings? His vegan food preferences? His Sixties idealism?

The adoration of his adoptive parents? His belief that he was chosen to "put a dent in the universe"?

Probably all that. But there's one more thing, and it's readily apparent in the conversation above: He was a prime contrarian. If you said the sky was blue, he said it was wide. If you said a trademark couldn't be printed in three colors, he would stamp his feet until he got six. As a designer, he was slow to recognize the potential of another person's idea. But after knocking it around in his head for a while he would often take ownership of it.

A key characteristic of an inventive mind is a strong *disbelief* system. Einstein and Picasso were dyed-in-the-wool skeptics. Einstein's physics professor once told him, "You are quite smart, but you have one big failing. You never listen to anybody." Similarly, Picasso's lithographer Fernand Mourlot once said, "Picasso looked, listened, and then did exactly the opposite of what was shown him." In science and art, as well as in other fields, innovation is an act of rebellion. You have to reject conformity if you're looking for brilliance.

The challenge, then, is how to put contrarian thinking to work without alienating the people you depend on. I have a few suggestions:

Learn to recognize judgments. Develop an ear for authoritative pronouncements about second-order reality—the world of meaning, not fact—and subject them to questioning. "Who says?" is a good place to start. Another is "So what? A third is "Why not?" You don't have to be rude, just curious.

Dare to be wrong. What would the answer be if you reversed one or more of the assumptions? What would happen if you did the opposite of what other people would do? As the saying goes, "If you only think what you've already thought, you'll only get what you've already got." Some groups and organizations place such a high premium on being right that there's no room for being wrong—even for a moment. These are the groups with the most severe cases of "infectious repetitis."

> A key characteristic of an inventive mind is a strong disbelief system.

Stay in the dragon pit. Entertain competing ideas for as long as possible, instead of scrambling to the safety of the known. It's common for managers and business leaders to think they have to have all the answers. This not only sets you up to fail, but undermines your credibility. Real innovators revel in the unknown. They love a mystery. As business advisor David Baker says, "An entrepreneur is someone who dives into an empty swimming pool and invents water on the way down."

Be disobedient. Don't play by the rules. If your goal is innovation, aligning with current practices is anathema. Alignment works well when the world isn't changing. But of course the world *is* changing. Rules can be helpful, but some rules are nothing more than scars from a previous bad experience.

Don't wait for research. Working without knowledge can feel like driving without headlights, but there's no law that says all the research has to come first. Sometimes it's better to grope your way toward an answer, then check it against reality when you have a specific hypothesis in hand.

Cannibalize yourself. Do what *The Atlantic* did when it found itself stuck in the dying world of print magazines: Pretend you're a venture-capital-backed startup in Silicon Valley whose mission it is to attack *The Atlantic* by disrupting the industry. Steve Jobs put it bluntly: "If you don't cannibalize yourself, someone else will."

Stand up for quality. The 20th century has been a triumph of quantity over quality, but in the 21st century we need to reverse the trend. "Be a quality detector," says systems thinker Donella Meadows. "Be a walking, noisy Geiger counter that registers the presence or absence of quality. If something is ugly, say so. If it is tacky, inappropriate, out of proportion, unsustainable, morally degrading, ecologically impoverishing, or humanly demeaning, don't let it pass."

What would happen if you did the opposite of what other people would do?

There you have it. Seven tips for being a contrarian without becoming a bully, a tyrant, or a curmudgeon. Ego-driven unpleasantness will always be a temptation for innovators. But how many inventions, masterpieces, and market disruptions would have happened without the researcher's hubristic ambitions, the artist's grand designs, or the entrepreneur's blithe disregard of risk?

"Here's to the crazy ones," intoned the announcer for Apple's comeback commercial. "They're not fond of rules. And they have no respect for the status quo. You can quote them, disagree with them, glorify or vilify them. About the only thing you can't do is ignore them…Because the people who are crazy enough to think they can change the world are the ones who do."

THE PLAY INSTINCT. How do you picture something that isn't there? What's the process for uncovering insights? Why do some people seem more inventive than others?

Hint: It's not because they work diligently. Instead, it's because they work *differently*. Imagination is the child of obstinacy and playfulness. It comes from a refusal to settle for the comfortable answer while having fun doing it.

During the Industrial Age, fun was discouraged. It took time to have fun, and time was the nonrenewable resource that needed to be managed, maximized, and measured. Employees were paid by the hour, the day, or the year. They were paid by number of pieces they could complete. Or they were paid by the predetermined function they performed. They were not paid by the number of new ideas they brought to the table or by the passion they brought to their work. Time was money and money was time.

After the clock came to Europe in 1307, it took less than a century for mechanical time to sweep the continent. With clocks you could agree on the delivery of a shipment, regularize the baking of bread, and estimate the completion of a brick wall. Clocks paved the way for sophisticated banking, transportation, mass production, and eventually computers. They brought precision to business. But they also brought an undue emphasis on quantity over quality.

The ancient Greeks understood that time came in two flavors: objective time, called *chronos*; and subjective time, called *kairos.* Chronos could be measured by the sun, the moon, or the seasons. Kairos could not be measured, only judged by the quality of one's experience. My kairos is different from your kairos, but our chronos is the same. Today we use the phrase *quality time* to describe the experience of living in unmeasured time. We find that as soon as we measure or limit quality time, it quickly turns into *quantity time.*

Think back to a day in your childhood when you were so busy playing that you lost track of the clock. The minutes and hours blended seamlessly, one into the next, while your mind focused on some absorbing project or engaging activity. As you grew older, your *play instinct* began to fade. The requirements of society demanded more attention to objective time—an adherence to deadlines, agreements, and social courtesies—until play became more and more associated with nonproductivity, a kind of time that had no commercial value.

Yet *quality time* is the state in which imagination flourishes best. You can't decide to produce an insight in 30 minutes or have an idea by 3:15. But you can decide to forget about the clock and focus on the challenge, in which case you may well have an idea by 3:15—or even five ideas. Imagination takes as long as it takes, and rushing it usually slows it down. This is the central conflict between the world of business and the world of creativity. They need each other, but can't seem to understand each other. They're working in two different kinds of time.

The solution to this dilemma, in my experience, is for business "doers" and creative "dreamers" to focus on goals instead of deadlines. Goals form the common ground that unites both workstyles. Focus on goals, take away the clocks, and start playing as soon as possible. What you'll find is that generating ideas "out of time" can produce results much faster than holding yourself to a deadline. If you wait until the last minute, however, leaving little opportunity for play, you'll find yourself clutching the first idea that floats by. Quantity time will enter the picture and force a mediocre result.

Goals are the common ground that unites business "doers" and creative "dreamers."

If you could pry the roof off of all the mediocre companies in the world, you'd see an army of adrenaline addicts working on perpetual deadline, madly checking boxes instead of thinking ahead. You can get an immediate buzz from getting things done, but innovation requires something more—it requires unmeasured time in the dragon pit.

But what should you be doing there? What are the rules of creative play? How do you know when you're winning? Here's where quantity plays a crucial role. The best creative thinkers are usually the most prolific thinkers, because innovation, like evolution, depends on variety. In fact, you could say that innovation is really just evolution by design. The more ideas you have, the better your odds that two will combine to make a useful third idea. In the parlance of creative theory, you're *fluent*. When ideas flow, the music of chance plays faster.

> The best creative thinkers are usually the most prolific thinkers, since innovation, like evolution, depends on variety.

In London's Highgate Cemetery, where ancient crypts lean out over twisted trails in silent competition for post-life prestige, one headstone stands in contrast. It's a small gray rectangle lying flat against the edge of the road to mark the grave of historian Jacob Bronowski. Bronowski was the narrator of an early PBS series called *The Ascent of Man*. On screen he spoke slowly and with a little trouble pronouncing the letter R, his stage-glasses flashing into the camera whenever he delivered his most fascinating insights. "A genius," he said, "is a person who has two great ideas." What he meant was that innovation often comes from connecting two thoughts that previously had been unconnected. These might be two ideas that had never been considered together, or two ideas previously thought to be in conflict, or one old idea plus one new idea. Einstein's term for this process was *combinatory play*.

While there may be nothing new under the sun, there's no restriction on combining old things in new ways. For an exhibition called "Making Connections," about midcentury designers Charles and Ray Eames, Ralph Caplan described their firm belief in combinatory play—the excitement of connecting disparate materials such as wood and steel, of connecting alien disciplines such as physics and painting, of connecting people like architects and mathematicians or poets and corporate executives. The connection point "is the crack in the wall, the point at which a designer can sneak past the limitations while no one is looking."

The importance of connections is also echoed by recent discoveries in neuroscience. The brain forms new ideas when two old ideas suddenly overlap. Cortical cells then make new connections, rewiring themselves into fresh networks. Once the insight has been formed, the prefrontal cortex can name it and claim it. But the real genius lies not in making interesting combinations, but in separating the great ideas from the merely crazy ones by applying the principles of aesthetics. Some connections offer a better fit than others.

Of course, it's easy to talk about fluency and variety and prolific imagination, but how do you start? What's the selection criteria? Where do combinable ideas come from?

Happily, they come from learnable techniques. While some people may be naturals in the realm of imagination, we can all improve our skills with deliberate practice. Here are ten strategies that can trigger new ideas.

Think in metaphors. A metaphor is a way of making a comparison between two unrelated things. "All the world is a stage" is an example. The world is not a stage, but it's *like* a stage in some ways. Shakespeare could have used a simile instead of a metaphor—"The world is like a stage"—and it would have had the same meaning, just not the same impact. By saying the world is a stage, a fresh idea is forced to emerge—that every person is merely playing a part.

Thinking about problems metaphorically moves your thinking from the literal to the abstract, so you can move freely on a different plane. To a literal thinker, a rose is a rose. To a metaphorical thinker, a rose could be a young woman's cheek, a seductive trap, or the morning sky before a storm. If your challenge is to invent a new name for a store that sells footwear to active girls, you could call it Active Footwear. Or you could think in metaphors and move beyond the first pasture. For example, maybe active footwear for girls is like the ballet slippers in *The Red Shoes*, or like a bouncy pop song from the sixties, or like—wait a minute. What if we call it Shubop?

When ideas flow, the music of chance plays faster.

Think in pictures. Many people assume Einstein was a logical, left-brain thinker, but he was actually the opposite. Rather than using mathematics or language to crack a tough problem, he preferred to think in pictures and spatial relationships. This is because visual thinking can strip a problem down to its essence, leading to profoundly simple conclusions that ordinary language might not be able to reach.

Visual thinking isn't just for graphic designers, artists, and illustrators. It's for anyone who can draw a stick figure, an arrow, and a talk balloon. Pick up a copy of *The Back of the Napkin* by Dan Roam to learn a few of the most useful tricks. You'll wonder why more people don't think like Einstein.

Start from a different place. Your brain builds up patterns of experience that act as attractor states, making it hard to think in new ways. Your best shot at clearing this hurdle is not to try and jump it but to go around it. Start from a different place. Start from a place that doesn't make any sense. Better yet, think of the worst place you could possibly start, and start there.

Let's say, for example, your task is to negotiate a peace treaty between warring states. (What? You don't have that on your calendar?) So far no amount of reasoning has been able to bring the two sides together. You could try more reasoning, or better reasoning, or perhaps the threat of draconian intervention, but these are likely to cause further entrenchment.

So you start from a different place. What would be the worst way to structure the talks? How about suggesting that the two leaders declare immediate, mutual, all-out war? Obviously, that's crazy. But at least it's different. Okay, what if you suggest it anyway, just to make a point about the absurdity of war? Then, when the two parties reject the idea, you can propose a less dramatic solution: Arm wrestling to the death, winner take all. No? How about this? Arm wrestling, and whoever loses buys the other a beer. Now we're getting somewhere. At least they'd have to be human, which would count as progress and make a great photo op as well.

The arm-wrestling photo op solution may not be the final idea, but you can see how difficult it would be to get there using the standard negotiating handbook. Next you might imagine other photo ops that could serve as clever backdrops for negotiation, and so on and so forth. By following the trail from the worst idea to a workable idea, you can avoid being imprisoned by old patterns.

Poach from other domains. Voltaire said, "originality is nothing but judicious imitation." What could be more judicious than steal-

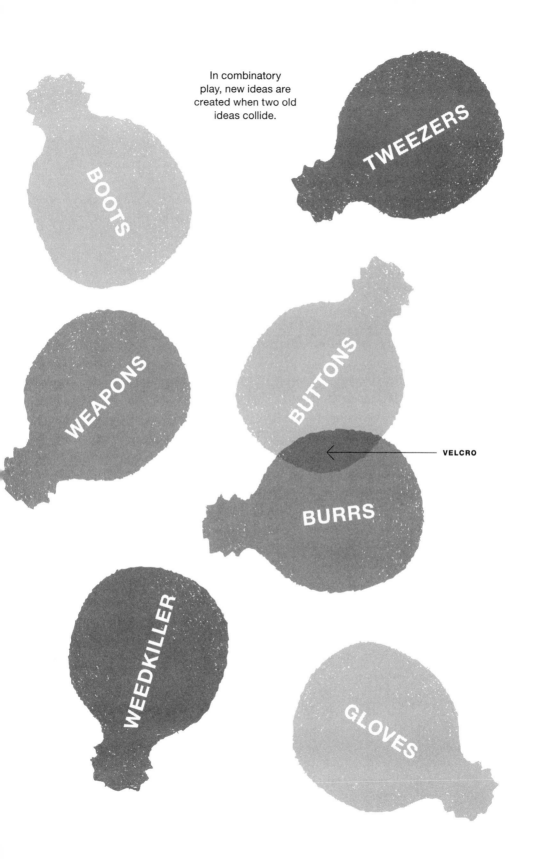

In combinatory play, new ideas are created when two old ideas collide.

BOOTS

TWEEZERS

WEAPONS

BUTTONS

VELCRO

BURRS

WEEDKILLER

GLOVES

ing ideas from other fields? While stealing is not the same as pure imagination, it still takes a mental leap to see how an idea from one industry or discipline might be used in another industry or discipline.

Gutenberg got the idea for the printing press from watching the mechanics of a wine press. This mental connection launched the book industry, and did no harm to winemakers.

One fine summer day in 1948, amateur inventor George de Mestral took his dog for a walk in the woods. Upon returning, he found his dog and his pant legs covered in pesky burrs. When he put them under a microscope he saw tiny hooks, perfectly suited for attaching themselves to fur and fabric. The result? Velcro.

In 1921, a 14-year-old Philo Farnsworth got the idea for the electronic television while tilling the family's potato farm. The back-and-forth plowing pattern suggested the back-and-forth scanning pattern for cathode ray tubes. Talk about stealing ideas from another field!

Arrange blind dates. The cases above show how a prepared mind can make novel connections under the right circumstances. But it's also possible to force connections by introducing two unrelated ideas. What do you get when you cross a bank with an Internet café? A shoe store with a charity? A Broadway show with a circus performance? Adhesive tape with a bookmark? You get successful business models like ING Direct, Tom's Shoes, Cirque du Soleil, and Post-it Notes.

Of course, you can also get the business equivalent of kitsch, as Clairol did when it crossed yogurt with hair care and got Touch of Yogurt Shampoo. Or as Omni did when it crossed a television hit with a carbonated drink and got Tru Blood soda. Don't fall in love with your first idea. Novelty and innovation are two different things.

Reverse the polarity. While it doesn't usually work with electronics, reversing the polarity in an assumption can release conceptual energy. Here's how you do it:

Let's say your challenge is to get your employees to wash their dishes instead of leaving them in the sink for someone else to do.

You can start by listing some assumptions about the problem.

1. Employees don't like doing dishes.
2. It's hard to tell whose dishes are in the sink.
3. The dishes are company property.
4. Dishes are easier to clean after they soak.
5. Dishes tend to pile up.

Now, reverse the assumptions to see what happens.

1. Employees love doing dishes.
2. It's easy to tell whose dishes are in the sink.
3. The dishes are employee property.
4. Dishes are easier to clean before they soak.
5. Dishes never pile up.

What would it take to make these true? Well, employees might love doing their dishes if they had a great music system at the sink. It would be easy to tell whose dishes were in there if each item were personalized with the employees' names or initials. Maybe employees could be allowed full kitchen privileges, but only if they agreed to use their own kitchenware. Or maybe you could install a large-capacity dishwasher that makes it just as easy to put dishes there as in the sink. Or maybe you could make your sink and sideboard so small that the dishwasher was the only logical place to put them. Of course, you could just lay down the law, then enforce it with a surveillance camera. But that seems a bit draconian.

Find the paradox. If you can describe the central contradiction within a given problem, you're well on the way to solving it. When designer Mitchell Mauk noticed a problem with the storm drains in San Francisco, he took it the initiative to propose a solution. The city had been concerned about people dumping motor oils and chemicals into the sewers, where they would flow into the bay and pollute the fish habitats. The usual warnings posted near the drains weren't working.

The central contradiction might have been stated like this:

People won't stop dumping toxins through the sewer grates unless they can read the signs, and they won't read the signs if they're too busy dumping toxins through the sewer grates. So Mauk asked the question another way. Can the sewer grates and the signs be one and the same? His elegant Gratefish sends an unambiguous message: Whatever you put down the drain goes right into the fish.

Give it the third degree. What else is like this, from which you could get an idea? Is there something similar that you could partially copy? What if this were somewhat changed? What can you eliminate? What can you substitute? Is this the cause or the effect? What if you changed the timing? In whose shoes should you put yourself? The questions are endless, but they don't take much time to ask.

Be alert for accidents. The great thing about creative play is that mistakes don't have consequences. You're free to follow any rabbit down any hole. While most of the time you won't find what you're looking for, sometimes you'll find what you *weren't* looking for, and that can be even better.

When mechanic John Hyatt was looking for a substitute for billiard-ball ivory, he accidentally invented celluloid, the plastic used in making movie film and hundreds of other products.

When Percy Spencer was working on radar for the military, he found a melted candy bar in his pocket, thus discovering the working principle for microwave ovens.

Steve Jobs, while trying to design a tablet computer, discovered a great set of features for the iPhone instead. The iPhone became the stepping stone back to the iPad.

Physicist Richard Feynman had a simple test for new ideas. "What did you discover that you didn't set out to discover?" If you only found what you expected to find, your idea probably isn't new.

Write things down. When I was a wannabe songwriter in my teens (who wasn't?), I never worried that I might forget a line of melody or snippet of lyric. I told myself if it were that good it would probably come back to me. Conversely, I believed if it didn't come back to me, it probably wasn't that good. There were two flaws in this logic. First, I *did* forget good musical ideas, and, second, the value of ideas often lies in their ability to trigger better ideas. If you don't capture them, you can't build on them.

"Ideas never stand alone," says Kevin Kelly. "They come woven in a web of auxiliary ideas, consequential notions, supporting concepts, foundational assumptions, side effects, logical consequences, and a cascade of subsequent possibilities. Ideas fly in flocks," he says. "To hold one idea in mind means to hold a cloud of them."

A cloud of ideas is a wonderful image. But my advice? Don't try to hold them all in your mind. Write them down. Record them. Get in the habit of taking notes, keeping a diary, carrying a sketchbook, or thinking out loud on a whiteboard. Just because play is fun doesn't mean your ideas aren't worth saving. This is especially true when the playground is collaborative.

DREAMING TOGETHER. Personal mastery can only have meaning in the context of group. None of us can succeed alone, even those whose work is mostly solitary. We all need society, culture, education, government, and industry to provide a framework in which mastery matters, and in which mastery can be learned. Furthermore, in a growing number of domains, nothing meaningful can be accomplished without the cooperation of a diverse set of players.

Creative collaboration, as a business competency, can't be confined to the R&D department. One reason industry has been less than creative during the last century is that innovation was disconnected from business strategy. It was locked in a small, windowless room in the basement, where it couldn't interfere with the running of the company.

In the Robotic Age, creative collaboration needs to escape the lab, linking people from top to bottom, beginning to end, across disciplines and over regional boundaries. It must become a day-one activity that's promoted and modeled by leaders, instead of a follow-on activity that only kicks in after a strategy has been endorsed.

The concept of brainstorming was introduced by Alex Osborn in *Applied Imagination*, a 1953 book that's still worth reading. He recommended that a brainstorm group consist of five to ten people, including both "brass and rookies." At least two people in the group should be self-starters, and they should be "sparking" from the moment the problem is stated. He observed that larger groups are better at getting buy-in on broad solutions, and smaller groups are better at solving specific problems. So far, so good.

> Creativity needs to escape the lab, linking people from top to bottom, beginning to end, across disciplines and over regional boundaries.

The key to brainstorming, believed Osborn, was to foster an atmosphere in which judgment was temporarily suspended. When participants fret over criticism, they hold back or edit their ideas to remove the threat of embarrassment. Most people take this principle as gospel, knowing from direct experience that a brainstorming session can quickly turn into a sniping session.

"The crazier the idea the better," he always said. "It is easier to tone down than to think up." In Osborn's version of the game: 1) judgment was suspended; 2) wildness was welcomed; 3) quantity was wanted; 4) combination and improvement were sought. The only problem: innovation was absent. Most of the early brainstorming groups that suspended judgment had a lot of fun but little success.

There's a big gap between good crazy and bad crazy. Good crazy is the kind of idea that seems crazy on the surface, but on closer examination is actually quite smart. Bad crazy is just crazy. Brainstorming groups that followed the rule of suspended judgment could often cover the walls with hundreds of ideas, but then they'd run out of energy before they could sort them and turn them into workable solutions. Crazy thinking can be frustrating when it turns into a tedious, thousand-monkeys exercise. This kind of session, in which all ideas are welcome and political correctness reigns, might be called *softball brainstorming*.

When the mission is critical and the time is short, however, what works best is *hardball brainstorming*, in which participants are experienced, well matched, and focused like a laser on the problem to be solved.

In hardball sessions, ideas are judged as they're pitched, producing not discouragement but more ideas, as thoughts bounce up against thoughts, deflecting minds into new areas of consideration. Instead of keeping judgment on a leash, hardballers apply *more* judgment. But it's creative judgment, based on the knowledge of what a great idea looks like as it moves through its various stages.

This is not to say that sessions like these are always pleasant. Stretching the imagination can be draining work, and tempers can flare. Therefore the main rule in hardball is to focus not on *who* is best but *what* is best. When everyone is working toward a shared goal, lightly bruised egos are quickly salved by group success.

In both kinds of brainstorming, hardball and softball, there's a necessary tension between contrariness and cooperation. Cooperation is essential for achieving an outcome, but without a certain amount of contrary input, the outcome is likely to be mushy. Studies by organizational psychologists have shown that individuals, not groups, tend to be better at divergent thinking, while groups are better at convergent thinking. When faced by complexity that tests the biological limits the brain, groups often default to a herd mentality instead of fighting for divergent ideas.

To guard against herd thinking, shared goals should be as bold as possible. They shouldn't be ordinary or safe. As Howard Schultz said about the challenge of engaging stakeholders at Starbucks, "Who wants a dream that's near-fetched?" The simplest way to develop bold goals is to start by wishing. When you get the members of a group to start wishing, their dreams can quickly become roadmaps. There's a reason people tell you to be careful what you wish for. It works.

For large design projects, especially those which benefit from multidisciplinary teams, there's an ongoing search for "T-shaped" people. A T-shaped person is one who has a strong descender (the vertical stroke of the T) and a well-developed crossbar (the horizontal stroke). The descender represents deep experience in a certain discipline, and the crossbar represents the ability to work with people across disciplines. Like rock bands, creative groups need specialists who can contribute something unique to the collaboration. The last thing they need is I-shaped people—specialists who have useful skills but can't work

> In hardball sessions, ideas are judged as they're pitched, deflecting minds into new areas of consideration.

with others.

Finally, both rock bands and creative groups need one more member: an X-shaped person. This is the one whose main role—though not the only role—is to bring the group together and facilitate progress toward a goal. X-shaped people are rare, because they usually have to prove their worth by first mastering a discipline. The leadership gene is an extra gene, a skill on top of a skill. John Lasseter has been a great creative leader for Pixar, but he developed his credibility and his deep-domain expertise by working first as an animator.

When X-shaped people attract the right T-shaped people to the mission, magic can happen. A surprising number of players will volunteer to dream together and work together if the goal is bold enough and the leader respected. This is especially true in an age of virtual collaboration. Anyone who has watched the exponential growth of Wikipedia can sense the power of collaboration. And while contributions to Wikipedia are voluntary, nothing would have happened without the passionate facilitation of its founder, Jimmy Wales.

Today there's a new variation of collaboration that takes advantage of widespread connectivity. *Swarming*, as it was originally termed by the military, is a method for attacking a problem or a project from a number of angles at once. Rather than structure a project as a linear exercise, the swarming method unleashes the full power of simultaneous collaboration. It lets you jumpstart the project by bringing a variety of minds together at the start, then tap the talents of a wide range of disciplines throughout the process.

Let's say you manage a design firm or an internal marketing department. As soon as you get an assignment, you might embark on the usual process of gathering executive interviews, doing customer research, brainstorming concepts, putting some initial thoughts on paper, making prototypes, testing them, refining them, and finally producing them. Because the steps are linear, each one depends on the one before, and the whole process takes ten weeks. Swarming, by contrast, lets you interview, research, brainstorm, sketch, and prototype in parallel, with each activity informing the

Great teams
are formed when
when T-shaped people
are joined by
X-shaped people.

others, while the team quickly builds up a rich understanding of the project's possibilities. Not only is it faster, but it skirts the danger of playing "telephone"—the children's game in which one kid whispers something quickly to a neighbor, who whispers it to the next neighbor down the line, who whispers it to the next neighbor, and so on, until "dancing on the lawn" becomes "Mrs. Johnson's dog." With swarming, the project has a better chance to come through in its purest, most focused form.

But let's be clear about collaboration. A team is only as good as the skills of the individuals in it. While you can learn a lot from working with great people, your value to the team comes from the quality of your own effort. Whether a T or an X, you still have to develop your own metaskills, create your own thought processes, and do battle by yourself in the dragon zone. A master's degree won't help you. Only mastery itself.

THE BOLT UPRIGHT MOMENT. The metaskill of dreaming brings with it a built-in reward: the glorious split second when the world suddenly reels, a thousand gears snap into place, and the long-hidden answer appears, shimmering, before your disbelieving eyes.

While not every epiphany packs this kind of punch, many do. It all depends on how difficult the problem was, how important the outcome is, and how long the solution has eluded you. And it also depends on the beauty—the sheer aesthetic elegance—of the final answer. Imagine the breathtaking moment when Einstein realized that the secret of relativity could be expressed in three letters and a number. He once likened the surprise of scientific discovery to a hen laying a golden egg. *"Kieks! auf einmal ist es da!"* Cheep! suddenly it's there!

I can honestly say that I'd rather have an epiphany than win the lottery. Okay, the lottery brings money, but it leaves you with the problem of how to turn your money into the kind of transcendent experience that makes life worth living. It's much easier to turn epiphanies into money than the other way around. Winning the lottery is like finding a golden egg; learning to dream is like raising a golden goose.

There's a good reason why people have reported sitting bolt upright in bed, suddenly awakened from slumber after weeks or months of wrestling with a problem. Their subconscious mind has been busy working behind the scenes to sort through the rational complexities that kept the solution hidden. This "dark time" is known as the *incubation* period, a stage when the problem, as it was originally framed, does not seem to yield to a solution. The solution can only come when the rational mind lets go so the dreaming mind can take over. It can happen during actual dreaming, but it can also show up anytime the rational mind lets down its guard—while taking a shower, driving a car, lying on the beach, or having sex (presumably with one's muse). Once, when Johann Sebastian Bach was asked where he found his melodies, he answered that the problem wasn't *finding* them—it was not *tripping* over them when he got up in the morning.

The bolt upright moment is the point at which a new idea clicks into the right criteria, even when the criteria are poorly understood. Sometimes what you think are the right criteria are not, and you find that your subconscious brain has reframed the problem. Other times, the criteria are so complex that your rational brain can't make sense of them, leaving the job to your dreaming mind.

Imagine criteria as a pile of pick-up sticks that happened to fall in a certain pattern. Each stick is a line item on your problem-solver's wish list. All you have to do is find a pattern where most of the pick-up sticks overlap. But there's a catch: Some of the sticks are hard to see, some are more important than others, and some won't stop moving. The shifting, now-you-see-it-now-you-don't landscape of criteria can overwhelm the focusing mechanism of your mind.

The bolt upright moment is the point at which a new idea clicks into the right criteria.

Have you ever pointed an autofocus camera into a moving crowd? The camera will have so much trouble deciding on the focal point that you'll miss your shot entirely. You'll hear the lens zooming in and out, but the shutter won't click. An autofocus camera is a little like your rational mind. It doesn't like ambiguity, so it will either take the first picture that comes into focus, or else become confused and freeze. This is the problem that the new

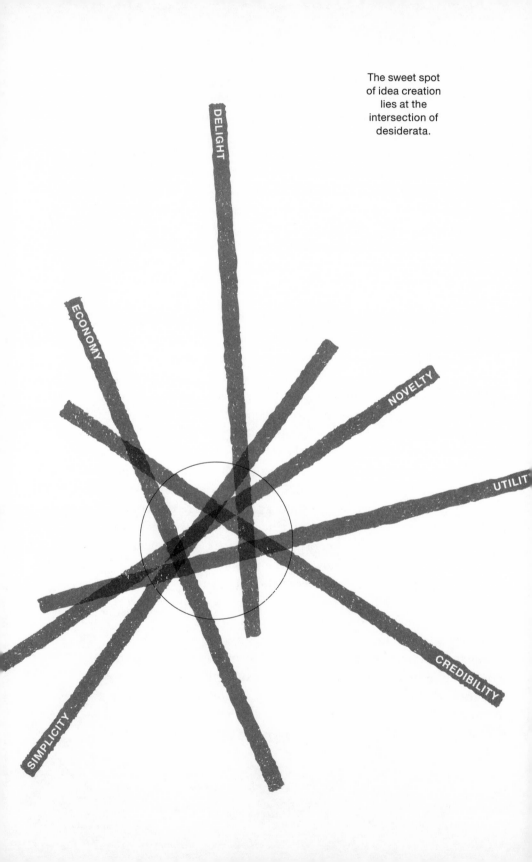

The sweet spot
of idea creation
lies at the
intersection of
desiderata.

DELIGHT

ECONOMY

NOVELTY

UTILIT

CREDIBILITY

SIMPLICITY

multifocus cameras solve. They capture all the information in the scene, but the leave the final decision on where to focus until later. In human terms, it's like allowing time for incubation.

When a fresh solution to a problem finally does come into focus, the emotional brain sends a signal to the rest of your body—sometimes described as a tingle, a flash, or a jolt—that tells you something remarkable has happened. Developing a sensitivity to these signals is an integral part of being creative.

SIX TESTS OF ORIGINALITY. The goal of dreaming is to produce an original idea. The idea can be new to you, new to your group, or new to the world. But how do you know which it is? And how do you know if it's any good in the first place?

In my experience, creative judgment comes with practice, maturity, and familiarity with the world of ideas. There's no short-cut. But there is a short*hand* for recognizing the potential of an idea at the point of epiphany. I've distilled it down to a list of six questions:

1. *Is it disorienting?* A great idea should be unsettling—not just to you, but to others in your group. Some people may reject it on the spot. This is not always a bad sign, since the potential of a new idea is often inversely proportional to its comfort factor.

Other people may simply find the idea baffling if it doesn't jibe with their existing beliefs. For example, when talking pictures became possible, H.M. Warner was firmly against it: "Who the hell wants to hear actors talk?" he roared. Some people believed air-planes would have no military value; that broadcast radio could not become popular; that no one would want a computer at home; and that educated people would never contribute to an encyclopedia without being paid. When you hear these kinds of comments, your antennae should tingle.

2. *Does it kill ten birds?* A good idea kills two birds with one stone. A great idea kills ten or twenty. This is the place where the pick-up sticks overlap, the pattern that tells you when a solution is elegant. The opposite of an elegant solution is one with too many trade-offs. In politics, trade-offs are often placed on a pedestal, held up

as examples of "the art of compromise." But great ideas don't come from compromise. They come from common ground.

Let's say you're trying to imagine a new product for your company. A great product idea would combine a dozen desirable traits in a single move. It might cost less to produce, use the existing supply chain, reposition the company's chief competitor, reenergize the workforce, attract more talent, inspire free publicity, deepen customer loyalty, increase annual revenues, produce higher profit margins, drive up the stock price, benefit the community, and create a platform for a whole new class of products. Twelve birds right there.

> The potential of a new idea is often inversely proportional to its comfort factor.

3. *Does it need to be proved?* Original ideas are unproven by definition—and therefore inherently risky. If an idea doesn't need to be tested, it's probably because it's not very original or not very bold. The skepticism that calls for a proof of concept is one of the signals of originality.

When my design firm was tapped by Apple in 1988 to rethink the packaging for the company's range of software products, one of the ideas we presented was a retail package with nothing on the front but a simple hand-drawn icon, a product name, a trademark, and a splash of color. At the time, no self-respecting software package would go out dressed in less than five colors, one or more photos of people using computers, at least three screen shots, and six or seven bullet points explaining its features—and this was just the front panel.

Bill Campbell, then president of the software business, was curious enough about the "white look" to test it with customers. As it turned out, this became the company's most successful format, increasing revenues by 40 percent across the product line in the first year, and inspiring the clean white packaging now associated with Apple. When your idea is bold enough to trigger the testing instinct, you might be onto something.

4. *Is it likely to force change?* Great ideas are not polite. They never say they're sorry. They don't try to fit in. On the contrary, they force the world around them to make changes in self-defense.

In the 1950s, a small advertising agency named Doyle Dane

Bernbach had a big idea: humor. In the hard-drinking, hard-selling days of Madison Avenue, humor was universally frowned on. The prevailing mantra was "the more you tell, the more you sell." The current voice of reason, David Ogilvy, maintained that "people do not buy from clowns." DDB's creative teams not only believed they did, but delivered their witty headlines and graphics with stark simplicity. Over the next decade any agency that couldn't create clean, humorous ads began to see its status sink like a stale olive in a cheap martini.

5. *Does it create affordances?* Affordances are the opportunities inherent in a new idea. Good ideas "come woven in a web of auxiliary ideas, consequential notions, supporting concepts, foundational assumptions, side effects, logical consequences, and a cascade of subsequent possibilities." An affordance of Twitter, for example, is to enable instant communication in places where communication is controlled, such as the Middle East during the Arab Spring rebellions. An affordance of democracy is that citizens can voice their opinions without the threat of reprisals. An affordance of baking soda is that it can soak up fridge odors in addition to making cakes rise.

The measure of a great idea is the number and quality of the affordances it throws off. If innovation is evolution by design, then the best idea is the one that affords the most choices.

6. *Can it be summarized?* Every innovation—whether a government, gadget, service, iPhone app, movie plot, or business model—can be reduced to a one-sentence description. The US government is a democracy of the people, for the people, and by the people. A Nano MP3 player puts four thousand songs at your fingertips. The Heathrow Express whisks you to London in 15 minutes flat. The Pages tablet application lets you be a writer one second and a designer the next. In *Talk to Her*, two men form an odd friendship while their girlfriends are in comas. Charles Schwab makes investing personal.

> The measure of a great idea is the number and quality of the affordances it throws off.

The reason a great idea can be described in a sentence is not because it's simple but because it has a strong internal order, one that answers to a clear and compelling purpose. The full idea may be quite complex. Complexity without order is an indescribable mess, while complexity with order appears simpler than it is. If you find it hard to describe your idea, don't fix your description. Fix your idea.

The metaskill of dreaming, the ability to cut ideas out of whole cloth, is not a subject currently taught in business schools—or any other schools. This seems odd in an age when innovation is the dividing line between success and failure. But the gap could grow even wider as aesthetics are asked to play a greater role the way ideas are realized.

The 20th century has made us believe that everything of value can be bought in a store; that the answer to the question lies at the back of the chapter; that design is something only designers do.

But now, in the 21st century, we're being nudged nervously forward—by our customers, by our employers, by our economy, and by the robots nipping at our heels—to be original. To innovate. To make things. Yes, *make* things.

MAKING

IL DISCORSO MENTALE. Leonardo was famous, or perhaps infamous, for taking months to complete a painting—if indeed he did complete it. Some say this is the reason there are so few Leonardo paintings extant. Whether that's true or not, he did leave quite a bit of time between layers of paint. He felt that *il discorso mentale*, the mental conversation, was more important than the actual painting. The extra time gave him the mental space to reflect on the details—what to include, what to exclude, and how the elements might fit together to make a unified whole. To Leonardo, an artist didn't learn to paint. He painted to learn.

This intimacy with craft would have been foreign to the ancient Greeks, who looked down on hand skills as dirty and degrading, a kind of manual labor fit only for the lower classes. Plato's elaborate taxonomy of human knowledge made no reference whatsoever to craft. To our present-day misfortune, Plato's way of thinking has had a much greater influence on our education models than Leonardo's. Today we hold academic schools in high regard, while placing trade schools on a much lower tier. What Leonardo understood is that imagination without experience is weak. Originality without craft, to a Renaissance artisan, would have seemed like marriage without sex—lofty but Platonic.

Creativity is more than imagination. It's imagination coupled with craft. It's the metaskill of *making*. It envisions, embodies, elaborates. It develops, shapes, solves. It advances, iterates, proves. Note the lack of passive verbs in this list. Making is action. Unless you're willing to get your hands dirty, your imagination will remain unrealized and uninformed.

Learning theorist Donald Schön took the idea of *discorso mentale* to a new level of understanding in his 1983 book, *The Reflective Practitioner*. He called craft knowledge "reflection-in-action," the result of thinking while doing. As the maker shapes an object or a situation according to an initial vision, the situation "talks back," and the maker responds to the backtalk. Our spontaneous reactions don't always work out, so we keep trying until we succeed. Schön believed that the starting point for reflection-in-action was "knowing-in-action," a dynamic way of knowing that stands in stark contrast to the kind of static knowledge we're taught in school.

Hungarian physicist Leó Szilárd, who conceived of the nuclear chain reaction in 1933, posed a simple question: Can we know all about the world without changing it? No, he finally said. Knowledge must come from action if it's to be deep enough and rich enough to drive lasting change. We can't reshape the world without a little trial and error.

Unless you're willing to get your hands dirty, your imagination will remain unrealized and uninformed.

Reflection-in-action goes a long way towards describing what we mean when we speak of a practioner's artistry. It's a capacity to combine thinking and doing in the middle of performing, often under stress, "while the train is running." We find this type of performance on the athletic field, where coaches literally coach their players to higher levels of skill, or in the music conservatory where performers, conductors, and composers use deliberate practice to stretch their musical muscles. We also find it in the clinic, the office, the lab, the studio, the shop—any place in which mentoring and apprenticeship are modes of learning.

The way designers approach a problem is to feel their way towards a solution, akin to how an athlete decides her next move. The decision is made more with the body than the mind. Only after a direction begins to feel right does the designer try to imagine specific aesthetics to make it tangible, visible, and functional.

Growing up in Denmark, Anders Warming loved to wash and polish his parents cars. He'd trace their subtle curves with his hands, marveling at the seamless progression of forms, one flowing into another, each in perfect harmony with the whole. "I touched them so many times that I could close my eyes and draw them," he later said. One of these cars was a mineral-blue Mini 850, a precursor of the new Minis he would end up designing for BMW in 2011.

Warming doesn't start a new design by going straight to CAD software. He also steers clear of verbal descriptions and PowerPoint presentations. Instead, he draws. He may make hundreds of sketches before even looking at a screen. "You probably need 90 sketches just to get warm, and after that, you're really in the flow. You're transcending the paper." He compares it to perfecting your serve so you can win at Wimbledon. "Maybe the 151st is the one."

All too often, says Julia Cameron in *The Artist's Way*, "we try to push, pull, outline, and control our ideas instead of letting them grow organically. The creative process is one of surrender, not control." By letting go our fears of looking foolish or wasting time, sketching or doodling can take us where we might not ordinarily go. Our experience with the subject we're drawing, or the idea we're pursuing, will be direct, undiluted, and free from the strictures imposed by our egos.

The concept of letting go is a theme running through all the creative disciplines. In design, sketching is the mother of invention. In science it's the experiment; in business it's the whiteboard diagram; in writing it's the rough draft; in acting it's the run-through; in inventing it's the prototype; in jazz it's jamming. Miles Davis once said: "Do not fear mistakes—there are none." Every step or misstep is provisional or correctable, a mini-lesson in the practice room of mastery. You go in not knowing so you can come out knowing.

THE NO-PROCESS PROCESS. There's a standard model that designers use to describe the creative process, usually with minor variations. Sometimes these are followed by a trademark notice, as if to say, "Hands off! This is *my* process, invented by *me*! By the way, did I mention it was *mine*?" Yet they all conform to the same progression that goes from a state of not knowing to a state of knowing, laid out in 4-10 logical steps.

The standard process looks something like this: 1) discovery, 2) definition, 3) design, 4) development, and 5) deployment. You could repeat some of these steps, or place them in a slightly different order, or add baby steps in between. You could also throw a step onto the front for getting the assignment, and another onto the back for launching the result. Most process diagrams are circular, suggesting that the end of the journey leads you right back to the beginning.

There's only one hitch. A truly creative process bears little resemblance to these models. In theory there's no difference between theory and practice. In practice there is. If it had to be circular, the real process of making things would look more like this: 1) confusion, 2) clutter, 3) chaos, 4) crisis, and 5) catharsis. But if designers presented this process as a diagram, they'd scare the bejeesus out of their bosses and clients. So instead they present the calm, confident progressions of the so-called "rational model."

The rational model of design is not exactly wrong. It's just not helpful. When used slavishly, it can lead to a significant waste of resources and a debilitating sense of hopelessness as originality and excitement turn to mediocrity and disappointment. Why would this happen? Because creativity doesn't respond to project management so much as passion management. Creative passion is the primary resource, so it needs to be nurtured and guarded. Designers may taxi to the runway with briefings, data, and deadlines, but they reach flying altitude with emotion, empathy, and intuition. By overemphasizing process, you can discourage greatness.

A better model for designing is the *no-process process*, an approach that recognizes the chaotic nature of creativity. In the no-process model, you start with a general understanding of the problem, the goals, the areas of concern, the milestones, and the criteria for success. But the steps for addressing these areas should grow from the particular nature of the challenge, the circumstances in which the work will be done, the skills and workstyles of the team members, and the insights revealed as the project unfolds. It shouldn't be forced to fit a diagram.

Listen to author Annie Dillard: "Rembrandt and Shakespeare, Bohr and Gauguin, possessed powerful hearts, not powerful wills. They loved the range of materials they used. The work's possibilities excited them; the field's complexities fired their imaginations. The caring suggested the tasks; the tasks suggested the schedules." While few of us are Rembrandts or Shakespeares, the principle is the same. You chain creativity to a wheel at your peril.

But if there's no process, where do you start? That's easy. Anywhere. Everywhere. Whatever place releases the most energy. "It doesn't matter where you start," said composer John Cage, "as long as you start." The important thing is that you cover all the bases by the time you're done. By bouncing around from dreaming to

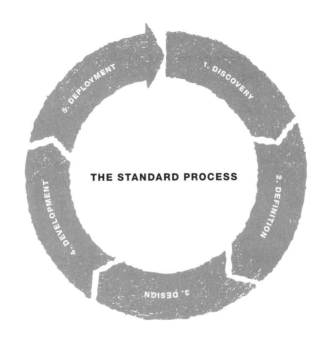

THE STANDARD PROCESS

1. DISCOVERY
2. DEFINITION
3. DESIGN
4. DEVELOPMENT
5. DEPLOYMENT

THE REAL PROCESS

1. CONFUSION
2. CLUTTER
3. CHAOS
4. CRISIS
5. CATHARSIS

research to model making to testing to walking to sketching to presenting to thinking to reading to arguing to sketching, you set off a chain reaction that a static process could never hope to match. The ideas virtually explode into being. The content determines the form, the form determines the content. Together they throw off clouds of surprising ideas.

The lifestyle stores known as Anthropologie have qualities of creativity and surprise baked into their business model. Each store has a large art room in the back where employees and contractors can experiment with new ways of displaying, merchandising, and creating products. As a result, no two stores are exactly alike, which allows them to keep their customers delightfully off-balance. The accepted notion that chain stores should aim for total consistency now seems hopelessly anachronistic.

As a believer in the magic of design, I have three fond wishes.

The first is that a greater number of creative people—designers, entrepreneurs, strategists, engineers, scientists—begin to embrace the true process of design, and abandon the comforting models that lead to mediocre outcomes.

The second is that educational institutions arrive at a similar understanding, making room for messy thinking and surprising ideas in the classroom. While I doubt I'll see real paint splattered on the walls of Harvard, Oxford, and the Sorbonne, metaphorical splatters would be a start.

The third is that the leaders and managers of companies encourage the real process of design in all of its chaotic splendor, trusting, even insisting, that the results be more than efficient— that they be surprising, amazing, and occasionally even world changing.

EVERY DAY IS GROUNDHOG DAY. Remember the movie with Bill Murray? The protagonist is forced to repeat the same day until he finally gets it right. He tries everything: manipulation, hedonism, theft, seduction, even suicide. Nothing works until he moves beyond his usual repertoire of cheap tricks and selfish tactics and realizes the only way out is up. He becomes more helpful to the townspeople—changing tires, saving children, helping old people. He even acquires new skills in jazz piano, ice sculpture, and chiropractic medicine. When at last he achieves the perfect day, he wins the girl and breaks the endless loop of repetition.

The experience of *Groundhog Day* is not unlike the experience of creativity. There are two main stages in innovation: 1) getting the right idea (dreaming), and 2) getting the idea right (making). As in *Groundhog Day*, getting the idea right is an iterative process. It doesn't happen overnight or in a sudden flash. It takes trial and error, aesthetic tinkering, and learning in action.

How many promising ideas have died after birth due to poor execution? I'd hazard a guess that the number is well over 50 percent. We'll never know, since they tend to disappear so quickly from the scene. A few which have stuck around long enough to notice are the Ford Edsel (died 1959), the movie *Ishtar* (died 1987), the Excite online network (died 2004), and the Bush-era Vision for Space Exploration program (died 2010).

And beyond this, how many innovations have managed to succeed temporarily, only to fall by the wayside as competitors outdesigned the original idea? The Betamax videotape format comes to mind (eclipsed by vhs), the Honda Insight (beat out by Toyota's Prius), and the BlackBerry smartphone (outclassed by Apple's iPhone). All of these are cases in which a first-mover advantage couldn't save a half-hearted execution.

Finally, how many of today's "successes" are vulnerable to more designful competitors? I'll nominate Facebook, Ryanair, Radio Shack, htc, Breville, Taco Bell, Oreck, Safeway, Hewlett-Packard, and Amtrak, just for starters. What seems to be missing in these organizations is a lack of sophistication about customer experience. You can see it more clearly when you compare them side by side with offerings from Pinterest, Southwest Airlines, Samsung, Nespresso, In-N-Out Burger, Dyson, Whole Foods, ibm, and tgv. The superior customer experience delivered by these brands is the direct result of design.

"The details aren't the details," said designer Charles Eames. "They make the product." Eames's every creative decision grew from "a tight and painful discipline" that brought him to grips with the most prosaic and minute problems. He obsessed about the way two different materials came together, and if they failed to provide a good aesthetic fit, he rejected them. "The connections, the connections, the connections."

Composer Philip Glass has a similar concern for integrity in his music. During an interview with his cousin, Ira Glass, he explained that one of the problems that occupied his attention early on was how to "collapse form and content into one condition, rather than pouring the content into a chosen form." In other words, instead of first selecting a musical genre and then "filling" it with his own music, he preferred to develop the format and the music together, creating a mutually supportive fit without regard to existing genres. It's easy to imagine a musician sitting in on a blues or folk performance without having heard the song before. It's harder to imagine a musician joining in on a quirky German *Lied* or a French *mélodie*. And it's impossible to imagine anyone sitting in on a new Philip Glass composition. By focusing on the fit instead of the genre, Glass has been able to get outside these categories and create unique musical forms and experiences.

You could dismiss this kind of attention to detail by saying, "Well, Philip Glass is a genius." But the same general process that makes Glass a genius is open to you, too, whether you're a business person, engineer, entrepreneur, student, designer, teacher, or supply chain manager. It just takes a willingness to learn through successive layers of effort. Alison Gopnik, a psychologist and author of

> **To improve, you have to push yourself beyond your limits, then pay attention to what trips you up.**

The Philosophical Baby, explains it this way: "You come to make better decisions by making not-so-good decisions and then correcting them. You get to be a good planner by making plans, implementing them and seeing the results again and again." To improve, you have to constantly push yourself beyond your limits, then pay attention to what trips you up.

In design circles this is known as *fast failing.* The successive drawings, models, and prototypes that designers make are not designed to be perfect solutions. They're designed to illuminate the problem, and in the process hone their intuition. In fact, the best designers are those who can keep the project liquid—allowing more iterations and more interaction among collaborators.

Undoubtedly, one of the world's finest examples of creative collaboration was the making of the *King James Bible*, first published 400 years ago. It took the work of 54 scholars and clergymen, organized into six nine-man teams called "companies," meeting over a period of seven years. Since they worked in successive iterations, sharing back and forth as they went, they were able to keep the project in a liquid state while they fashioned one of the purest masterpieces in the history of English prose.

When the project is physical, like a product or a movie or a building, sometimes the biggest challenge is to keep the gestural feeling of the original drawings alive as you work through the iterative process. One way to accomplish this feat is to work physically as long as possible, making mockups, acting out stories, or building models instead of heading straight to the computer.

The temptation in design is the same as in *Groundhog Day*. To look for the quick answer, skip the tedious effort, go right to the gratification of closure. But that would defeat the whole purpose of the exercise. Making, if it's to be meaningful, is a journey to your best self. If you want more, pay more. The effort to imbue objects with integrity is the reason some things are more valuable than others.

THE DISCIPLINE OF UNCLUDING. Many people can *include*. Even more people can *exclude*. But very few people know how to *unclude*. Uncluding is the art of subtracting every element that doesn't pull its weight. Or, as artist Hans Hofmann said, "eliminating all but the necessary so the necessary may speak."

We live in a time of unprecedented clutter: visual clutter, verbal clutter, product clutter, feature clutter, conceptual clutter. *Clutter* is any element that doesn't contribute to meaning or usefulness—a form of pollution that makes life harder to navigate. If life were a garden, clutter would be the weeds that block our paths or obstruct our views. Yet a weed is simply a plant you don't want in your garden, so one person's weed might be another's treasured specimen. And herein lies the wiggle room for many an abuse.

We seem to be addicted to addition. Adding, collecting, stacking, extending, building up, building out—these are activities that come naturally to us. Perhaps there was once a genetic advantage in acquisitiveness, which simply grew stronger over time. We have an urge to build shelters, store food for the winter, add to our knowledge, add to our wealth, and add to our personal power. In some people this addiction devolves into a pathology known as hoarding, causing them to fill their houses to the rafters with old newspapers, used pie tins, odd scraps of plastic, pieces of cardboard—always collecting, never discarding. We shake our heads at this behavior, but maybe we should simply view it as human, only more so.

Companies, also, have a tendency toward hoarding. They build up a tangle of products, services, brands, subbrands, features, departments, offices, and the bureaucratic rules to manage them. They only cut them back when the weeds begin to strangle their profits.

Suzanne Heywood, a consultant for McKinsey, divides business complexity into four types: 1) Dysfunctional complexity, in which irrelevant practices are perpetuated, or relevant activities are duplicated in the wake of mergers or reorgs; 2) designed complexity, created in the expectation that the benefits will outweigh the costs; 3) inherent complexity, part and parcel of the work itself; and 4) imposed complexity, shaped by industry regulators, NGOS, and trade unions. The first two are self-inflicted, while the second two come with the territory.

Heywood interviewed executives at 900 companies, and found that certain types of complexity were causing employees to experience high levels of stress and confusion, which in turn were affecting their performance. They cited things like merger pressures, collaboration challenges, and product proliferation as growing problems.

Of course, complexity isn't always bad. There can be value in having multiple business units, addressing multiple segments, and offering multiple product lines. But there's a difference between complexity and clutter. Complexity, if well organized, is healthy. Clutter is a sign of dysfunction. Companies tend to forgive product proliferation, even embrace it, in the pursuit of growth. And they excuse overgrown product lines on the basis of giving customers more choice.

Customers do want choice, but they want *optimum* choice, not *maximum* choice. A technique called conjoint analysis—a way to study the trade-offs customers are willing to make in a purchase decision—has taught researchers that the most number of choices is rarely the best number of choices. The human brain resists "overchoice"—a word used by Yankelovich Partners to describe the baffling number of options in the marketplace today. They recommend instead that companies offer customers "one-think" shopping as a way to simplify the buying experience.

One-think shopping is actually the number-one goal of branding. It creates the shortest, most efficient path to potential satisfaction and tension release for stressed-out customers. In an age of extreme clutter, the strongest brands are simplifiers.

So why isn't clutter going away? What are the forces arrayed against simplicity? Let me suggest the following:

A need for growth. Most businesses are driven by a desire to keep expanding, which can overshadow the desire to stay lean and profitable. When CEO Ken Constable took over Smith & Noble, an online window-covering company, the product team had been adding new styles of woven blinds at an alarming pace. They named every new product after an Asian city. "I knew we were in trouble," said Constable, "when they told me they were running out of cities." He quickly cut the number of products to the most popular destinations.

> Customers do want choice, but they want optimum choice, not maximum choice.

A search for synergy. As companies grow, they branch out in directions that sometimes aren't profitable. Rather than accept this as a setback and retrace their steps, they add more elements to create "synergy" with the elements that weren't working. In essence, they fight complexity with more complexity, usually making the problem worse. The same thing can happen when a company whose revenues are declining tries to create synergy by merging with another company in the same situation. It's like tying two stones together to see if they'll float. They usually sink to the bottom in a sorry tangle.

A lack of discipline. Simplifying is hard work. It takes vision and courage to fight ambiguity and clutter. It's easier to let customers sort through the mess themselves, then justify it as "customer choice." Only a warrior like Jobs would insist on total simplicity. While other technology companies loaded up their products with functions and buttons, he treated buttons like blemishes, and had them removed.

Market opportunism. When a chance to increase revenues comes along, many companies grab at it, despite the effect on long-term strategy. With every opportunistic grab, complexity increases and focus decreases. This is particularly true with companies who chase fashion over function, as Dell did with its recent line of overtly designed computers, most of which placed style above substance. Hemlines go up, hemlines go down.

Personal fear. Companies are collections of individuals, and individuals can make little decisions that have large cumulative effects. Various fears, including the fear of embarassment, the fear of being singled out, and the fear of being fired, can cause people to hide behind a smokescreen of ambiguity. "All erroneous ideas would perish of their own accord if expressed clearly," said the writer Luc de Clapiers. Better to be unclear than unemployed. This may explain a lot of overblown language, like on the sign next to security at Gatwick Airport: "PASSENGER SHOE REPATRIATION AREA ONLY." *Put your shoes on here* might have been clearer, but not nearly as important sounding. Now imagine a whole company talking like that.

Just as the marketplace is suffering from clutter, so is the English language. Writing expert William Zinsser once said, "We are a society strangling in unnecessary words, circular constructions, pompous frills, and meaningless jargon." In other words, verbal clutter.

Even before Zinsser, Will Strunk gave this advice in *The Elements of Style*: "Omit needless words. Vigorous writing is concise.

A sentence should contain no unnecessary words, a paragraph no unnecessary sentences, for the same reason that a drawing should have no unnecessary lines and a machine no unnecessary parts. This requires not that the writer make all his sentences short, nor that he avoid all detail and treat his subjects in outline, but that every word tell."

A newspaper editor recently received this tweet: "Big story here on natural disaster. Shall I send?" The editor replied, "Send 600 words." The young reporter issued another tweet from the field: "Can't be told in less than 1200." The editor shot back, "Story of creation told in 600. Try it."

Hemingway supposedly bet someone in a bar that he could write a complete story in less than ten words. "No one can do that!" cried the bartender. Hemingway thought for a minute. On the back of the bill, he wrote six words: "For sale. Baby shoes. Never worn."

Creativity consultant Andy Stefanovich found an even more concise expression of a big idea: an insurance company in Norway named If.

When critics complain that something is "overdesigned," what they mean is that it's underdesigned and overdecorated. You can't really overdesign something, because design is the process of improvement. You never hear people complain that something is overimproved. You do hear them complain that something is frilly, pompous, confusing, or unnecessary. Adding decorative elements to an underperforming object is not design but clumsy obfuscation. More is never enough.

> When critics say that something is "over-designed", they usually mean it's under-designed and over-decorated.

"Many of my favorite dishes are those based on the fewest ingredients," said superchef Mario Batali. "And when there are fewer members in the choir, each element must sing perfectly, or harmony is lost." The reason too many elements are dangerous to design is that they become hard to control. Some will cancel others out, some will add irritating noise, and others will drain the vitality from the original concept. These vampire elements may not kill the project, but they can quickly reduce it to zombiehood.

Zombie designs are everywhere, although you don't always

notice them until they get in your way. Take the Swiss Army Knife, a classic metaphor for the value of "more." The $260 Victorinox WorkChamp XL bristles with 28 clever blades, including a scissors, corkscrew, tweezers, toothpick, pliers, metal saw, hoof cleaner, belt cutter, and shackle opener. It's a whole toolshed in a single product. While impressive as a brand symbol, it's not the product that sells the most. Instead, it's a much simpler knife—with only a few tools. Most people view the extra blades in the WorkChamp as costly clutter.

Uncluding is the art of subtracting every element that doesn't pull its weight. over-decorated.

How do you know what should be included and what should be uncluded? Where do you draw the line? Here are five little principles to help you simplify:

1. *Think big, spend small.* When Acorn Computers' Hermann Hauser led the effort to design an elegant processing chip in the early 1980s, he made two crucial decisions. "I gave them no people, and I gave them no money. There was no way they for them to come up with a complex chip."

2. *Kill ten birds with one stone.* Find the place where several problems line up, then knock them down in a single move. For example, organize potential solutions into lists of what's cheap, what's new, what's available, what's different, what's compelling, what's proprietary, and so on, then choose the solution that makes the most out of the least.

3. *Be clear.* Create solutions that are deliberate, single-minded, and free of conceptual noise. "If a man writes clearly enough," said Hemingway, "anyone can see if he fakes." The same applies to all creative disciplines. It's harder to fool yourself when you can clearly see what you're doing.

4. *Look for the obvious.* When presented with two explanations, prefer the simpler. This is the conceptual tool called Occam's Razor, named after medieval philosopher William of Ockhan. Often the best answers are hidden plain sight, so when you slap yourself on the forehead, you've probably found it.

5. *Keep subtracting.* After you've included everything you think is necessary, start uncluding. Remove one element at a time to see

whether it hurts the balance, the proportion, or the unity of the solution. You may be surprised how much energy is released with every subtraction. When you've finally removed the last scrap of clutter, you can then improve what's left.

All the lessons of invention come down to this: The best design tool is a long eraser with a pencil at one end.

THE ART OF SIMPLEXITY. We tend to view simplicity and complexity as opposites, like two sides of a teeter-totter: when one goes up the other goes down. But this isn't true. The enemy of simplicity isn't complexity, but messiness. Likewise, the enemy of complexity isn't simplicity, but also messiness. Complexity and simplicity are both fighting on the same side—the side of increasing order. While complexity seeks order through addition, simplicity seeks it through subtraction. Together they produce richness and usability, two complementary values that have driven the whole of evolution.

The phrase "To be or not to be" is a simple string of words, and each word in it is equally simple. But the meaning behind the phrase is profoundly complex. Namely, why is life worth living? It's not only the basis of a great play, but of the world's great philosophies and religions. Therefore, is "To be or not to be" a simple question, or a complex one?

As I write this sentence on my MacBook Air, I can't help but notice how effortless the interface is. The keyboard is delicate and responsive to the touch; the screen reports back instantly with perfect fidelity; and the whole machine performs like an extension of my mind and fingertips. Yet I'm perfectly aware that this is a complicated machine. It's jam-packed with processors and memory chips and controllers and batteries and cards and cables and LEDS and speakers and other miracles of miniaturization, and each of these is the product of many minds and many years of cooperation and competition. So, is a MacBook Air a simple product, or a complex one?

It may be helpful to think of simplicity and complexity as a combo-concept called *simplexity*. Simplexity stands in opposition to disorder, to entropy, to the messiness that has no meaning.

There's nothing valuable about a mess. It offers complexity without clarity. How do you describe the rubble left by the path of a tornado? The only way to describe it is by calling it a mess, since only the actual mess can describe itself. The problem with messes is that one looks a lot like another. One cluttered website looks a lot

SImplexity stands in opposition to disorder, to entropy, to the messiness that has no meaning.

like another cluttered website. One "comprehensive" product offering looks much like another comprehensive product offering. One convoluted business model is no different—nor more valuable—than any other one. A mess is counterproductive when you're trying to create meaningful differentiation or a competitive advantage.

You know you've found simplexity when you can describe a complicated entity using just a few words, a brief formula, or a clearly conceived diagram. When JetBlue says every passenger flies business class for the price of coach, they've encapsulated their entire value proposition in one sentence. But when American Airlines says passengers can fly without putting their lives on hold, they're unable to find a competitive advantage other than wi-fi. One unfocused airline looks a lot like another to most people. American's difficulty in expressing a clear value proposition reveals a lack of simplexity.

In *The User Illusion*, Tor Nørretranders introduces the term *exformation* to describe how meaning is created. He says that the real value of a message or a product doesn't come from its final content, but from the content that's been discarded along the way—its exformation. The more exformation, the more valuable the information.

For example, by writing 500 words off the top of my head to describe a new product, I could quickly create a page of text. But I'd also be creating a more difficult task for my reader, who now has to sift through my rambling sentences to extract any useful ideas. In systems terminology, I'd be *shifting the burden* to my reader; in the language of economics, I'd be *externalizing* the costs of communication. The value of my work would be low.

But let's say I labored a bit longer on my text, making sure I had the key ideas in place, that they were revealed in a logical order, that the language was crisp and clear, and that all needless words and ideas had been stripped out as exformation. Even though my text has shrunk to only 200 words, it's now many times more valuable than the original 500-word mess. My reader will be able to quickly read it and digest it, and easily remember it and act on it.

When you apply the principle of exformation to a message, you increase its meaning, and therefore its value. The amount of meaning that can be easily extracted from a message is called its *logical depth*. According to IBM Fellow Charles Bennett, the more "calculating time" a sender invests—either in his head or on a computer—the more meaning the receiver will get from it, and the greater its logical depth.

In the world of fashion, Tomas Maier works hard to eliminate all the unnecessary elements in his designs. He doesn't stop until a shirt or a dress reaches a state he calls "a certain nothingness." Sometimes, he says, "you look at a piece of abstract art and it's just, like, a line, and somebody standing next to you says, 'I could do that.' Well, actually—no." Not unless you first spend a decade or so absorbing the lessons of your discipline, then bring your work to a high level of simplexity.

Simplexity does not imply subtraction alone. If you threw out half the parts in a laptop, you might achieve simplicity, but the product wouldn't work. To retain the richness of simplexity, you need compression, not reduction. You need to figure out how to squeeze all the goodness of a complex solution into a package that's easy to use. Think about the electrical grid that brings power into your house. The grid itself is

> You know you've found simplexity when you can describe a complicated entity in only a few words, a brief formula, or a clearly conceived diagram.

fairly complex, but you don't have to worry about that. All you do is flip the switch. The rest of the system is hidden on the other side of the wall.

Apple's lead designer, Jonathan Ive, says his task is "to solve incredibly complex problems and make their resolution appear inevitable and incredibly simple, so that you have no sense how difficult it was." Maybe this is what Leonardo meant when he called simplicity the ultimate sophistication.

A REALITY CHECK. The no-process process is not a license to play around endlessly, any more than the standard process is a license to do mediocre work on time. If the goal is excellence, you have to finish, and you have to do great work. This begs the question, What is great work? How do you know when you're finished? Here are ten simple tests:

1. *Is it surprising?* Will it scare some people? Does it challenge notions of what's normal? Did it reframe the problem? Did you learn something new in the process? The heart of innovation is novelty. So if your solution doesn't disrupt expectations, it has little chance of disrupting a category, a marketplace, or an industry.

2. *Does it have fitness for duty?* Does it fill the "answer-shaped hole"? Is there a good match between what it is and what it does? Is it economical to produce, launch, maintain, and use? Does the solution seem inevitable? Billy Baldwin, one of the last century's most influential interior designers, believed that nothing was in good taste unless it suited its purpose. "What's practical is beautiful," he said.

3. *Are the underlying assumptions true?* Which ones must be correct for the outcome to be a success? Is there a way to test the assumptions using the prototype? If the assumptions prove untrue, in what ways must the solution change?

4. *Does it have a clear focus?* Is it single-minded? Is there a key subject, a central theme, or a main benefit to anchor the proposed solution to its purpose? If it seems like it's trying to satisfy too many goals, or too many people, go back to the drawing board.

5. *Are the elements in harmony?* Are they in the right balance? Is each one necessary? Do they create a unified whole? Is it beautiful? When the choir is singing together, it should sound bigger and richer than the number of singers would suggest.

6. *Will the right people love it?* Will it inspire loyalty? Will it attract talent to your mission? If you try to please everyone, you'll end up pleasing no one. If you please the wrong people while leaving the right ones unmoved, you may wish you had done a little testing before going public. Henry Ford didn't believe in testing, and found out too late that the 1958 Edsel was a car without a market.

7. *Is it courageous?* Even testing won't take all the risk out of innovation. At some point you'll need to stick your neck out. Luckily, most people admire risk taking, which is why so many bold ideas have managed to attract fanatic followings. Courage reads as authenticity to most people.

8. *Is it valuable beyond the near and now?* Does it link up with other great ideas? Will it provide a platform for further innovation? Does it take other people into consideration—not just you and your company, but your customers and society at large? Does it accept responsibility for future consequences?

9. *Does it have depth?* Does it connect on more than one level? Does it appeal not only to people's senses, but to their rational minds, their emotions, their associations, their sense of identity?

10. *Is it as simple as it should be?* Have you eliminated all the unnecessary features, buttons, and colors? Stripped away the excess flourishes, surfaces, and angles? Removed gratuitous scenes, chapters, and symbols? Cut out extra steps, operations, and costs? This is not to say you need to strip out all the quirky details, but that any quirkiness should pull its weight.

How much simplifying is right? It's a question of informed intuition; you need to develop an eye for it. The best way to teach your intuition how to judge simplicity—and aesthetics in general—is the same way everyone makes good judgments. You compare. You consider the merits of one feature, or one solution, relative to another. You weigh the pros and cons, turning it in your hand to look at it from every angle. Without the ability to compare, you're floating in the fog.

Think of comparison as the "eye test" of aesthetic judgment.

Think of comparison as the "eye test" of aesthetic judgment. When you visit the optometrist to get your vision checked, you view the eye chart on the wall through a phoropter, a futuristic-looking machine that lets the doctor switch lenses in and out to find the optimum correction for each eye. With every change of lens he'll ask, "Which looks sharper, this one...or this one?" Just when you think the letter Z looks pretty sharp, the next lens makes it look even sharper. Without the benefit of comparison, you'd probably end up with a suboptimal pair of glasses.

Most of us, given enough time and enough choices, will select for better aesthetics. But we don't always have enough time or enough choices. We need to make decisions on the fly, without sufficient context.

What gives professionals their value is experience—they've worked through so many situations that they've developed a repertoire of aesthetic choices. They don't need as much time because they've already put in their time. The relevant options are hardwired into memory.

SELL IN, NOT OUT. The same skill that allows professionals to make quick, intuitive judgments also creates a knowledge gap that gets in the way of broader adoption. *Asymmetrical knowledge*—a situation in which one person or group knows less about a subject than another person or group—creates fear in the first group and frustration in the second. This is because appreciating a new idea is a kind of journey. Those who've taken the journey, the innovators, forget that the others will need a little more time to catch up.

Imagine being shown a map of the world, only upside down, and being told that this is how all maps will be displayed in the future. Even though you know it's the same map you've seen a thousand times, it suddenly seems unfamiliar. It feels wrong, like your first day in a new school. It takes a bit of effort to accept the idea that Australia is "up over" instead of "down under."

Now imagine being presented with an idea that's guaranteed to turn your actual world upside down. It could be a radical new business initiative, a sweeping organizational change, or an unexpected proposal of marriage. Your first reaction might easily be resistance. You might cast around for logical arguments against it. You might even shoot the messenger. The truth is, most people love change until it affects *them*. Scott Berkun says, "The secret tragedy of innovators is that their desire to change the world is rarely matched by support from the people they hope to help."

What often happens when a new idea hits strong resistance is on-the-spot compromise. The presenter simply "sells out" in order to salvage some of the work or avoid conflict. Yet discounting the integrity of an innovation is like buying an airline ticket halfway to China—you save some money, but you never arrive. A better idea is to take your audience on the same journey you went on, but without the detours and discomforts.

The first step in selling a concept into an organization is to understand what geneticist J.B.S. Haldane knew when he charted the "four stages of acceptance." Whenever a game-changing idea is presented, the first reaction of colleagues is to call it "worthless nonsense." As it begins to slowly take hold, the same colleagues label it "interesting, but perverse." Later, when the idea is all but proven, they admit that it's "true, but unimportant." Finally, after success is assured, they'll claim it as their own: "I always said so." This pattern is so common that you can almost use it as a test for promising ideas. Extreme resistance can be a portent of extreme success.

The second step is to condense the four stages into a shorter time span. If you can take your audience on the journey from "this is worthless nonsense" to "I always said so" in a few minutes or days instead of a few months or years, you'll be able to keep the integrity of your idea and still launch it in a timely fashion. The best way to condense the journey is with a story. The story can take the form of a fable, a comic strip, a children's book, or any other narrative vehicle. The main thing is to keep it simple. Fact-laden PowerPoints will not win hearts and minds. Dr. Spencer Silver spent five fruitless years trying to persuade 3M of the value of his adhesive because he couldn't tell a simple story about what would later become Post-it Notes. If he had imagined this particular use of his adhesive, he could have turned the prototype itself into a vivid story vehicle.

When your goal is to describe a vision for the future, information is not enough. People are up to their necks in information. What they need is a way to imagine life after the change, and compare it with life today. That's why it's called a vision and not a plan. Managers get frustrated when employees say their company has no vision. "Of course, we have a vision," the manager sputters. "It's to be a $5 billion company in five years!" Actually, that's not a vision.

A vision is an image, a picture, a clear illustration of a desired end state. When Microsoft started up, the company's vision was "a computer on every desktop and in every home." That was something everyone could visualize.

When you lead people from *what is* to *what could be* using a simple story, they can more easily visualize themselves playing a role. And if you give them a clear illustration of the happily-ever-after moment, they'll carry it in their minds as they forge onward. Where there's a way, there's a will. A clearly articulated story inspires people to volunteer for a mission instead of waiting for orders.

ACCEPTANCE THRESHOLD

The final challenge in selling into an organization is to shepherd the concept through the "valley of death." This is the bog between the original vision and its commercial deployment, where many a promising idea has met its untimely end. New ideas are fragile. They can be trampled by a word, a glance, or a noncommittal shrug. The job of the shepherd is to shield the idea until it becomes strong enough to fend for itself.

One way to deflect the sticks and stones of naysayers is through a deft use of metrics. When you can counter doubts with concrete numbers, you'll find it has a calming effect on people's nerves.

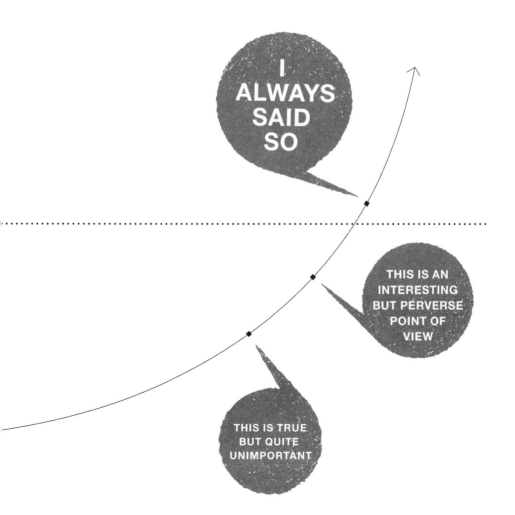

Conventional wisdom says that innovation is difficult to measure. But that's only true if you believe measurement must have an exact value. A more practical approach is to look for "quantified uncertainty reduction," a handrail for the faint of heart. Bayes' Theorem is one such approach. It's a mathematical formula that expresses how a belief should change to account for new evidence. While Bayes' Theorem and other formulas are guesses, they can remove enough doubt to make room for courage.

Another way to keep the naysayers at bay is to find a powerful sponsor. The leaders of organizations usually aren't the innovators. But they can be influential in shifting the norms of the group. In the words of social psychologist Deborah Prentice, "leaders are high-status superconformists, embodying the group's most typical characteristics or aspirations." They're in a good position to support an innovative concept if they can see its value to the goals they've set.

What leaders and designers have in common is a shared interest in positive change. If design is the process of changing an existing situation to an improved one, then in a sense all leaders are designers, and all designers are leaders. Even politicians long for positive change, but the way the political system is set up, they aren't free to promote unproven ideas. They have to wait until ideas gain traction at the grassroots level before they can embrace them.

Dreams don't become innovations overnight. They require visualizing, nurturing, refining, protecting, proving, improving, and selling in. Even smaller dreams—such as writing a great app,

A clearly articulated story inspires people to volunteeer for a mission instead of waiting for orders.

filming a taut documentary, designing a new product, creating an iconic ad campaign, inventing a new dance—must go through the same stages. Lawrence Summers, a former president of Harvard University, said that a good rule in life is that "things take longer to happen than you think they will, and then happen faster than you thought they could."

To me, launching an innovation is like giving birth: it's painful, it seems to last forever, and afterwards you don't get much sleep. Of course, I'll never know for sure. I can only imagine that giving birth is like launching an innovation: you wonder what you were thinking, you wish you'd never started, and when it's over you feel very proud.

THE BIG TO-DO LIST. Recently a group of astronomers in Geneva announced the discovery of a promising Goldilocks planet. What's a Goldilocks planet, you ask? Well, it's one that's not too big, not too small, not too hot, not too cold. One that's *just* right. It's a planet in the so-called habitable zone, orbiting at the right distance from its sun, with earthlike temperatures, liquid water, a rocky surface, and a decent atmosphere.

This particular Goldilocks planet (with the endearing name of HD 85512b) is 3.6 times as massive as the earth and circles its sun at about one-fourth of the distance that our own planet does. It takes only 58 days to complete one orbit (so you could celebrate your birthday six times as often). Its sun is orange and only one-eighth as bright as ours. But the good news is this: It's only 36 light-years from Earth, located in the constellation Vela. That means if we could figure out how to travel at the speed of light, then find our way to Vela, we could reach the surface in less than four decades ("Dad, are we there yet?").

When I was eight years old I led a neighborhood effort to build and launch our first rocket ship to Mars. It ran into technical difficulties almost immediately. We finished the hull on the first day, but we were lacking a means of propulsion, a guidance system, and a way to make the ship spaceproof. At this point it was just wood with an open-air cockpit. We put the project on hold until we could crack the few remaining problems.

Is this the same kind of project? Why would we need a list of Goldilocks planets anyway? Is it because the world's scientists are, at heart, only eight years old? Or is it because enough people believe we'll need to move?

Around two million years ago, at the time of *Homo erectus*, the planet Earth played host to billions of animals, but only a few thousand of them were humans. The human population stayed fairly stable—until approximately fifty thousand years ago when Cro-

Magnon man launched the first cultural revolution, a steady acceleration in the use of tools, fire, bipedal walking, and, most important, spoken language. The population began to surge, and, armed with these new skills, humans began to venture up from Africa to Europe and around to Australia. It was the Cro-Magnons who left us the cave paintings.

The second surge began about ten thousand years ago. First we figured out how to produce food using a predictable system of agriculture, then we invented writing so we could pass our knowledge down and across to others. This was a tipping point at which "our ability to modify the biosphere exceeded the planet's ability to modify us," says Kevin Kelly. In other words, our technology was evolving faster than our DNA. By the year 1 AD, the population had grown to 300 million.

The third surge coincided with the Industrial Revolution about 200 years ago. The mass production of books, starting just after the Renaissance, had begun to democratize science and technology. By the year 1800 we had grown to one billion human beings. Only 127 years later, two billion. We hit three billion in the next 33 years, and four billion in only 15 more. Today we're at a teeming seven billion.

This exponential population growth lies at the heart of our fears about the future. How many humans can the earth support? Are we good for the planet, or just a virus that will eventually run its course and leave the damaged biosphere to recover on its own? This sort of runaway population growth is known as a Malthusian crisis. Thomas Malthus was the economist who, in 1798, wrote "An Essay on the Principle of Population." In it he warned, "The power of population is so superior to the power of the earth to produce subsistence for man, that premature death must in some shape or other visit the human race." He imagined a cascading failure in which widespread famine led to the spread of disease and the decimation of the human race.

Today's Malthusians have generalized the problem of feeding an outsized population to include all natural limits, such as using up our fossil fuels, exhausting our forests, compromising our air, contaminating our water, shrinking our biodiversity, and stripping out our minerals. In their view we're like children who, given a priceless collection of gold coins, spend them all in gumball machines. It took the earth 4.5 billion years to accumulate the resources we now enjoy, yet we're tearing through them like there's no tomorrow. "We do not inherit the earth from our ancestors," says the proverb. "We borrow it from our children." Unfortunately, most of today's talk about natural resources revolves around whether we can extract them. One wonders if the earth will collapse when it's finally hollowed out. Clearly, if we go on as we are, we won't be able to sustain our evolutionary progress.

"But we won't go on as we are," says Matt Ridley, author of *The Rational Optimist*. "That's what we never do." He says we'll try to invent new technologies and new systems and new philosophies to take us to the next level. Just because we *don't* know how doesn't mean we *won't* know how. We'll muddle through.

Let's start by compiling our to-do list. What are the grand challenges facing us in the 21st century? Which problems, if addressed, could unleash a new wave of health and prosperity?

For one, we could slow the extinction of animal and plant life. Losing a species is not only sad, it weakens the overall resilience of our ecosystem. Biodiversity is a key factor in sustaining a healthy planet.

We could make cities more livable. Researchers predict that 75 percent of the world's population will live in them by 2050. Cities offer huge advantages, including the sharing of resources, knowledge, and talent. But does that mean we have to give up trees, quiet streets, and clean air?

Let's get a handle on our food problem. Half of the world is growing obese while the other half is going hungry. We don't seem to know how to feed ourselves. Figuring out the food situation is not only worthy work, but urgent work.

Global warming is nearing condition red. Despite the naysayers, we have cause for alarm. Rising oceans and the loss of animal populations are bad enough—we shouldn't compound the problem with denial. We need to act.

Energy. The fuel that drove us here won't get us where we're going. Everyone knows that, but it's still a challenging problem. Wouldn't it be sad if we poisoned our own atmosphere with fossil fuels, then discovered we didn't have enough to get us to a Goldilocks planet?

On the subject of pollution, we need to clean up the oceans. The thing that makes our own planet the best possible Goldilocks planet is our water. It's the envy of the universe.

We also need to reduce the waste stream. If we're really smart and determined, we should be able to design our products so they can be recycled instead of downcycled or thrown away. Of course, nothing can actually be thrown away. There is no "away" in a closed system.

Let's democratize medicine. This is more than a humanitarian cause. As long as medicine doesn't reach every corner of the planet, the human race is in danger of fast-moving viruses and other contagions. As we become more connected, we become more exposed.

Then there's war. While war is generally on the wane, we need to outgrow it entirely. War is the very essence of entropy. Under the strain of seven billion people, we can no longer afford the wholesale waste that comes from large-scale, mechanized violence. It's a drain on resources and a drain on the human spirit.

These are a few of the urgent items. Once we cross them off the list, we can tackle the really advanced ones, such as how to get around the speed of light. Then traveling to those Goldilocks planets will be more than a fairy tale.

Obviously, huge challenges like these are beyond the reach of a single person, no matter how many metaskills he or she masters. So-called wicked problems can only be addressed through collaboration. Yet the people who will make the most difference in tomorrow's groups are those who can foster a shared vision, then pursue it with a passion, using a combination of feeling and seeing, dreaming and making. If this sounds like you, there's one more metaskill you'll want—*learning*, the opposable thumb of the five talents.

Complex problems like these can only be addressed with metaskills, networked tools, and a shared vision of the future.

GRAND CHALLENGES

INCREASE BIOLOGICAL DIVERSITY
MAKE CITIES MORE LIVABLE
REVERSE OBESITY
IMPROVE LARGE-SCALE FARMING
INVENT RENEWABLE ENERGY SOURCES
CLEAN UP THE OCEANS
REDUCE THE WASTE STREAM
STANDARDIZE REUSABLE MATERIALS
ABOLISH WAR
RESTORE THE MIDDLE CLASS
REPAIR THE OZONE LAYER
HUMANIZE THE PENAL SYSTEM
REDUCE THE OCCURRENCE OF DISEASE
ALLEVIATE HUNGER
FIX THE HEALTH SYSTEM
IMPROVE INTERNATIONAL COOPERATION
DESIGN CLEAN WATER
STREAMLINE MONEY FLOWS
FOSTER STRONGER COMMUNITIES
DEMOCRATIZE BEAUTY
IMPROVE PUBLIC TRANSPORTATION
REDESIGN EDUCATION
OPTIMIZE POPULATION LEVELS
MINIMIZE POVERTY
REINVENT GOVERNMENT
INCREASE HAPPINESS
OUTRUN THE SPEED OF LIGHT

LEARNING

5

IMPOSSIBLE IS NOTHING. Our school system was built on the belief that education is a form of programming. It presumes people will need to follow standardized modes of thought if they're to contribute profitably to society. So the game that guidance counselors play is one of prediction. They ask themselves, In the near future, which jobs will be most abundant?

This leads to the kind of advice we received at my college-preparatory high school: Aim for a degree in accounting or law, since these are prestigious, high-paying professions. Guess what? A large number of graduates ended up in accounting and law. The rest of us drifted off into nonsanctioned roles and workaday jobs, or simply fell off the grid, resigned to the view that we weren't very valuable.

Okay. It was the '60s. But the pressure to conform is still palpable a half-century later. I often hear students make statements like, "I guess I'll be going into social media, since that's where the money is." Or, "It looks like economic power is shifting to China, so I'm learning Mandarin." Or, "Biology is the new black." There's an air of fatalism about these pronouncements, a sense that one's future is both determined and limited by the job market *du jour*.

The future doesn't belong to the present. And we don't belong to our education. It belongs to us. We need to take responsibility not only for *what* we learn, but *how* we learn. As Howard Gardner said, "We need to be able to formulate new questions, and not just rely on tasks or problems posed by others." More importantly, we need to be able to transfer learning from one context to another and not settle for rote answers.

"If you answer questions on a multiple-choice test in a certain way," he says, "or carry out a problem set in a specific manner, you will be credited with understanding. No one ever asks the further question: But do you really understand?" The unspoken agreement is that a certain level of performance is adequate for this particular class. Gardner's view is that even honors students suspect that their knowledge is fragile, which contributes to the uneasy feeling that they—and even the educational institution itself—are somehow fraudulent.

Today's students are not only rewarded for shallow learning, they're punished for deep learning. Genuine learning requires going "offroad," spending as much time as necessary to really understand a subject or a discipline. Traditional schools are simply not set up for this. If an ambitious student decides to buck the system and seek a genuine level of understanding, the outcome is likely to be a bad scholastic record.

Here's my advice for serious students: Instead of expecting traditional schools to do what they can't do, take your education into your own hands. Use traditional courses for what they can do—introduce you to what's broadly known—and use other vehicles to explore what's not broadly known, what's special to your own deep interests, and therefore more valuable to you. These vehicles might include apprenticeships, workshops, special projects, non-credit classes, online tutorials, or self-prescribed reading regimens. When you shift your focus from getting grades to gaining understanding, you set yourself on the road to mastery. You begin learning how to learn.

Self-directed learning, or *autodidacticism*, is a powerful practice because it lets you build a new skill on the platform of the last one. Learning to learn is personal growth squared. It gives you the ability to move laterally from one skill to another by applying deeply understood principles to adjacent disciplines. The faster the world changes, the more fluidly you need to adapt. "The illiterate of the 21st century will not be those who cannot read and write," said

Self-directed learning, or autodidacticism, is powerful because it lets you build a new skill on the platform of a previous one.

Alvin Toffler in *Rethinking the Future*, "but those who cannot learn, unlearn, and relearn."

When you're able to learn something at will, nothing seems impossible. Your confidence swells and any feelings of fraudulence recede. Your knowledge is completely authentic because you've lived it, earned it, claimed it. Whenever you take on a new subject or skillset, your brain reconfigures itself to accommodate the new knowledge. You're literally a different person than you were before. "New ideas capture and possess the mind that births them," said Robert Grudin in *The Grace of Great Things*. "They colonize it and renew its laws."

A 30-year study published in 1999 by the National Institute of Mental Health found that people who take on new and difficult problems tend to perform better than people whose jobs require less thought. Most of us assume that learning difficult subjects requires a higher IQ, but it's more likely that a higher IQ comes from confronting harder problems. In a way, we don't solve problems—problems solve us. They help us complete the puzzle of who we are, asking us to stretch beyond our boundaries and confront what we don't know.

THE JOY ZONE. Erik Demaine became MIT's youngest-ever professor at age 20. If you think this is an accomplishment, consider that he was homeschooled by his single-parent father, started college at 12, and graduated with a bachelor's degree in computer science at 14. A few years later, after getting his PhD from the University of Waterloo, he was awarded a MacArthur "genius" fellowship, an honor that comes with a $500,000 grant to work on whatever strikes you as amusing. For Demaine, it was the mathematics of origami. "I fold paper because it's fun," he says. "That's the driving force." But now he's tackling one of the toughest problems in biology: learning how protein molecules fold themselves into the shapes that dictate their individual functions.

"If you look really close at any living thing, deep inside are lots of little proteins running around, making life happen. Each type of protein folds into a special shape. When proteins fold into the wrong shape," he says, "you get a disease, like Alzheimer's or Mad Cow." The problem for science is that protein folding has been impossible to observe in real time. By developing a mathematical model based on his deep knowledge of origami, Demaine hopes to make the design of synthetic proteins possible.

What kind of person does this? "I'm a geek," he says with a grin. His interests read like the to-do list of a precocious ten-year-old: card magic, juggling, string figures, video games, paper folding, improvisational comedy, and glassblowing. "I blow glass because it's fun. I do improv because it's fun. I fold paper because it's fun. Initially, I did it because the mathematics was fun. Now when I get time I fold paper, because, actually, folding paper is fun."

So here's the $500,000 question: Does Erik Demaine get time to play because he's a genius? Or is he a genius because he gets time to play? The MacArthur committee clearly believes it's the latter, since they referred to Demaine as "moving readily between the theoretical to the playful" in his effort to coax scientific insights from his personal interests.

This is what some would call *ludic* learning, or learning by playing. What makes it so effective is the space it allows for positive emotions. Emotions drive attention, and attention drives learning. "Learning," said Richard Saul Wurman, "is just finding out more about what you're interested in." Wurman has worked variously as a cartographer, architect, graphic designer, author, publisher, and founder of the TED conferences. "I look for subjects that I find particularly interesting but don't completely understand."

Renowned circus juggler Serge Percelly said much the same thing. "I'm just trying to do the act that I would have loved to see."

Filmmaker Jane Campion put it this way: "Playing in your work is the way to find your energy." There's a reciprocal relationship between playfulness and joyfulness. Creative play is thought to release endorphins, those little molecules that put you in a good mood. Conversely, studies have shown that when you're in a good mood, you're usually more creative. Happiness and creativity are therefore mutually supportive. You enter a *joy zone* in which learning accelerates, sometimes by a factor of five or ten. The time seems to fly by, and before you know it you've learned something that becomes deeply embedded in your psyche.

When you enter the joy zone, your learning can accelerate by a factor of five or ten.

The joy zone is traditional education's best-kept secret. After all, if it were widely understood that learning is a product of passion and not test taking, society would have to embrace a more difficult educational model. Schools would have to become facilitators of passion instead of directors of course material. Their efforts would be unmeasurable by current standards, since individual passion can't be standardized. The only measurement of any importance would be the happiness, achievements, and sense of fulfillment of graduates over time.

Pipe dream? No. I believe this is exactly the model we're moving toward. But for many people it's too late. They're either fully occupied in the workforce or just completing their formal education. If this is you, your best bet—which is still a good one—is to take control of your education from here on out. To realize that every day is opportunity to enter the joy zone, the place of autotelic learning, where the thing being learned is its own reward. All this requires is that you know what you love to work at, that you embrace "what you're interested in."

> When you're in your element, mastery follows a simple formula: practice x passion = skill.

When you're in your element, mastery becomes a simple formula: practice × passion = skill. It takes both factors to produce deep learning. If you remove practice from the equation, all you have is aimless enjoyment. If you remove passion from the equation, you're left with shallow learning. While you can still acquire a certain amount skill with one of these factors absent—think of kids who are forced to play the violin—it takes much longer, and your skill will be in some way lacking. But practice and passion together? Magic. Your learning accelerates, your joy shoots off the charts, and over time mastery is inevitable.

Let's go back to Mihaly Csikszentmihalyi (ME-high CHEEK-sent-me-HIGH-ee, remember?). Professor C. is the acknowledged expert on *flow*, a term he uses to describe the mental state of being truly creative. It's a state of optimal experience—the feeling of being in control of your actions, master of your fate. It happens in the narrow space between boredom on one hand, and anxiety on the other. If a task is too easy, what happens? You lose interest. If it's too hard, what happens? You give up. The space in the middle—where a task is neither too easy nor too hard—is the joy zone.

Most of our optimal experiences occur with activities that are goal directed, not aimless, and are bounded by rules. They require an investment of psychic energy, and can't be done without the right skills. They can be competitive, but only if the competition is a means to perfect our skills; when competition becomes an end in itself it ceases to be fun.

The best moments, he says, are when your body or mind is stretched to the limit in a voluntary effort to accomplish some-

When your skills are equal to your challenges, you enter the "flow channel," a zone of joyful engagement.

thing difficult and worthwhile. "It is what the sailor holding a tight course feels when the wind whips through her hair," he says. "It is what a painter feels when the colors on the canvas begin to set up a magnetic tension with each other, and a new thing, a living form, takes shape in front of the astonished creator."

The optimization of creative experience assumes freedom—the freedom to find the right balance between challenge and personal ability. This kind of freedom is not likely to come from a standardized curriculum or test-based educational model. You have to give it to yourself. You have to find your strengths, discover the right medium in which to express them, and allow yourself the necessary time to experiment and push the limits of your understanding. As Joseph Campbell said, you have to "follow your bliss."

WHAT'S THE MISSION? Passion is powerful, yet not always strategic. We live in a society where competition often determines winners and losers in accordance with the Competitive Exclusion Principle. This is the Darwinian rule that says when two or more species compete for a limited resource, one of them will win, eventually squeezing the others out of the picture. It's a cruel world. But it doesn't have to be if you apply the opposite lever—the Strategic Differentiation Principle. This is the principle of dominating a valuable niche that's unavailable or uninteresting to others.

"I'm not the sort of person who likes a lot of competition," said Jack W. Szostak, a Nobel Prize winner who's now researching the origins of life. "I particularly don't like the feeling that if I weren't around doing certain work, it wouldn't make any difference. If it's going to be done anyway," he said, "what's the point?" Exactly. Why invest so much time into your skills if you have to fight everyone else for the privilege of applying them? And why work hard at something the world doesn't need?

At the beginning of the book, I hinted at the potential of purpose to drive personal success. My view is that we're not born with a purpose, but that nature has equipped us with goal-seeking minds that perform better in the context of purpose, or the sense that life *means* something. The American Psychological Association defines learning as the natural process of pursuing one's personal goals, in which we construct meaning by filtering information and experiences through our unique perceptions, thoughts, and feelings. According to Professor Csikszentmihalyi, "The age-old riddle—What is the meaning of life?—turns out to be astonishingly simple. The meaning of life is *meaning.*"

Yet meaningful purpose, even when fueled by passion, is not enough to ensure success in the face of serious competition. Purpose needs to be coupled with strategy, a deliberate plan to own and defend a niche that matters. The world doesn't really need another software designer, artist, actress, economist, athlete, attorney, food writer, activist, or TV host. But it does need Jack Dorsey, Ai Weiwei, Viola Davis, Muhammad Yunus, Buster Posey, Almudena Bernebeu, Amanda Hesser, Camila Vallejo, and Stephen Colbert. These are people who have found a unique mission to express their life's purpose. Some have stumbled into it, some have simply followed their bliss, and others have designed a deliberate path.

A *mission*, simply stated, is a plan to fulfill a purpose. Having a mission doesn't guarantee success, but it does make it more than an accident. A mission isn't permanent. It can change as you learn more about your discipline, your competition, and who you are in relation to the larger world. Its value doesn't derive from rigidity but from focus. It keeps you from running off in a hundred directions at once in the mistaken belief that more is better.

"There is no evidence that quantity becomes quality in matters of human expression or achievement," said Jaron Lanier. "What matters instead, I believe, is a sense of focus, a mind in effective concentration, and an adventurous individual imagination that is distinct from the crowd." When you're focused on a mission, your mind becomes magnetized. It collects only the information and experiences you're likely to need, arranging them into a flexible hierarchy. The purpose determines the mission, the mission determines the strategy, the strategy determines the tactics, the tactics determine the tasks.

When you're focused on a mission, your mind becomes magnetized.

But what *is* the mission? What should I do? Where do I start?

These are important questions, but they don't have to tie you in knots. The liberating answers are "you decide," "whatever you like," and "start anywhere." The reality is, you can't know the ultimate shape of your mission. You have to begin the journey someplace and correct course as you go. But it does help to set off with a rough map of the territory.

Your map can be as simple as two overlapping circles. One circle represents the world, or, more precisely, what the world values. The other circle is you, including all the passion and skills you can bring to it. Where the two circles overlap is the most fertile area for growth. It's the place where your mission can most easily take root, and where you'll find the success and appreciation you'll need to thrive. You may long to be a musician, for example, but the world doesn't need more musicians. It needs certain kinds of musicians, with certain skills, who can make certain kinds of music, and address certain audiences. Finding out where these special areas are, and which ones overlap with your passion and skills, is the biggest challenge.

Once you've found the overlaps, you can decide where to focus your energies. My advice is to choose a direction that lets you work with your whole heart instead of a divided heart. In today's fragmented world, wholeheartedness confers a distinct advantage upon those who can offer it, because it turns ordinary work into extraordinary work.

Psychologists Howard Gardner, Mihaly Csikszentmihalyi, and William Damon led a collaborative effort to discover the key properties of extraordinary work. Members of the GoodWork Project conducted 1200 interviews in nine professional spheres, and came up with what they called the three *E*s. "Good work is *excellent*," said Gardner. "It meets the technical standards of the relevant profession or craft. It is personally *engaging*. Carrying out good work over the long haul proves too difficult unless that work remains inviting and meaningful to the practioner. The third *E* is *ethical*," he said. "The good worker constantly interrogates herself about what it means to be responsible."

Whenever you engage in good work that aligns with your mission, your progress accelerates. You can see firsthand that your

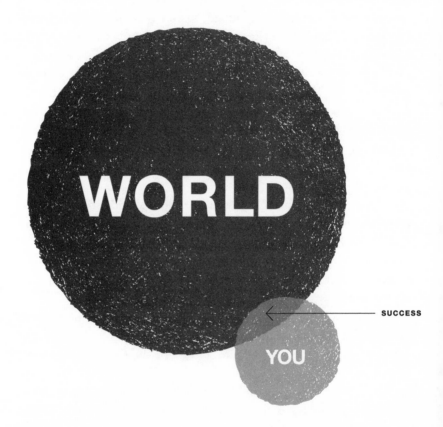

WORLD

YOU

SUCCESS

The most fertile
area for growth
is the overlap between
what the world
needs and what you
have to give.

work matters. You learn more quickly, and you learn more deeply. You get the short-term rewards of being in the flow, and you get long-term rewards of eudaimonic well-being, the happiness that comes from fulfilling your potential.

A THEORY OF LEARNING. The talent of learning is a form of meta-cognition, or knowing about knowing. It's the self-awareness that comes from observing what you think while you're thinking it. It tells you when and how to use a particular strategy to solve a problem or address a challenge.

We learn skills in a predictable sequence. We begin with the *cognitive* phase, in which we intellectualize the task and invent tactics to accomplish it with the fewest number of errors. Then we move to the *associative* phase, in which we worry less about errors than applying our skill to a specific task. Finally, we reach the *autonomous* phase, when we're just about as good as we need to be. Our skills have become habits—foundations on which we can build new skills.

William Edwards Deming was the American statistician and consultant who taught Japanese manufacturers how to compete with the rest of the world. Remember Toyota's advertising tagline? "The quality goes in before the name goes on." This was more than a boast. It was the reason Americans began buying Japanese cars instead of those made in Detroit. When Ford Motors finally got around to analyzing the difference between Japanese cars and American cars, they found that the only variation lay in the tolerances of the parts. The Japanese simply put more effort into precision and efficiency. That was the influence of Dr. Deming, whose advice had fallen on deaf ears in his own country.

Yet Deming was no bean counter. He was a teacher who understood that the most important things in life couldn't be measured. Profound knowledge can't be taught, he said, only learned through experience. While many people would agree that "experience is the best teacher," he believed that experience by itself teaches nothing. You need to interpret your experience against a theory. Only then can you understand learning in the context of a system.

A theory is a model of reality that can be used to explain, predict, or master a particular phenomenon. It provides a framework for experience, so you can understand what happens, not at the event level, but at the systems level. It helps you answer the question: What does this *mean?* Becoming an autodidact requires that you develop your own theory of learning, a personal framework for acquiring new knowledge. While everyone's framework is unique, here are 12 timeless principles you can borrow to construct it:

Learn by doing. First-hand experience offers the richest fuel for creativity. We learn better and faster when we use our senses, our hands, and our whole bodies in addition to our brains. You can certainly read about dancing, but there's no substitute for getting out on the floor.

> **We learn better and faster when we use our senses, our hands, and our whole bodies in addition to our brains.**

Find worthy work. A journey of a thousand miles begins with a single step. Make sure the first one, and each one thereafter, offers new and valuable lessons on the path to your purpose. Try not to settle. It's too hard to work with one hand holding your nose.

Harness habits. The brain forms habits when routines are shoved from the frontal cortex down to the basal ganglia. They allow you to perform familiar tasks with very little conscious thought, freeing up mental resources to concentrate on new challenges. Consistency and repetition recruit your neural networks to turn experiences into automatic skills. Of course, habit works both ways.

Focus on your goals. Of the eight conditions for creative flow, five are concerned with focus. You must be able to 1) define clear goals for yourself, 2) concentrate on the task at hand, 3) become so deeply involved that 4) your sense of time is altered, and 5) all concern for the self disappears. You'll find that with practice you'll develop a ready capacity for intense focus.

Learn strategically. You can learn *anything,* but you can't learn *everything.* Read specifically on your subject. Appreciate great ideas with felonious intent. Keep a file of every idea you wish had been yours, and you'll begin to absorb the lessons of your heroes. Über-restaurateur Reed Hearon said, "If you read two books on a subject written by knowledgeable people, you will know more than 95% of the people in the entire world know about that subject."

Cultivate your memory. Memory is like a garden. It you don't tend it, your knowledge will wither from a lack of nutrients, or starve from a lack of light. While general knowledge is readily available online, knowledge that's specific to your craft or discipline needs to be available right when you need it. This is possible through neuroplasticity, the ability of the brain to connect new ideas to old ones. "Nerve cells that fire together wire together," says educator Stephanie Marshall. By the same token, you need to continually weed out obsolete knowledge by forgetting.

Increase your sensitivity. What makes artists different from non-artists is their ability to make subtle distinctions between outcomes. This takes place in the associative phase of learning, after you've mastered the basics of your discipline. But it doesn't happen by itself. You need to consciously identify the nuances that separate the great from the merely good.

Stretch your boundaries. Personal growth demands that you constantly aim beyond your capabilities. When someone says he's had 15 years of experience, you wonder if he's actually had one year of experience 15 times. Masterful practitioners are those who constantly stretch into new areas, even at the risk of failure. When Alexander Bell was imagining the telephone, he talked to an electricity expert named Professor Joseph Henry. Bell told Henry he didn't have the electrical knowledge to bring the invention into existence. The professor replied, "Get it."

Customize your metaskills. For purposes of this book, I've focused on five abilities I feel are missing from our current educational models. But the metaskill of learning requires that you develop a personalized list to address your own situation and the requirements of your discipline. For example, Dr. Gerald Grow of Florida A&M University offers this list of six metaskills for budding journalists: clarity, compassion, commitment, context, creativity, and centeredness. What are the metaskills that will drive success for you?

> **What makes artists different from non-artists is their ability to make subtle distinctions between outcomes.**

Feed your desire. I once asked my mentor, painter Robert Overby, what he thought was the secret of creative success. He said, "The

Big Want." It's the burning desire that can't be extinguished with failure, lack of sleep, lack of money, or loss of friends. When you want something so bad you'll never give up, no matter what kind of setbacks you encounter, success will eventually surrender to you. The Big Want is not a hardship. It's the vision that carries you forward, and all you have to do is keep it alive.

Scare yourself. Courage is not the same as fearlessness. Instead, it's the ability to move ahead *despite* your fear. When you confront your demons, you often find they're more mirage than monster, and you advance by leaps and bounds. Every day your to-do list should contain this item: "Scare self."

Practice. There's practice, and then there's practice. Deliberate practice is the only kind that makes a difference. Training a skill involves performing an action over and over, deliberately and mindfully, until it becomes part of your muscle memory. Only then can you move on to higher levels of creativity and nuance. Shortly after Michelangelo died, a scrap of paper was found in his studio that contained a note to his assistant: "Draw, Antonio, draw, Antonio, draw and do not waste time." Practice is the scaffolding of magic.

Though these principles may seem demanding, you can probably conquer the ones you need in several years. That's not long in the context of a career. And as you begin to absorb their lessons, you'll find yourself quickly scaling the heights of mastery.

CLIMBING THE BRIDGE. One way to think about career learning is to conceive it as a bridge that's built on a series of spreading columns. Each column represents a path that leads from a specific skill at the bottom up to more general skills at the top. The base of each column is *craft knowledge*, the entry level for your journey upward. From there you acquire *disciplinary knowledge*, the skillset that qualifies you as a competent professional. Higher up is *domain knowledge*, a broader understanding of the environment in which you practice your discipline. And at the very top is *universal knowledge*.

Universal knowledge is the level that connects all the domains, including all their supporting disciplines and crafts. It's domain-independent, meaning that the same knowledge is applicable to any skill you care to learn. There's no express elevator to universal knowledge. The only way to reach it is by working your way up from the bottom, tier by tier. Once you get there, however, it's fairly easy to move across to new domains, where you can drill down into the supporting disciplines and crafts from a position of experience. Here are some stories to illustrate this.

On her fifth attempt, a young accountant finally passes the CPA exam. Her craft skills are minimal, but they're enough to land her a job with a good firm. Within a few years she demonstrates a solid understanding of the laws and procedures governing state and federal income taxes, and gains fluency with QuickBooks and other tools of the trade. As her confidence grows, her domain knowledge lets her reimagine the tax accounting business. She takes over a small firm and transforms it by applying new processes and cutting-edge technology cobbled together from reading, seminars, workshops, and conferences. Soon after this, she decides to sell the firm and reinvent herself. With the benefit of generalized knowledge, she's able to move directly across into a CEO position with an exciting electronics firm. Today she smiles when she thinks about her CPA exam.

In middle school, a boy becomes a Guitar Hero expert. He borrows a beat-up Stratocaster, and begins learning riffs and chord sequences by imitating what he hears on recordings. In a few years he gets a job with a bar band, where he's exposed to a variety of genres and quickly expands his repertoire. By now he can play just about anything after hearing it once or twice. He learns to combine musical ideas, invent his own, and even compose whole songs from scratch. His latest band begins performing and recording his original music, during which time he learns the business side of rock and roll. He takes up other instruments, including piano, bass, and drums, and makes the deliberate move of learning musical notation. This frees him to write and arrange music for other groups. He then embarks on a successful career as a composer, creating music for movies, commercials, and well-known artists. Lovingly displayed on his studio wall is his old Guitar Hero controller.

A socially challenged Trekkie reads voraciously about anything technical. He does math for kicks, thinks his college classmates are stupid, and can't seem to get a job. He finally gets hired as a bug hunter for a software firm. While not exactly his dream job, it lets him distinguish himself from the hundred or so programmers in his group. He begins to realize that there are other smart people in the world, and that "smart" comes in different flavors. He gets a chance to manage a small team of developers working on a pilot application for mobile computing. It doesn't go well. The other members resent his abrupt manner and become frustrated with his lack of people skills. Over the years he grapples with this problem, consciously focusing on communication, group dynamics, and marketing theory. Eventually he leads a team that invents a language translation application. It becomes the standard system for simultaneous translation, which opens up millions of new channels for commerce, culture, and idea sharing around the world.

The simplified bridge model is useful because it emphasizes how leaders in any field are more effective when they bring the req-

UNIVERSAL KNOWLEDGE

DOMAIN KNOWLEDGE

DISCIPLINARY KNOWLEDGE

CRAFT KNOWLEDGE

uisite craft and disciplinary knowledge with them. I'm always suspicious of job applicants who define themselves as "concept people." Concepts about what? Based on what? Who's going to execute these concepts? A concept is only as valuable as the knowledge, experience, and skills behind it. Real idea people are those who have paid their dues at the bottom of the bridge, where the crucial details are tested, refined, and proven.

Yet the top of the bridge is where evolutionary progress is made. This is the level where domains are joined, ideas are shared across disciplines, and vocabularies are cross-translated in ways that invigorate art, science, business, and education. Biologist E.O. Wilson uses the word *consilience* to describe this phenomenon. It literally means "a jumping together" of knowledge from different fields of endeavor.

The pathway to the top is not a ladder but a lattice. It's made up of people and opportunities that offer multiple routes for learning, advancement, and contribution. There's no predetermined course, no guided tour, no golden ticket. It's up to you to choose your steps.

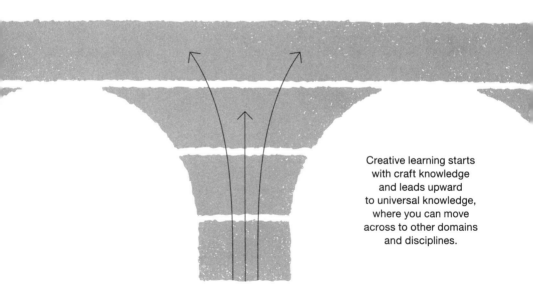

Creative learning starts
with craft knowledge
and leads upward
to universal knowledge,
where you can move
across to other domains
and disciplines.

CREATIVITY LOVES COMPANY. You can be a genius all by yourself, but a genius without a community is less powerful than a genius within a latticework of kindred spirits. As with any kind of lattice, whether physical, chemical, or social, it's the connections between the parts that determine the collective power of the whole, and therefore its value to the parts.

In social networks, there's a qualitative difference between bridging and bonding. *Bridging*, to paraphrase political scientist Robert Putnam, is the process of making friends with like-*spirited* people, people with different views and skills but similar ethics and goals. *Bonding*, in contrast, is making friends with like-*minded* people—people of the same political party, the same religion, the same nationality, the same age group, or the same race. Both kinds of connections, bridging and bonding, are necessary to be successful and happy. But bridging is the activity that brings the highest rewards, and the one that pushes society forward. Social bridging and career bridging run in parallel.

Social bridging makes use of what sociologist Mark Granovetter calls "weak ties." He found that weak ties *between* groups can be stronger than the strong ties *within* groups. If you're seeking new information or fresh insights, you need to look beyond your clique, since a clique is a closed system that acts more like a mirror than a window. For example, the workers at Google are a fairly diverse group of people, but they spend a lot of time together at the Googleplex in Silicon Valley, reading the same great books, eating together in the same great cafeterias, working on the same fascinating problems. When CEO Larry Page was asked what he thought the biggest threat to his company was, he replied: "Google."

The antidote to the clique is to open the window. Connect with groups outside your own. Put yourself in the way of meeting like-spirited people, not just like-minded people. This is the underlying principle of social networks like LinkedIn and Facebook, which facilitate weak ties with people outside your group. It's also the driving force behind social venues like Fritz Haeg's Sundown Schoolhouse in Los Angeles, where filmmakers, technologists, and other professionals freely share their knowledge, and the Secret

Science Club in Brooklyn, where everyone is welcome and speakers are paid in "beer and applause."

There's a popular saying that came from a Frank Sinatra song. It goes: If you can make it in New York, you can make it anywhere. While this may be flattering to New Yorkers, the opposite is more likely to be true: If you can't make it somewhere else, you can probably make it in New York. Large populations provide the social and business networks necessary for professional success, especially when the profession is highly specialized, or the professional has rarefied skills. You can perform in musicals in the state of Nebraska, but you'll learn much faster on the stages of New York.

Moreover, studies show that people are often happier in social networks. Happiness appears to be contagious. When one person is contented, their friends have a 25% greater chance of being contented themselves. People near the center of the network tend to grow happier over time than those at the periphery. This shouldn't be surprising, since people in networks tend to share knowledge more frequently than loners. When you continually give away what you know, you learn to replenish your knowledge as you go, and you also benefit from the knowledge of others. People who hoard knowledge simply don't get much knowledge back. "He who receives an idea from me," said Thomas Jefferson, "receives instruction himself without lessening mine; as he who lites his taper at mine receives lite without darkening me." Jefferson would have been right at home with social media. (Especially with that funky spelling.)

Yet the strong ties that exist within groups can also be powerful, especially when you're trying to accomplish a creative task that demands a high degree of both skill and collaboration. Frank Stephenson, the designer of the BMW Mini and the Fiat 500, is proudest of his work on the McLaren MP4, since the tight-knit design team was able to create a cohesive look for the body styling. "A lot of times when you get a car out there," he said, "it looks like you had somebody working on the front, somebody working on the sides, and somebody working on the back—and they were all mad at each other."

> People near the center of a network tend to grow happier than those at the periphery.

I was hiking one day when I saw another hiker with a T-shirt that said: "Small animals make first paths." That seemed like an apt metaphor for innovation. Most of the world's breakthroughs have been the work of small companies or small teams, working closely together with a shared vision for changing the world. We know Apple as a company with thousands of designers on the payroll, but the company's key products were conceived by a small, intimate team, working closely in a small space with great tools.

Talent isn't something we have, but something we do. We can believe we have talent in private, but we can't prove it unless we exercise it in public. Excellence thrives in a network.

UNPLUGGING. To be creative, whether alone or in a group, you need the ability to pay attention. "Paying attention" is the right phrase, because it costs something to focus on a task, or a train of thought, or another person's words. The price of attention is psychic energy. Most of us can pay attention to a difficult task for a few seconds or a few minutes, but it's real work to stay focused much longer than that. Our minds tend to wander, looking for an escape. We can almost feel our brain squirming in its seat.

This attention deficit isn't new, but it seems to have gotten worse during the Industrial Age. As life sped up, our attention spans got shorter. Now we have a situation called *continuous partial attention*, meaning that our consciousness is so fragmented, so chopped up and balkanized that the pieces are nearly unusable. We hope that somehow the bits and bytes of partial attention will reconnect, like data packets over the Internet. But they rarely do. We're left with partial thoughts, partial experiences, and partial understandings.

This is the trap of the always-on, always-on-ya culture. Mobile computing offers a built-in escape from sustained focus. At the same time, it provides a ready excuse for avoiding conversation with the strangers, neighbors, and colleagues who might expand our thinking. If we're always on, then our creative brains are always off. Creativity requires sustained concentration, the ability to stick with a problem long enough to get beyond shallow, multiple-choice answers. Instagram, the photo-sharing program, makes you feel creative when you apply "artistic" filters to your images, but it's multiple-choice artistry. The real artistry was in the design of the business model. The users are merely components.

Does this sound critical? It should. This is the road that leads to robotic people instead of humanlike robots. A recent New York Times article reported the story of a 14-year-old girl at Woodside High School, in California, who sends and receives 27,000 texts per month, "her fingers clicking at a blistering pace" as she holds up to seven conversations at a time. "I can text one person while talking on the phone to someone else," she says.

Once we get past our admiration for anyone who can develop such arcane skills, we can see this is not so much a skill as an addiction. With her day taken up with texting, it's unlikely that she has time for focused schoolwork or homework, much less quiet reflection. In fact, there's a good chance she's even uncomfortable being alone with her thoughts. The *Diagnostic and Statistical Manual of Mental Disorders* even has a new term for it: Internet use disorder.

"When people are alone, even for a few moments, they fidget and reach for a device," says Sherry Turkle, psychology professor at MIT. "Here connection works like a symptom, not a cure." We believe constant communication will make us feel less lonely, she says, but the opposite is true. "If we are unable to be alone, we are far more likely to be lonely." Psychologist put some of this down to "FOMO," or the "fear of missing out." It's a flammable mixture of anxiety, inadequacy, and irritation that can flare up while using Facebook, Twitter, Foursquare, or Instagram.

Creativity requires sustained concentration, the ability to stick with a problem long enough to get beyond shallow, multiple-choice answers.

Some people blame the situation on information overload. Technology pundit Clay Shirky disagrees: "It's not information overload. It's filter failure." The traditional boundaries built into our social norms have been breached by technology, and we haven't figured out where to build new boundaries. We're still in the gee-whiz phase of social media, in which everything is exciting and seductive. Yet creativity and self-directed learning demands that we periodically wall ourselves off from the always-on culture, so we can spend quality time with our thoughts.

"Without solitude," said Picasso, "no serious work is possible." Leonardo found the same thing to be true. By all accounts he was a highly social creature—dressing in the latest fashions, hobnobbing with royalty, attending and designing glittery social events—but he would also disappear for weeks a time, completely *incommunicado*, to pursue a line of questioning without interruption. Steve Wozniak, designer of the original Macintosh, said that "most inventors and engineers I've met are like me—they live in their heads. They're almost like artists. In fact, the very best of them *are* artists. And artists work best alone."

You can't switch off the world. But you can block it out while you work. You can carve out quiet time to work things through by yourself, so that when you return to the world you have something deep and pure to show for it. Working alone doesn't mean being lonely. It doesn't even mean being alone. But it does mean paying attention, listening to your own voice, and listening to the voices of others with sustained focus. Only when you've mastered this skill can you embark on the long journey of creative self-discovery.

THE SCENIC ROAD TO YOU. There's no set route to self-mastery. You can't print out directions from MapQuest or follow the instructions of your GPS device. There's no app for that. You can't ask Siri. The only voice that really matters is the little voice in your head, the one telling you to take this opportunity, avoid that trap, wait and see on that situation. In the pursuit of mastery, as in the geometry of nature, there are no straight lines—only curving, broken, sketchy, or tentative ones. The kind of learning that feeds your talent requires that you go the long way instead of taking the shortcut. As Jaron Lanier said, "Being a person is not a pat formula, but a quest, a mystery, a leap of faith."

That doesn't mean you're without resources. A hiker may not know what kind of weather lies in ahead, or what kind of terrain to expect, but she can start out with a general plan, be prepared with a backup plan, pack the right equipment, and arm herself with survival skills. Every step or misstep is provisional and correctable, a mini-lesson on the path to mastery.

We used to think of higher education as the four years following secondary education. You put in your time, you pass your tests, and *ta-da!* You're educated. They slap a diploma on your back and ship you off to work. Yet tomorrow an education will look less like a package and more like journey. It's estimated that by 2025, the number of Americans over 60 will increase by 70%. This means occupational changes will become more commonplace, requiring new habits of lifelong learning.

In the pursuit of mastery, as in the geometry of nature, there are no straight lines.

Brain scientists are finding that older minds can compete quite well with younger ones, albeit in different ways. Younger minds can retain information better and retrieve it more quickly, while older minds can solve problems better and put information in perspective. What the oldsters lack in quickness, they make up for in wisdom. This is good news for both ends of the spectrum, since the young and the old make excellent partners, each supplying what the other lacks.

The trend toward multiple careers is not lost on what's been called Generation Flux. GenFluxers are a psychographic group made up mostly—but not entirely—of young people who understand that the race goes not to the swift but to the adaptable. They embrace instability and revel in the challenge of new careers, new business models, and shifting assumptions. Robert Safian notes that the vast bulk of our institutions—educational, corporate, political—are not built for flux. "Few traditional career tactics train us for an era when the most important skill is the ability to acquire new skills." GenFluxers are undeterred.

The Robotic Age seems tailor-made for GenFlux. Jeremy Gleick is a sophomore at UCLA who majors in both neuropsychology and engineering. Recently, while his friends were out partying, he stayed back and logged the 1,000th hour of his self-study program. He's been using the Internet to teach himself an eclectic range of subjects from alchemy to Zulu, from left brain to right brain, for no other reason than they interest him. Jeremy is not a nerd. He's not socially challenged. He's just on fire with curiosity. His spreadsheet shows 17 hours on art history, 39 on the Civil War, and 14 on weaponry. He's taken up juggling, glass blowing, banjo, and mandolin, working on each in turn for one hour a night.

Learning like this is liberating. It's not part of a curriculum, and there's no certificate, no graduation day. Just the satisfaction of following your bliss until you become the person you're capable of being. When you learn like this, you defy everyone who tells you to be practical, to get with the program. As Nicholas Humphrey put it, once you harness your ambitions to this unique thing called *me*, you become the kind of person who aspires not just to *be* yourself but to make *more* of yourself—through learning, creativity, expression, influence, and love. You become the story you tell about yourself. Your story becomes your map.

What makes us happiest is getting where we want to go. The quality of our attention shapes us, then we in turn shape the world. The ones who do it best, most beautifully, most lovingly, most imaginatively, are the crazy ones—the ones who think they can. As John Maxwell said in *The Difference Maker*, "Impossible is just a big word thrown around by small men who find it easier to live the world they've been given than to explore the power they have to change it. Impossible is not a fact. Impossible is not a declaration. It's a dare. Impossible is potential. Impossible is temporary. Impossible is nothing."

When you find the joy zone and stay in it, you embark on a journey to the center of yourself. You carry with you the five tools that define your humanness—*feeling, seeing, dreaming, making,* and *learning.* You join a small party that set out 50,000 years ago from the caves of Africa, and is now on its way to the stars.

We're not human beings; we're human *becomings.* We're not the sum of our atoms; we're the potential of our spirit, our vision, and our talent. We delight in feeling alive, in seeing what's possible, in putting our mark on the universe.

This hand made this drawing.

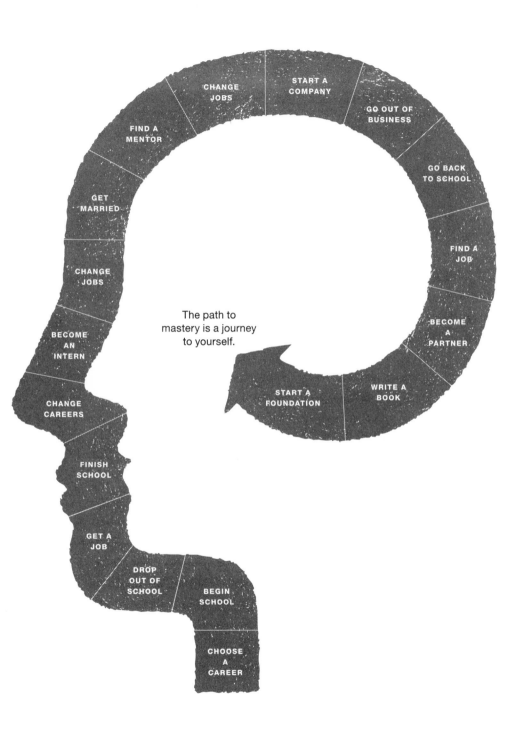

The path to mastery is a journey to yourself.

A MODEST PROPOSAL

I wrote *Metaskills* primarily for professionals already in the workplace—those of us whose education didn't prepare us for the rigors of the Robotic Age. But what about the generations coming up? Shouldn't these higher-order skills be built into their education? Possibly even the foundation for it? Anyone born after the year 2000 will face a much different world than we did, and will require a different kind of education. Tellingly, the need for transformation is coming at a time when the cost of traditional schooling is spiraling out of reach, causing students and parents to question the cost-benefit ratio. We've reached a point where disruptive innovation can trigger a sweeping change.

In the commercial arena, when products get so fancy that their prices start to strain the pocketbook, not-so-fancy products and services with lower cost-structures can easily disrupt the marketplace. People adopt them—not because they're better—but because they're more immediate and affordable than the older alternative. Examples include shopping on Amazon, getting around town with a Zipcar, holding meetings on Skype, and making movies on an iPad. Over time, disruptive products get fancier and more expensive, making them ripe for the next round of disruption. There's no reason to exclude education from this cycle of improvement.

In 1729, Jonathan Swift wrote a satirical essay called "A Modest Proposal" in which he suggested that the solution to poverty and overpopulation in Ireland was for the Irish to eat their children: "I have been assured by a very knowing American of my acquaintance in London," he said, "that a young healthy child, well nursed, is at a year old a most delicious, nourishing, and wholesome food, whether stewed, roasted, baked or boiled; and I make no doubt that it will equally serve in a fricassee or ragout." Good one. But by feeding our children to the factory, we did pretty much the same thing. We sacrificed our offspring to the gods of mass production.

So to round out the book I'd like to offer an opposite proposal, laid out in seven steps.

1. SHUT DOWN THE FACTORY. I propose—modestly, of course—that we dismantle the educational factory and replace it with an educational garden. Like the best gardens, it should combine both organic and man-made components, be designed to serve the twin goals of beauty and function, and be open to the widest possible public.

At a time when the Industrial Age is coming apart at the seams, school reformers have doubled down on the factory model, insisting on standardized courses, standardized testing, and standardized views of human resources. They're busy producing graduates for standardized jobs that may not exist in a few years, and that offer little in the way of satisfaction, fulfillment, or joy. If we had set out to pry our children from their human natures, dampen their passion, and keep them from constructing a meaningful story for their lives, we couldn't have designed a better system.

"Why can't Johnny and Susie read, write, and count?" is the mantra of reform, says Stephanie Marshall. "Why aren't we at least equally troubled by why Johnny and Susie can't think, can't slow down, can't sit still, can't imagine, can't create, and can't play? Why aren't we deeply saddened that they can't dance, or paint, or draw, or make up a story? Why aren't we worried that they can't cope with frustration and conflict?"

Every learner possesses a unique and vibrant constellation of unknowable learning potentials, she says. But all we worry about is what college our kids will get into. In 1972, according to a recent study, high-income families were spending five times as much on education as low-income families. It said that by 2007 the gap had grown to nine to one as spending by upper-end families doubled. The pattern of privileged families is "intensive cultivation," it concluded, set against a background of extreme competition.

In a recent article, "The Escalating Arms Race for Top Colleges," Jennifer Moses said, "My husband and I shelled out a small fortune over the past year for SAT and ACT tutoring for our 17-year-old twins, a son and a daughter. If we hadn't, what if—God forbid—some other kid who went ahead and got the tutoring inched his or her SAT score up just enough to bump our kids out of the running?" This general perception of scarcity has only strengthened the business of the educational factories. Except now they're disguised to look more like resorts than factories, with relaxed course loads, nonscholastic amenities like climbing walls and dining facilities, handsome buildings by famous architects, expansive sports complexes, and celebrity professors spread too thin, all of which adds to the cost but not the quality of education. Meanwhile, fewer and fewer students can afford them, and of those who can, many will be saddled with so much debt that they have to follow the money instead of their dreams. There will always be a market for luxury learning experiences. But we'll need affordable and flexible alternatives if we hope to prepare society for the Robotic Age.

In an educational garden, the gates are open to everyone. There's a wide variety of learning options. New concepts are cultivated and tested every year. Special memberships and paid events are available for those who can afford them, while the basic entrance fees are kept to a minimum for those who can't. An educational garden replaces replication with imagination, reductive thinking with holistic thinking, passive learning with hands-on learning, and unhealthy competition with joyful collaboration. A garden is not only more soul stirring than a factory, it costs much less to maintain—especially when the factory is all dolled up with inessential frills.

2. CHANGE THE SUBJECTS. Anatole France said, "Let our teaching be full of ideas. Hitherto it has been stuffed with only facts." Facts are useful when they serve as fuel for the mind, but the problem is that the number of useful facts keeps growing. To accommodate them, schools keep reducing the depth of their teaching. Facts look like towns flashing past on a speeding train, and courses are souvenir decals on a suitcase. "Rome—isn't that where we had the gelato?"

Subjects like language, history, chemistry, geography, civics, biology, and algebra are chock full of factual information, so they give the impression of contributing to a thorough education. In reality they're taught with too much detail and not enough depth. It's a "speed grazing" strategy that leaves students with very little to show beyond a diploma. "In real life, I assure you," said Fran Lebowitz, "there is no such thing as algebra." Real life certainly demands some of this knowledge (including algebra), but rarely in the form or the proportions in which the subjects are taught. And by the time you need them, 95% of the actual facts are gone, lost in the mists of memory.

With the exception of language and math basics, the subjects we now teach in school are the wrong subjects. The right subjects—the ones that will matter in the 21st century—are metaskills. Students today should be learning social intelligence, systemic logic, creative thinking, how to make things, how to learn. What we now think of as subjects—sociology, trigonometry, physics, art, psychology, and scores of others—should become "drill-downs" from the metaskills, specific disciplines designed to explore the high-order subjects. By the time of secondary education, the drill-downs should be as flexible as possible, so that students can follow their personal interests instead of learning disciplines *en masse.*

Flexible pathways through the five metaskills would turn education into a strategic exercise. It would put students in charge of their own learning, allowing them to tap into their own interests and discover who they are. It would leverage emerging technologies, including new repositories of factual knowledge like Wikipedia, and social learning tools like those from Inkling and Pearson, which enable interactive, collaborative learning. It will free up time spent on short-term memorization so it can be invested in long-term pursuits, that leave deeper understanding in their wake.

Educator Sheldon Rothblatt did a study of 19th-century Cambridge University that described the successful strategies the dons employed to keep classical studies dominant over the retrograde "useful studies." They believed, not unlike the ancient Greeks, that any subject that could be turned to practical use or might benefit business did not deserve the imprimatur of the university. Of course, this ruled out science and technology, as well as the technical aspects of art. You could study these fields as an observer, but not truly engage in them. That would get your hands dirty.

Most of the subjects we now teach in school are the wrong subjects.

Refocusing education on metaskills means transforming the educational experience. It means balancing academic learning, or learning through analysis, with generative learning, or learning through synthesis. In other words, reintegrating the left and right sides of the brain. Happily, Cambridge is no longer focused on the left side alone. There's a growing recognition within the university that students also need affective-emotional skills, cognitive-intellectual skills, aesthetic-artist skills, physical-manual skills, and personal-social skills.

Changing the course of traditional education is no easy task. Derek Bok, a former president of Harvard, once likened the difficulty of reforming a curriculum to the difficulty of moving a cemetery. But it's possible if you begin at the edges, in the crevices, or at the bottom, where traditional education can't reach.

3. FLIP THE CLASSROOM. Salman Khan may have accidentally started a revolution. In trying to teach his cousin a little math, he stumbled onto the biggest educational idea since the textbook.

He began tutoring young Nadia with fairly good results. But when he moved out of town, his only option for continuing to teach her was through online videos. So he asked himself an odd question: "How can an automated cousin be better than a cousin?"

The answer turned out to be the Khan Academy. Founded in 2009, the website now offers thousands of free 10-minute videos, spanning a wide range of educational subjects from math to history and science to English, to anyone who cares to access them. His bare-bones tutorials have been watched an average of 20,000 times each by high-school and middle-school students as a supplement to live teaching.

But why did the Academy catch on in such a big way? Sure, it's free, but since when did free education ever inspire such fanaticism? There are four good reasons for Khan's success, all of them suggestive for the future of education.

1. Sal is a charming presenter. He knows his stuff, and can infect students with his passion. He can also attract other knowledgeable presenters to his mission.

2. The videos are accessible round the clock, not just during daylight hours, so students can learn whenever their schedule or

energy permits.

3. They can learn at their own pace, repeating lessons or parts of lessons as many times as needed.

4. And teachers can direct their students to the Khan Academy to help them work on problem areas, or even build a course around the videos.

This last benefit has triggered a phenomenon called "flipping the classroom." With this approach students listen to the "lecture" on YouTube at night, freeing the teacher to help them with their "homework" in class the next day. With the old model, the classroom lecture was a waste of collaborative time; students sat in their seats quietly taking notes, straining to stay awake and up to speed during the monologue. In a flipped classroom, teaching time is given over to activities that allow individual mentoring, communal learning, and even physical movement around the classroom. The students who understand the material can also act as teaching assistants, gaining another level of experience instead of becoming bored and tuning out.

The flipped classroom is not yet the standard, because the cemetery doesn't easily move. But it's getting traction in the crevices (students who are left behind), at the bottom (autodidacts who can't afford tuition), and at the edges (schools that innovate).

At first glance, this looks like the Robot Curve in action—teachers being replaced by videos. But it's actually an opportunity for instructors to stop being "the sage on the stage" and start being flesh-and-blood mentors and coaches. It's the point at which education becomes inspiration.

In the future we're likely to see more superteachers with their own courses.

Charismatic presenters like Khan have the additional opportunity of becoming "superteachers," celebrated educators who can deliver lecture material on video with memorable performances. Think about video presenters like Kenneth Clark, Carl Sagan, James Burke, David Attenborough, Isabella Rossellini, and Neil deGrasse Tyson.

In the future we're likely to see superteachers with their own courses, their own teaching assistants, and their own promotional campaigns. They might be syndicated across a number of institu-

OLD SCHOOL	NEW SCHOOL
FACTORY MODEL	HUMAN MODEL
MECHANISTIC	CREATIVE
LECTURES	WORKSHOPS
TRANSMITTING	MENTORING
FACT-BASED	IDEA-BASED
STANDARDIZED	PERSONALIZED
HOMEWORK	PROJECTS
TEXTBOOKS	SUPERTEACHERS
COMPETITIVE	COLLABORATIVE
MONOLOGUES	DIALOGUES
BUNDLED CLASSES	UNBUNDLED CLASSES
REDUCTIVE	HOLISTIC
PASSIVE LEARNING	DYNAMIC LEARNING
ANALYTICAL	GENERATIVE
LEFT BRAIN	WHOLE BRAIN
MEMORIZING	MAKING
DUTY-DRIVEN	PASSION-DRIVEN
COMPLETION CREDITS	ACHIEVEMENT CREDITS
SUBJECTS	METASKILLS

tions, and even offer certificates for completing their modules. It's possible to imagine a professor on the faculty of a traditional university, and at the same time deriving income from videos and online courses. A world-famous instructor could only be an asset to a traditional institution.

A final advantage of the flipped classroom is that, with thousands or even tens of thousands of learning modules online, helping a student to follow her special interests in pursuit of a metaskill can become a reality. A single teacher cannot have mastery over thousands of specialized skills, but he can have mastery as a guide, a facilitator, and an expert in personalized teaching.

4. STOP TALKING, START MAKING. Harvard Law School introduced the "case method" of learning in 1870, designed to cultivate a student's capacity to reason, and simultaneously elevate the practice of law to more than a craft. Unfortunately, this widely copied method teaches little about the quotidian work of being a lawyer. It's unlikely that a class on contracts, for example, will offer students much experience in creating contracts. "What they taught us in law school," said a recent graduate of George Washington University, "is how to graduate from law school."

A friend of mine, a writing professor at Stanford University, confided that he found his job deeply unsatisfying because his students couldn't actually write. All they could do was argue the merits of other writers and postmodern philosophers. The principles of a well-constructed sentence eluded them.

This is the legacy of academic education. An academic subject is one that teaches knowledge about knowledge, or knowledge about knowledge about knowledge. It doesn't teach students how to create knowledge, which can only be accomplished by manipulating things, by getting your hands into them. The mistake that traditional education makes is thinking that knowledge ignites creativity. Surely it's the other way around. Creativity, the process of experimenting with things, ignites knowledge.

Piaget's "stage theory" of child development didn't help matters. It implicitly supported the bias toward academic superiority by suggesting that "sensorimotor intelligence" was important only during the first two years of life, and was later superseded by more intellectual ways of knowing. The job of educators, then, was to pry children from their reliance on intuition and their senses as soon as possible, and encourage them to become analysts and explainers. Today in our business schools, says Roger Martin, creativity is not merely ignored but actively disdained as frivolous. "Analytical thinking is presented as not just logically superior but *morally* superior."

It literally took an act of Congress to break academia's tight grip on higher education in America. In 1862, after being vetoed by President James Buchanan, the Land Grant College Act was signed into law by his successor, Abraham Lincoln. It supported the heretical idea that agriculture and machinery skills were fit subjects for formal education. One educational journal said these were "schools where hayseeds and greasy mechanics were taught to hoe potatoes, pitch manure, and be dry-nurses to steam engines." What happened to these pathetic excuses for education? They became the Massachusetts Institute of Technology, Cornell University, and the University of California campuses, among others.

In a windowless classroom on the campus of Triton College, 16 girls from 11 to 15 years old are designing and constructing a cat feeder, a candy dispenser, and a music box using various pieces of foam board, fiberglass, metal, and PVC pipe. Antigone Sharris founded this all-girls program, which she calls Gadget Camp. "Not letting children learn the hands-on component of science is killing us as a nation," she said. "You have to stop giving kids books and start giving them tools."

Doreen Quinn, a treatment therapist for the New Haven Youth and Family Services in Vista, California, took on the thankless task of helping at-risk boys in gang-prone Hispanic neighborhoods, many of whom had severe emotional problems, learning disabilities, or a lack of English skills. She found it almost impossible to get through to them. On the brink of giving up, she had an epiphany: Boys learn better on their feet.

She hurried down to Lowe's and bought some wood, glue,

Creativity, the process of experimenting with things, ignites knowledge.

nails, paint, and simple hand tools. She laid them out next to a plan to build a birdhouse. The boys were transfixed. They became fascinated with the problem of building their own structures, suddenly paying attention, cooperating, and asking detailed questions. Her conversations with them began to flow naturally, giving the therapeutic process a chance to unfold. Not only that, building a birdhouse, or anything else, requires skills such as reading (plans and instructions), math (measurements and geometry), economics (budgeting and buying), and interpersonal skills (cooperating and collaborating).

Quinn's success led New Haven to found a tuition-free public charter school for kids with learning challenges, called North County Trade Tech High School. Trade Tech now has 28,000 square feet of classroom and workshop spaces, and harbors a dream to expand into a community college, adding specialties such as auto-tech, the culinary arts, and sports and recreation hospitality.

While most people assume trade school is the end of the educational line, Quinn has found that many of the kids go on to traditional colleges. Along with real-world technical training, they learn core academics, including math and English. A daily fixture of the curriculum is a 30-minute, campuswide period of "sustained silent reading" (no comics allowed), and students are required to write "reflections" about what they've learned or how they might solve a particular problem. She calls this kind of education "back-dooring."

But what if the back door is really the front door? What if project-based learning is superior to subject-based learning in the Robotic Age?

Technology innovator Ray Kurzweil thinks it is. "The best way to learn is by doing your own projects," he says. Project-based learning, also called problem-based learning, has become a hot topic. It was discussed with excitement at a string of European conferences in 2009, as part of the European Year of Creativity and Innovation. In China, a country long thought a bastion of non-innovation, educational reforms are underway to extinguish the drill-and-kill teaching style and replace it with problem-based learning.

Problem- and project-based education is a dynamic process

that reconnects students with their emotions, with their senses, with their concept of what's possible in life. Instead of only taking in, they're asked to give out, to contribute something new. Creative achievement requires an act of courage, which in turn builds character. It fosters hard work, integrity, self-control, honesty, and persistence, virtues that have been eroded by our culture of easy multiple choice.

I once had a college instructor who would shout, "Shut up and design!" He knew that if your goal was to make something, there was no substitute for getting on with it.

5. ENGAGE THE LEARNING DRIVE. Why can't Johnny and Susie sit still? Ken Robinson offers an interesting hypothesis. He noticed that attention-deficit disorder has been spreading in lockstep with standardized testing, showing up first in places where schooling is the most regimented, such as the eastern United States. He says in some ways ADHD is a "fake disease." Not that there aren't legitimate cases, of course, but that the cause of most hyperactivity and lack of focus is the nature of our schooling, not an outbreak of neurological difficiencies.

He draws a contrast between two kinds of experiences: aesthetic and *anaesthetic.* An aesthetic experience is one in which your senses are operating at their peak, when you're in the moment, when you're fully alive, when you're resonating with the excitement of what you're learning. An anaesthetic experience is one in which your senses are deadened. He believes we're getting our kids through school by anaesthetizing them with Ritalin and other interventions. "We shouldn't be putting them to sleep," he says. "We should be waking them up to what they have inside themselves."

A special issue of *Newsweek* titled "The Creativity Crisis" blamed the decline of creativity, in part, on the number of hours kids now spend in front of the TV and playing videogames instead of engaging in creative activities. That's one way to look at it. The other way is that, given the state of creativity in schools, videogames seem like a blessed relief from alternating bouts of boredom and stress. Most students, if offered a choice between the fun of playing a videogame and the fun of designing one, would choose the latter. So why not create a videogame project for the classroom? Engage kids in real-world challenges such as concepting, game theory, planning, storyboarding, motion graphics, sound design, programming, writing, and teamwork.

"It's very important for people to continue to develop their feeling world" according to psychotherapist Anat Baniel. When a child has to ignore his kinesthetic and perceptual world to learn about things "out there," he has to disassociate from himself to do it. As a result, an understanding of aesthetics never develops. To appreciate any kind of art or skillful achievement, you need to relive or "mirror" the making of it. If you've never played a sport, it's hard to appreciate the physical and mental inputs that make it remarkable. If you've never played music, it's hard to appreciate the intricately layered sounds or the tradition that gave birth to them. If you've never written a story, it's hard to appreciate the rhythms, symbols, and structure of someone else's story.

A hands-on, minds-on project can make the difference between shallow learning and deep learning. In a typical textbook lesson, such as memorizing word pairs or historical events, most students can only recall an average of 10 percent of the material after 3 to 6 days. The other 90 percent goes away. In contrast, hands-on learning has a way of sticking around much longer, since it engages students at a deeper level, the level of emotion and personal interest.

Shallow learning results from a reductionist use of rational drivers such as memorization, extrinsic rewards, objective truth,

A hands-on, minds-on project can make the difference between shallow and deep learning.

formulas, observation, reason, skepticism, and expertise. Deep learning comes from the addition of emotional drivers such as imagination, intrinsic rewards, experiential truth, aesthetics, intuition, passion, and wonder. When you mix these together, you can achieve a kind of spontaneous combustion—an explosion of questions and creative activity that makes traditional learning seem tame by comparison.

A 2010 Gallup poll showed that, although students begin to form ideas about what they can and can't achieve by age 7 or 8, only 42 percent of students between ages 10 to 18 say they're energetically pursuing their goals. Only 35 percent believe they can find ways around obstacles to their goals. This doesn't mean that they're not learning. It just means that part of what they're learning is that their dreams aren't achievable. If the goal of education is self-confidence, 35 percent is a pretty dismal score.

A reporter from NBC was doing a story on a fifth-grade class using the Khan Academy videos as course material. She noticed a fifth grader doing trigonometry, and sat down beside her. "Do you think this is fifth-grade math?" she asked. The little girl whispered conspiratorially: "No—I think it's *sixth*-grade." There's nothing like believing you're special to light a fire under your learning.

Specialness, the feeling that you matter, is what creative projects bring out. They give you a chance to locate your passion, your joy, your personal source of energy. When you know your name will be connected to a creative work, your mind becomes magnetic to knowledge, attracting every grain of information that could possibly lead to a better result. It doesn't matter whether the project is a birdhouse, a videogame, a trigonometry problem, a blog entry, a cartwheel, or a smile on the faces of an audience.

6. ADVANCE BEYOND DEGREES. There's nothing wrong with extrinsic rewards if they help you focus on what's important. But if test scores, grades, credits, rankings, or degrees become ends in themselves, they divert valuable energy towards inauthentic goals. Real advancement can't be measured in merit badges and gold stars.

Interestingly, as the market value of a college degree rises, students aren't the only ones trying to game the system. So are the educators, who are tempted to deliver less and charge more, secure in the knowledge that the credential, not the education, is what the marketplace values. While most educators would never consciously cut back on what they deliver, there's nevertheless a subtle market pressure to lighten up on class time. The average number of hours college students spend on educational activities is about two per day. A third of students do less than five hours of studying per week and yet manage, on average, to earn Bs. I still remember my shock a few years ago when I complimented a friend on earning his MBA from Northwestern. He replied, "It's nothing. It's a check box."

This is the lingering effect of the Industrial Age on education. Getting a good test score has come to mean progress. Listening to a lecture has come to mean understanding. Finishing a course has come to mean proficiency. And getting a degree has come to mean expertise. Meanwhile, cheating has reached epidemic proportions.

Real advancement can't be measured in merit badges and gold stars.

Remember Dr. Deming? The man who improved the quality of Japanese cars by measuring operations down to the tiniest detail? "Our educational system would be improved greatly by the abolishment of grading," he said. "No one can enjoy his work if he will be ranked with others." The idea of being ranked at the top of your class is out of sync with how learning works. Anyone at the top of his class, according to the principle of flow, is necessarily underchallenged. The proper place to be is somewhere in the middle, grappling with tasks that are neither too hard nor too easy.

The long, slow slide to conformity seems to begin in K–12 (ages 6-17) with standardized textbooks. Kids learn that the answer is in the back of the book, there's nothing important that hasn't been written down, and the highest goal in life is to be correct. This is what educational psychologist Donald Treffinger referred to as "right-answer fixation." Students who fear mistakes are the ones who avoid the dragon pit. They can't abide failure. Yet real advancement is measured in mastery, not correctness. As you master a topic, a skill, or a discipline, you can feel your confidence grow. The feeling itself is the measurement.

What does the route from student to master look like? More than anything, it looks like apprenticeship. For most of our history, children have learned skills from experienced workers a very early age. Apprenticing *was* schooling. But even today, the shortest path to well-honed, finely tuned skills in most disciplines is working alongside a master. Mastery can't be reached without guidance and sustained focus. It can't be assembled from thin, 50-minute classes spaced apart by days.

Quest University in British Columbia has attacked this deficiency head-on. Instead of the usual curriculum of several subjects spread over 16 weeks, Quest uses the "block system." Students take one course for four weeks straight, no interruptions, before moving on the next one. This means the students are together with their instructor every day for the duration of the course. Instead of juggling, they focus. Instead of grazing, they dive. Instead of piling up credits, they collect skills, knowledge, and experience.

Quest's president, David Helfand, was a traditional educator who began to see cracks in the system. One day when he was teaching a class at Columbia, he asked the students why they weren't more curious, why they didn't ask more questions. The answers fell into three categories. Answer 1: "There's so much to learn, and it's all on Google anyway." Answer 2: "This is a seminar; asking questions could be a sign of weakness." Answer 3: "You have to understand, I'm paying for a degree, not an education." Soon after, Quest University was born.

I'm not suggesting we eliminate degrees, or the tests and textbooks that define them. I'm only suggesting that we make mastery more important than merit badges by giving students of a taste of authentic joy.

7. SHAPE THE FUTURE. Today we find ourselves caught between two paradigms, the linear, reductionist past and the spiraling, multivalent future. The old world turned on the axis of knowledge and material goods. The new one will turn on the axis of creativity and social responsibility. To cross the gap we'll need a generation of thinkers and makers who can reframe problems and design surprising, elegant solutions. We'll need fearless, self-directed learners who embrace adventure. We'll need teachers, mentors, and leaders who understand that mind shaping is world shaping—who give learners the tools they'll need to continually reinvent their minds in response to future challenges.

The cold rationality of the assembly line has denied us access to the most human part of ourselves. It made us believe that if a thing can't be counted, weighed, measured, or memorized, it can't be important. It caused us to narrow our experience of life, leaving little room for feeling, seeing, dreaming, making, or learning.

There's a theory called *cognitive recapitulation* that says children learn by retracing the steps of human evolution. As toddlers, we resemble nothing so much as monkeys, absorbed with climbing and clinging and touching. By six years old we've acquired the cognitive skills of Lucy, *Australopithicus afarensis*. One year later we're passing through the world of early *Homo erectus*, and by eight we're racing past the genius level for *erectus*, well on the way to *Homo sapiens*.

In the 21st century it seems as if we're straining towards a new stage of evolution. Our "fourth brain"—the shared, external brain we're building in the technology sphere—is rebalancing the load so that our right brain can rejoin our left as an equal partner. It now seems possible, even necessary, to reconnect art with science, synthesis with analysis, magic with logic. By taking the gains of the Industrial Age and infusing them with the humanity already encoded in our genes, we can reclaim our humanness and create dazzling arrays of technological wonders. We can begin to lighten our step and lengthen our stride as we make way on once impossible problems such as sustainability, poverty, war, injustice, and ignorance. The Robotic Age, if we want it, can be more than a grainy blowup of the Industrial Age.

How should our educational system accommodate the fact that the hand is not merely a metaphor for humanity, but the actual cause of it? How should we develop this lever, this launching pad, this wielder of tools and shaper of worlds?

For our ancestors, the beautiful animals carved into bone, stone, and ivory, and the paintings in the caves of the Midi-Pyrénées, of the Dordogne, of Spain, and of Australia and Africa, are the remaining traces of a culture so profound that it lasted 20,000 years. These drawings were not just their art, but their history and religion and science. They rendered the world comprehensible, gave meaning to their lives, and expressed the heartbreaking beauty they saw all around them. The evolutionary relationship between brain and hand is written in our DNA. It's living proof that we're not only *Home sapiens* but *Homo creatis*.

I *make*, says the hand on the wall, therefore I am.

NOTES

PROLOGUE

Southern France

XIII Hand stencils: *The Cave Painters: Probing the Mysteries of the World's First Artists,* by Gregory Curtis (Knopf, 2006).

North America

XIV Watson on *Jeopardy*: Wikipedia, en.wikipedia.org/wiki/Watson_(computer)

XIV 33 billion operations per second: "What Is Artificial Intelligence," by Richard Powers, *The New York Times*, February 6, 2011.

XIV Massively parallel processing: "Can a Computer Win on Jeopardy?," by Stephen Baker, *The Wall Street Journal*, February 5-6, 2011.

TEN QUESTIONS

XVII Why do we create? *The Cave Painters: Probing the Mysteries of the World's First Artists*, by Gregory Curtis (Knopf, 2006).

XVIII What is a human? "Androids to Bring Surrogates Closer to Reality," by Tim Hornyak, *CNET News*, April 5, 2010, tinyurl.com/y8wgltc

XX Why do we work? *The Gardens of Democracy*, by Eric Liu and Nick Hanauer (Sasquatch Books, 2011).

XXV What is a sin? "Municipal Solid Waste Generation, Recycling, and Disposal in the United States: Facts and Figures for 2010," EPA (2011).

XXVI What is beauty? "Runway to Poise or Problems?" by Karen Mansfield, *Observer-Reporter* (Washington and Greene Counties, Pennsylvania), January 26, 1997.

XXVII Who will we worship? "The Celebrity 100", *Forbes*, May 2012, www.forbes.com/profile/lady-gaga

XXVIII Who will we educate? "Student Protests Spread throughout Region," *Nation of Change*, November 26, 2011, tinyurl.com/bvkh2ze

XXIX How will we eat? From a personal conversation with designer Mitchell Mauk in 2012.

XXXI Where will we live? "World Population," *Wikipedia*, en.wikipedia.org/wiki/World_population

XXXIII What makes us happy? "Giant Smiley Indicates Mood," Roos Bros., January 10, 2012, www.roosbros.com/?p=2830

THE MANDATE

The arc of human talent

2 Extropy: "Principles of Extropy," by Max More, www.extropy.org/principles.htm

3 The hands of *Homo erectus*: *The Hand: How Its Use Shapes the Brain, Language, and Human Culture,* by Frank R. Wilson (Vintage Books, 1999).

3 Transhumanists: "Transhumanism: Toward a Futurist Philosophy," by Max More, www.maxmore.com/transhum.htm (1990)

3 The Singularity: *The Singularity Is Near: When Humans Transcend Biology,* Ray Kurzweil (The Viking Press, 2005).

4 Information has grown at 23% per year: "The World's Technological Capacity to Store, Communicate, and Compute Information," by Martin Hilbert and Priscilla López, *Science,* February 10, 2011.

4 Information increases tenfold every five years: *The Economist,* February 27, 2010.

4 Five exobytes of information every two days: *Think Quarterly,* issue 02, from the introduction, July 23, 2011.

4 Total amount of information is 1.27 zettabytes: *The Economist,* February 27, 2010.

4 Every book every printed: "Amazon CEO Jeff Bezos Unveils Kindle DX in New York," by Chris Dannen, *Fast Company,* May 6, 2009.

4 Self-awareness of computers: *Who Says Elephants Can't Dance?,* by Louis V. Gerstner (Collins, 2003).

5 IBM's cognitive computer chips: "IBM Announces Brainy Computer Chip," *The New York Times,* by Steve Lohr, August 18, 2011.

5 Technium: *What Technology Wants,* by Kevin Kelly (Penguin, 2011).

5 iPod in 1961: conversation with Kurt Kwok, director of marketing for chip maker Applied Materials.

5 28th doubling of computer power: *Radical Evolution: The Promise and Peril of Enhancing Our Minds, Our Bodies—and What It Means to Be Human,* by Joel Garreau, (Doubleday, 2005).

6 Law of Accelerating Returns: *The Singularity Is Near,* Kurzweil.

6 Genes evolving 100 times faster: *What Technology Wants,* Kelly.

6 Evolution as a play in four acts: Ibid.

6 Heaven, hell, and prevail scenarios: *Radical Evolution,* Garreau.

6 A long way from paintings on cavemen's walls: "Michael Eisner," interview by Alan Deutschman, *The New York Times,* December 2, 2010.

The innovation mandate

9 Information age: *The Third Wave*, by Alvin Toffler (Morrow, 1980).

10 Paradigm shift: *The Structure of Scientific Revolutions*, by Thomas Kuhn (1970).

10 Creative destruction: *Capitalism, Socialism and Democracy*, by Joseph Schumpeter (1942).

11 Innovation areas: "The Ten Types of Innovation," from the Doblin Group, www.slideshare.net/markoh/doblin-ten-types-of-innovation-presentation

11 They copied all they could follow: "The Mary Gloster," by Rudyard Kipling (1896).

Where are the jobs?

12 Supply-side economics: *The Gardens of Democracy*, by Eric Liu and Nick Hanauer (Sasquatch Books, 2011).

12 Horse-and-sparrow theory: Wikipedia, en.wikipedia.org/wiki/Trickle-down_economics

12 Financial sector became the master instead of the servant: "The Limping Middle Class," by Robert Reich, *The New York Times*, September 3, 2011.

13 Consumer hourglass effect: "As Middle Class Shrinks, P&G Aims High and Low," by Ellen Byron, *The Wall Street Journal*, September 12, 2011.

13 The top one percent: *That Used to Be Us: How America Fell Behind in the World It Invented and How We Can Come Back*, by Thomas L. Friedman and Michael Mandelbaum (Farrar, Strauss & Giroux, 2011).

13 Universal opinion of economists: "With Prospect of U.S. Slowdown, Europe Fears a Worsening Debt Crisis," by Steven Erlanger, *The New York Times*, August 7, 2011.

15 American pay has only risen 6 percent: "The Limping Middle Class," Reich.

The Robot Curve

18 IBM experiment led to WellPoint contract: "IBM Watson's Next Job: WellPoint Health Insurance," by Tom Murphy, *The Huffington Post*, September 12, 2011.

18 First knowledge-industry workers to be put out of work: Wikipedia, en.wikipedia.org/wiki/Watson_(artificial_intelligence_software)

19 Companies report difficulty in filling jobs: ManpowerGroup press release, May 19, 2011.

19 Gap between workers and jobs: From an interview with Kathy Smith, HR Manager, Kaman Composites, 2011.

A crisis of happiness

20 Yardstick for progress: "Redefining What No. 1 Means,"
by David J. Rothkopf, *The New York Times*, October 9, 2011.

21 The Well-Being Index: "Discovered: The Happiest Man in America,"
by Catherine Rampell, *The New York Times*, March 6, 2011.

21 Making progress at meaningful work: *The Progress Principle: Using
Small Wins to Ignite Joy, Engagement, and Creativity at Work*, by Teresa
Amabile and Steven Kramer (Harvard Business Review, 2011).

22 Being the richest man in the cemetery doesn't interest me: "What's
Next? Steve Jobs's Vision, So on Target at Apple, Now Is Falling
Short," by G. Pascal Zachary and Ken Yamada, *The Wall Street Journal*,
May 25, 1993.

22 Eudaimonia and self-actualization: "Our Imperfect Search for
Perfection," by Carina Chocano, *The New York Times*, March 18, 2011.

The obsolete industrial brain

24 I bought a bus and it sank: *Out of Our Minds: Learning to Be Creative*,
by Ken Robinson (Capstone, 1998).

24 King Ammon and Theuth: *Phaedrus, by Plato*, translated by Harold
N. Fowler (Harvard University Press, 1925).

25 Unconscious memory of human experience: *Archetypes and the
Collective Unconscious*, by Carl G. Jung (1959).

25 Three-brain model: *The Triune Brain in Evolution: Role in Paleocerebral
Functions*, by Paul D. MacLean (Springer, 1990).

Wanted: Metaskills

27 Today's robots are primitive: "In Search of a Robot More Like Us,"
by John Markoff, *The New York Times*, September 11, 2011.

27 Higher-level understanding: "In Pursuit of the Perfect Brainstorm,"
by David Segal, *The New York Times*, December 16, 2010.

28 Push harder on STEM subjects: "Why Education Without Creativity
Isn't Enough," by Anya Kamenetz, *Fast Company*, September 14, 2011.

29 Six drivers of change: "Future Work Skills 2020," by The Institute
of the Future on behalf of Apollo Research Institute,
tinyurl.com/7b3orkw

Congratulations, you're a designer

30 Wicked problems: coined by Horst Rittel in 1967, Wikipedia,
en.wikipedia.org/wiki/Wicked_problem

31 If you want to innovate, you have to design: *The Designful Company:
How to Build a Culture of Nonstop Innovation*, by Marty Neumeier
(New Riders, 2009).

31 Design and design thinking: "Secrets of Design: Rebellion," by Marty Neumeier, Critique: *The Magazine of Design Thinking*, issue 2 (Neumeier Design Team, 1996).

33 Definition of a design: *The Sciences of the Artificial*, by Herbert Simon (MIT Press, 1969).

33 Designers are in the miracle business: from a talk by Dr. Carl Hodges at the Ringling School of Art and Design, 2010.

33 Design can bring back value: "Sustaining the Dream," interview with James P. Hackett, president and CEO of Steelcase, by Maha Atal, *BusinessWeek*, October 4, 2007.

33 Good design is serious business: "Delivering Delight," by A.G. Lafley with Christine Canabou, *Fast Company*, June 1, 2004.

The future in your hands

34 Language was the turning point in human evolution: "Biography of Richard G. Klein," by Erica Klarreich, www.pnas.org/content/101/16/5705.full

34 Baby's first words: *Thought and Language*, by Lev Vygotsky (MIT Press, 1986).

35 Nouns as stones and verbs as pulleys: *The Hand: How Its Use Shapes the Brain, Language, and Human Culture*, by Frank R. Wilson (Vintage, 1998).

FEELING

Brain surgery, self-taught

39 Calculating feats of savants: "A Genius Explains," by Richard Johnson, *The Guardian*, February 11, 2005.

39 Allan Snyder, Centre for the Mind: Ibid.

40 *Cogito ergo sum vs. sentio ergo sum: Soul Dust: The Magic of Consciousness,* by Nicholas Humphrey (Princeton University Press, 2011).

40 Horse and rider: *The Ego and the Id*, Sigmund Freud (W.W. Norton, 1969).

41 Purpose of the OFC: Wikipedia, en.wikipedia.org/wiki/Orbitofrontal_cortex

41 A brain that can't feel: *How We Decide*, by Johah Lehrer (Houghton Mifflin 2009).

42 Accumulating wisdom through error: Ibid.

43 Reflection-in-action: *The Design Studio: An Exploration of Its Traditions and Potentials*, by Donald Schön (1985).

43 Mirror neurons: *Emergence: The Connected Lives of Ants, Brains, Cities, and Software*, by Steven Johnson (Scribner, 2001).

When the right brain goes wrong

46 The limits of intuition: *Thinking, Fast and Slow,* by Daniel Kahneman (Farrar, Strauss and Giroux, 2011).

46 Cognitive biases: *Principles of Visual Perception,* by Carolyn M. Bloomer (Design Press, 1990).

47 The Stroop Test: "The Stroop Effect." Wikipedia, en.wikipedia.org/wiki/Stroop_effect

The magical mind

49 Mental state of flow: *Flow: The Psychology of Optimal Experience,* by Mihalyi Csikszentmihalyi (Harper, 2008).

49 Consciousness as information: *The User Illusion: Cutting Consciousness Down to Size,* by Tor Nørretranders (Penguin, 1999).

49 Evolutionary advantages of consciousness: *Soul Dust: The Magic of Consciousness,* by Nicholas Humphreys (Princeton University Press, 2011).

52 Hard problem of consciousness: "Facing up to the Problem of Consciousness, by David Chalmers, *Journal of Consciousness Studies,* 2(3): 200-19, 1995.

52 Plato's cave: "Allegory of the Cave," Wikipedia, en.wikipedia.org/wiki/Allegory_of_the_Cave

52 Cartesian model of consciousness: "Meditations on First Philosophy," by Réne Descartes (1641).

Leonardo's assistant

54 Butterfly effect: "Does the flap of a butterfly's wings in Brazil set off a tornado in Texas?," a speech given by Edward Norton Lorenz to the American Academy for the Advancement of Science, 1972.

54 100,000 drawings and 13,000 pages of notes: *The Science of Leonardo: Inside the Mind of the Great Genius of the Renaissance,* by Fritjof Capra (Doubleday, 2007).

54 Leonardo's assistant: "Francesco Melzi," by Cynthia Phillips Ph.D. and Shana Priwer, Netplaces, tinyurl.com/6wqqodn

55 Fracture between art and science: *The Science of Leonardo,* by Fritjof Capra.

56 Exile of emotion: *Out of Our Minds,* Ken Robinson.

56 Factual knowledge was an invention: *What Technology Wants,* Kevin Kelly.

56 Split between science and life: "Neurology and the Soul," by Oliver Sacks, *New York Review of Books,* November 22, 1990.

57 Codex Leicester: *The Science of Leonardo,* by Fritjof Capra.

The uses of beauty

58 Conceive yourself stripped of emotion: *The Varieties of Religious Experience: A Study in Human Nature*, by William James (Longman, Green, 1902).

60 Way-it-should-be-ness: *Connections: The Work of Charles and Ray Eames*, with an essay by Ralph Caplan (UCLA Art Council, 1976).

60 Optimal closure: From a personal conversation with Carolyn M. Bloomer in 2012.

63 Mini spends one percent on design: *Glimmer: How Design Can Transform Your Life, and Maybe Even the World*, by Warren Berger (Penguin, 2009).

63 Most evolved things are beautiful: *What Technology Wants*, Kevin Kelly.

Aesthetics for dummies

63 Ten definitions of aesthetics: *Which Aesthetics Do You Mean?*, Leonard Koren (Imperfect Publishing, 2010).

64 Universal or personal: *The Principles of Aesthetics*, by Henry Parker DeWitt (1923).

68 Good taste is learned: *Truth, Beauty, and Goodness Reframed: Educating for the Virtues of the 21st Century*, by Howard Gardner (Basic Books, 2011).

69 Primary illusions: "The primary illusions and the great orders of art," by Susanne K. Langer, *The Hudson Review*, Summer, 1950.

72 Difficulty of aesthetics: *The Elements of Style*, by William Strunk and E.B. White (Macmillan, 1959).

73 Meaning and interpretation are at the heart of all creative processes: *Out of Our Minds*, Robinson.

73 Satisficing: "Rational choice and the structure of the environment," by Herbert Simon, *Psychological Review*, volume 63, number 2, 1956.

It's not business—it's personal

75 80/80 rule: from a talk by Oliver King of Engine Service Design (London), at DMI Remix, 2008.

75 Brand as commercial reputation: *The Brand Gap: How to Bridge the Distance Between Business Strategy and Design*, Marty Neumeier (New Riders, 2003).

75 Brand momentum as a leading indicator: *The Brand Bubble*, by John Gerzema and Ed Lebar (Jossey-Bass, 2008).

75 Zappos: "The Brand Bubble in the Digital Era," an interview with John Gerzema by Gabriel Rossi, Slideshare, tinyurl.com/y9kggmq

76 Starbucks: "A Changed Starbucks. A Changed CEO," by Claire Cain Miller, *The New York Times*, March 13, 2011.

76 Ryanair pricing: "Costs Out at All Costs," by Todd Sattersten, *Fixed to Flexible* (ebook), March 29, 2010.

77 They will only forget to do it once: "Prevent Nickel-and-Diming," by Arthur Frommer, *San Francisco Chronicle*, October 18, 2009.

78 Bags fly free: "Pushing 40, Southwest Is Still Playing the Rebel," *The New York Times*, November 20, 2010.

79 Nespresso: "Nestlé Stakes Its Grounds in a European Coffee War," by Christina Passariello, *The Wall Street Journal*, April 26, 2010.

80 Innovative ideas are rarely rejected on their technical specs: *The Myths of Innovation*, by Scott Berkun (O'Reilly, 2007).

80 Dirty towers on windswept plains: *Glimmer*, by Warren Berger.

80 Katrina cottages: Ibid.

82 Social skills: *Emotional Intelligence: Why It Can Matter More Than IQ*, by Daniel Goleman (Bantam, 1997).

On what do you bias your opinion?

84 Confirmation bias: "How to Ignore the Yes-man in Your Head," by Jason Zweig, *The Wall Street Journal*, November 19, 2009.

85 BlackBerry's mental model: "RIM Loses Marketing Chief", by Phred Dvorak and Stuart Weinberg, *The Wall Street Journal*, June 25, 2011.

86 Giordano Bruno: Wikipedia, en.wikipedia.org/wiki/Giordano_Bruno

87 We define first, then we see: "Defining the Facebook Deal," by Holman W. Jenkins, Jr., *The Wall Street Journal*, January 15, 2011.

87 Culture is not defined by what we argue about: *The Future of Ideas: The Fate of the Commons in a Connected World*, by Lawrence Lessig (Random House, 2001).

88 Replace beliefs with knowledge: *The Big Questions: Tackling the Problems of Philosophy with Ideas from Mathematics, Economics, and Physics*, by Steven Landsburg (Free Press, 2009).

SEEING

The tyranny of or

92 Civilizations based on opposition face gridlock: *The Watchman's Rattle: Thinking Our Way Out of Extinction*, by Rebecca Costa (Vanguard Press, 2010).

94 Integrative thinkers: *The Opposable Mind: How Successful Leaders Win through Integrative Thinking*, by Roger Martin (Harvard Business School Press, 2007).

94 Niels Bohr and paradox: *Niels Bohr: The Man, His Science, and the World They Changed*, by Ruth Moore (1966).

Thinking whole thoughts

95 Painter Robert Irwin: *Seeing Is Forgetting the Name of the Thing One Sees*, by Lawrence Weschler (University of California Press, 1982).

95 The father of holistic invention: *The Science of Leonardo*, Capra.

96 Macroscopes: *In the Bubble: Designing in a Complex World*, by John Thackara (MIT Press, 2006).

97 I have yet to see any problem: *Thinking in Systems: A Primer*, by Donella H. Meadows (Chelsea Green Publishing, 2008).

97 Don't get involved in partial problems: *Notebooks 1914-1916*, by Ludwig Wittgenstein, edited by G.E.M. Anscombe and G.H. von Wright (University of Chicago Press, 1984).

How systems work

98 Elements, interconnections, and purpose: *Thinking in Systems*, Meadows.

98 Latency: Ibid.

100 Feedback types: *The Fifth Discipline: The Art and Practice of the Learning Organization*, by Peter M. Senge (Doubleday, 1990).

100 Unfamiliar shower: Ibid.

102 State government raises taxes: *Applied Economics: Thinking Beyond Stage One*, by Thomas Sowell (Basic Books, 2003).

102 Overvaluing the short term: "When Our Brains Short-Circuit," by Nicholas D. Kristof, *The New York Times*, July 1, 2009.

Grandma was right

103 First rule of systems: *Thinking in Systems*, Meadows.

104 Systems create archetypes: *The Fifth Discipline*, Senge.

105 Rick Perry on global warming: "Global Warming Based on Scientists Manipulating Data," by Dina Cappiello, *The Huffington Post*, August 17, 2011.

107 Cold War escalation: *The Better Angels of Our Nature: Why Violence Has Declined*, by Steven Pinker (Viking, 2011).

108 Obama drone program: "Coming Soon: The Drone Arms Race," by Scott Shane, *The New York Times*, October 8, 2011.

108 Archetype 5: "The Tragedy of the Commons," by Garrett Hardin, 1968, tinyurl.com/6p33g

109 Three ways out of the trap: *Thinking in Systems*, Meadows.

111 The United Nations' carbon credits: "Carbon Credits Gone Awry Raise Output of Harmful Gas," by Elisabeth Rosenthal and Andrew W. Lehren, *The New York Times*, August 8, 2012.

113 IBM's transformation: *Who Says Elephants Can't Dance?*, by Louis V. Gerstner (Collins, 2003).

113 Kodak's loss of momentum: *The Designful Company,*
by Marty Neumeier (New Riders, 2009).

114 Competitive Exclusion Principle: *The Struggle for Existence,*
by Georgii Frantsevich Gause (Williams & Wilkins, 1934).

115 No Child Left Behind Act: *Standards: Recipes for Reality,*
by Lawrence Busch (MIT Press, 2011).

116 Obvious yet subversive: *Thinking in Systems,* Meadows.

The primacy of purpose

117 Organizing purpose of a company: *The Designful Company,* Neumeier.

117 To create a customer: *The Practice of Management,* by Peter Drucker
(Heinemann, 1967).

118 Some people just got too big-headed: "Toyoda Concedes Profit Focus
Led to Flaws," by Norihiko Shirouzu, *The Wall Street Journal,*
March 1, 2010.

118 European Dream: *Dress to Kill,* by Eddie Izzard (Vision Video, 1998).

120 Robert F. Kennedy presidential election address: University of
Kansas, March 18, 1968, tinyurl.com/3btkx7n

120 Positive psychology: *Flourish: A Visionary New Understanding of
Happiness and Well-Being,* by Martin E. P. Seligman (Free Press, 2011).

120 Purpose and Alzheimer's: "Effect of a Purpose in Life on Risk of
Incident Alzheimer Disease and Mild Cognitive Impairment in
Community-Dwelling Older Persons," by Patricia A. Boyle, PhD;
Aron S. Buchman, MD; Lisa L. Barnes, PhD; David A. Bennett, MD;
Archives of General Psychiatry, March 2010.

Sin explained

122 Enlightenment vs. Postmodernists: *Consilience: The Unity of Knowledge,*
by Edward O. Wilson (Knopf, 1998).

122 New Enlightenment: *The Gardens of Democracy: A New American Story of
Citizenship, the Economy, and the Role of Government,* by Eric Liu and
Nick Hanauer (Sasquatch Books, 2011).

123 Dangerous flaw built into the brain: *How We Decide,* by Jonah Lehrer
(Houghton Mifflin, 2009).

123 Freedom isn't free: *The Gardens of Democracy,* Liu and Hanauer.
Rule for good behavior: *The Big Questions,* Landsburg.

125 Rules for belonging together: *The Power to Transform, Leadership that
Brings Learning and Schooling to Life,* by Stephanie Pace Marshall
(Jossey-Bass, 2006).

125 Axiology: Robert Schirokauer Hartman, www.hartmaninstitute.org.

126 Exaggerated present: *Thinking in Systems,* Meadows.

126 Living successfully in a world of systems: Ibid.

DREAMING

153 Cannibalize yourself: *Steve Jobs*, Isaacson.

153 Be a quality detector: *Thinking in Systems*, Meadows.

153 Here's to the crazy ones: "Think Different," Wikipedia, en.wikipedia.org/wiki/Think_Different

The play instinct

154 Chronos and kairos: *In the Bubble: Designing in a Complex World*, by John Thackara (MIT Press, 2006).

154 The play instinct: *A Designer's Art*, by Paul Rand (Yale University Press, 1985).

156 A person with two great ideas: *The Ascent of Man*, by Jacob Bronowski (Ambrose Video Publishing, 2007).

156 Combining old things in new ways: *Ralph Caplan, Making Connections: The Work of Charles and Ray Eames*, by Ralph Caplan (UCLA Art Council, 1976).

157 Think in metaphors: *I Is an Other: The Secret Life of Metaphor and x How It Shapes the Way We See the World*, by James Geary (Harper, 2012).

158 Anyone who can draw a stick figure: *The Back of the Napkin: Solving Problems and Selling Ideas with Pictures*, by Dan Roam (Portfolio, 2008).

160 Idea for the printing press: *Creativity: Genius and Other Myths*, by Weisberg (W.H. Freeman, 1986).

160 Idea for Velcro: "Velcro," Wikipedia, en.wikipedia.org/wiki/Velcro

160 Idea for the electronic television: "Electrical Engineer Philo Farnsworth," by Neil Postman, *Time*, March 29, 1999.

160 Touch of Yogurt shampoo: "Hall of Shame," *Time*, October 22, 1984.

160 Tru Blood soda: "Tru Blood and More: Entrepreneur Brings Fictional Products to Life," by Vanessa Rancaño, Oakland Local, April 13, 2012.

161 Find the paradox: *Getting to Innovation: How Asking the Right Questions Generates the Great Ideas Your Company Needs*, by Arthur B. VanGundy (Amacom, 2007).

162 Idea for celluloid: "Celluloid," Wikipedia, en.wikipedia.org/wiki/Celluloid

162 Idea for the microwave oven: "Microwave Oven," The Great Idea Finder, tinyurl.com/2mshpe

162 Idea for the iPad: "The iPad" Past, Present, Future," an interview of Steve Jobs by Walter Mossberg, *The Wall Street Journal*, June 7, 2010. Richard Feynman's test of new ideas: *Genius: The Life and Science of Richard Feynman*, by James Gleick (Vintage, 1993).

163 Ideas never stand alone: *What Technology Wants*, Kelly.

The no-process process

180 Rational model of design: *The Sciences of the Artificial*, by Herbert A. Simon (MIT Press, 1996).

180 Annie Dillard: "Write Till You Drop," by Annie Dillard, *New York Times*, May 28, 1989.

Every day is Groundhog Day

183 The details aren't the details: *Connections*, Caplan.

184 Composer Philip Glass: Interview with Ira Glass on NPR, September 21, 1999.

184 Learning through successive efforts: *The Philosophical Baby: What Children's Minds Tell Us about Truth, Love, and the Meaning of Life*, by Alison Gopnik (Picador, 2010).

185 King James Bible: "Why the King James Bible Endures," by Charles McGrath, *The New York Times*, April 23, 2011.

The discipline of uncluding

186 Four types of business complexity: "Too Big to Manage," by Julian Birkinshaw and Suzanne Heywood, *The Wall Street Journal*, October 26, 2009.

187 Optimum choice, not maximum choice: *The Paradox of Choice: Why More Is Less*, by Barry Schwartz (Harper, 2005).

187 One-think shopping: *Simplicity Marketing: End Brand Complexity, Clutter, and Confusion*, by Steven M. Cristol and Peter Sealey (Free Press, 2000).

188 Jobs treated buttons like blemishes: "Freedom from the Press," by Nick Wingfield, *The Wall Street Journal*, July 25, 2007.

188 Fashion over function: "PCs Take a Stylish Turn to Tackle Apple," by Robert A. Guth, Justin Scheck, and Don Clark, *The Wall Street Journal*, January 4, 2008.

188 A society strangling in unnecessary words: *On Writing Well*, by William Zinsser (HarperCollins, 1985).

188 Omit needless words: *The Elements of Style*, by William Strunk and E.B. White (Macmillan, 1959).

189 Baby shoes. Never worn: Most likely an apocryphal story, used in the play "Papa." Snopes.com, www.snopes.com/language/literary/babyshoes.asp

189 Fewer members in the choir: *Simple Italian Food*, by Mario Batali (Clarkson Potter, 1998).

190 Swiss Army Knife: "Defeating Feature Fatigue," by Roland T. Rust, Debora Viana Thompson, and Rebecca W. Hamilton, *Harvard Business Review*, February 1, 2006.

190 Acorn computer chip: "Getting an ARM up on Intel," by Rolfe Winkler, *The Wall Street Journal*, March 17, 2011.

190 Occam's Razor: *The Agenda: What Every Business Must Do to Dominate the Decade*, by Michael Hammer (Three Rivers Press, 2003).

The art of simplexity

192 Exformation: *User Illusion*, Nørretranders.

193 Logical depth: Ibid.

193 A certain nothingness: "Just Have Less," Tomas Maier, interviewed by John Colapinto, *The New Yorker*, January 3, 2011.

193 Jonathan Ive: "Radical Craft: The Second Art Center Design Conference," by Janet Abrams, *Core77*, tinyurl.com/743uhnq

The reality checklist

194 Heart of innovation is novelty: "Inspiration: Where Does It Come From?" Arthur Lubow, *The New York Times*, November 30, 2003.

194 What's practical is beautiful: *Billy Baldwin Decorates*, by Billy Baldwin (Chartwell, 1972).

194 Henry Ford didn't believe in testing: *The Brand Gap: How to Bridge the Distance between Business Strategy and Design*, by Marty Neumeier (New Riders, 2003).

Sell in, not out

196 The secret tragedy of innovators: *The Myths of Innovation*, Berkun.

197 Four stages of acceptance: *Big Bang: The Origin of the Universe*, by Simon Singh (Harper, 2005).

197 3M Post-it Notes: "Spencer Silver," Wikipedia, en.wikipedia.org/wiki/Spencer_Silver

199 Deft use of metrics: *How to Measure Anything: Finding the Value of Intangibles in Business*, by Douglas W. Hubbard (Wiley, 2010).

200 Bayes Theorem: *The Theory That Would Not Die: How Bayes' Rule Cracked the Enigma Code, Hunted Down Russian Submarines, and Emerged Triumphant from Two Centuries of Controversy*, by Sharon Bertsch McGrayne (Yale University Press, 2011).

200 High-status super-conformists: "Under the Influence: How the Group Changes What We Think," by Shirley S. Wang, *The Wall Street Journal*, May 3, 2011.

200 Things take longer to happen: "What You (Really) Need to Know," by Lawrence H. Summers, *The New York Times*, January 20, 2012.

The big to-do list

201 Goldilocks planet: "36 Light Years from Here, New Hope for an Earth-like Planet," by Dennis Overbye, *The New York Times*, September 12, 2011.

202 Population growth in three surges: "Human Population Growth and the Accelerating Rate of Species Extinction," by Gary W. Harding, www.earthportals.com/extinct.html

202 Malthusian crisis: "Linear Resources + Exponential Demand = ?", by Andrew Revkin, *The New York Times*, August 13, 2011.

203 That's what we never do: *The Rational Optimist: How Prosperity Evolves*, by Matt Ridley (Harper, 2010).

203 75 percent of the world will live in cities: "A New Gear," by Jeffrey Ball, *The Wall Street Journal*, March 6, 2011.

LEARNING

Impossible is nothing

207 Formulate new questions: *Truth, Beauty, and Goodness Reframed: Educating for Virtues in the Twenty-First Century*, by Howard Gardner (Basic Books, 2011).

208 Learn, unlearn, and relearn: *Rethinking the Future: Rethinking Business, Principles, Competition, Control and Complexity, Leadership, Markets, and the World*, by Rowan Gibson, Alvin Toffler, and Heidi Toffler (Nicholas Brealey, 1998).

208 New ideas capture the mind: *The Grace of Great Things: Creativity and Innovation*, by Robert Grudin (Ticknor & Fields, 1990).

209 Problems solve us: "Ways to Inflate Your IQ," by Sue Shellenbarger, *The Wall Street Journal*, November 29, 2011.

The joy zone

209 Erik Demaine: "Independent Lens: Between the Folds," (PBS, 2010).

209 I'm a geek: "Calculating Change: Why Origami Is Critical to New Drugs," by Unmesh Kher, *Time*, September 4, 2005.

210 Richard Saul Wurman: "Smart Yellow Pages," *Communication Arts*, January/February, 1988.

210 Serge Percelly: *The Hand: How Its Use Shapes the Brain, Language, and Human Culture*, by Frank R. Wilson (Vintage Books, 1999).

211 Mental state of flow: *Flow: The Psychology of Optimal Experience*, by Mihaly Csikszentmihalyi (HarperCollins, 1990).

What's the mission?

213 Competitive Exclusion Principle: *The Struggle for Existence*, Gause.

213 Jack W. Szostak: "From Telomeres to the Origins of Life," by Claudia Dreifus, *The New York Times*, October 17, 2011.

214 The meaning of life is meaning. *Flow*, Csikszentmihalyi.

214 No evidence that quantity becomes quality: *You Are Not a Gadget: A Manifesto*, by Jaron Lanier (Knopf, 2010).

215 GoodWork Project: www.goodworkproject.org

A theory of learning

217 We learn skills in a predictable sequence: "Secrets of a Mind-gamer," by Joshua Foer, *The New York Times*, February 15, 2011.

217 Experience by itself teaches nothing: *The New Economics: For Industry, Government, and Education*, by W. Edwards Deming (MIT Books, 1994).

217 Profound knowledge: Ibid.

218 The brain forms habits: "A Quest to Understand How Memory Works," by Claudia Dreifus, *The New York Times*, March 5, 2012.

218 Focus on your goals: "Secrets of a Mind-gamer," Foer.

219 Nerve cells that fire together: *The Power to Transform*, Marshall.

219 Bell and Henry: *Your Creative Power: How to Use Imagination*, by Alex Osborn (Scribner's, 1948).

219 Metaskills for journalists: "The Metaskills of Journalism," by Gerald Grow, PhD, Gerald Grow's Website, tinyurl.com/82hlmkk

220 Deliberate practice: *The Genius in All of Us: Why Everything You've Been Told About Genetics, Talent, and IQ Is Wrong*, by David Shenk (Doubleday, 2010).

220 Draw, Antonio, draw: "Write Till You Drop," by Annie Dillard, *New York Times*, May 28, 1989.

Climbing the bridge

223 A jumping together: *Consilience: The Unity of Knowledge*, by Edward O. Wilson (Knopf, 1998).

Creativity loves company

224 Bridging and bonding: *Bowling Alone: The Collapse and Revival of American Community*, by Robert D. Putnam (Simon & Schuster, 2000).

224 Weak ties: "The Strength of Weak Ties," by Mark S. Granovetter, *American Journal of Sociology*, volume 78, issue 6.

224 Biggest threat to Google: "Google's Chief Works to Trim a Bloated Ship," by Claire Cain Miller, *The New York Times*, November 9, 2011.

224 Sundown Schoolhouse: *Glimmer: How Design Can Transform Your Life, and Maybe Even the World*, by Warren Berger (Penguin, 2009).

224 Secret Science Club: "Continuing Education, at the Bar," by Jennifer Schuessler, *The New York Times*, January 6, 2012.

225 He who receives an idea from me: "Why Technologists Want Fewer Patents," by L. Gordon Crovitz, *The Wall Street Journal*, June 15, 2009.

225 Frank Stephenson: "Video: McLaren Designer Details Latest Masterpiece," *Motor Trend*, tinyurl.com/7akzr5n

Unplugging

226 Attention deficit: "Continuous Partial Attention—Not the Same as Multitasking," by Linda Stone, *Bloomberg Businessweek,* July 14, 2011.

226 Always-on culture: *In the Bubble,* Thackara.

227 Woodside High School girl: "Growing Up Digital, Wired for Distraction," by Matt Richtel, *The New York Times,* November 21, 2010.

227 Internet use disorder: "Silicon Valley Says Step Away from the Device," by Matt Richtel, *The New York Times,* July 23, 2012.

227 Fear of missing out: "Feel Like a Wallflower? Maybe It's Your Facebook Wall," by Jenna Wortham, *The New York Times,* April 9, 2011.

227 It's filter failure: Clay Shirky at Web 2.0 Expo, September 17, 2008, www.youtube.com/watch?v=LabqeJEOQyI

228 Picasso: *Quiet: The Power of Introverts in a World That Can't Stop Talking,* by Susan Cain (Crown, 2012).

228 Leonardo: *The Science of Leonardo,* Capra.

228 Wozniak: "The Rise of the New Groupthink," by Susan Cain, *The New York Times,* January 13, 2012.

The scenic road to you

228 A person is not a pat formula: *You Are Not a Gadget,* Lanier.

229 Older minds, younger minds: "Thinking and Remembering: The 2008 Progress Report on Brain Research," The Dana Foundation, tinyurl.com/72ycdoj

229 Generation Flux: "Meet the Pioneers of the New (and Chaotic) Frontier of Business," by Robert Safian, *Fast Company,* January 9, 2012.

229 Jeremy Gleick: "Renaissance Man," by Diana Kapp, *The New York Times,* January 22, 2012.

230 This thing called me: *Soul Dust,* Nicholas Humphrey.

230 Impossible is nothing: *The Difference Maker: Making Your Attitude Your Greatest Asset,* by John Maxwell (Thomas Nelson, 2006).

A MODEST PROPOSAL

Introduction

233 Disruptive innovation: *The Innovator's Solution,* by Clayton M. Christensen and Michael E. Raynor (Harvard Business School Press, 2003).

233 Johnathan Swift: "A Modest Proposal: For Preventing the Children of Poor People in Ireland," by Jonathan Swift (1729), Wikipedia, en.wikipedia.org/wiki/A_Modest_Proposal

1. Shut down the factory

234 An educational garden: *The Power to Transform*, Marshall.

234 The factory model of learning: *Out of Our Minds*, Robinson.

234 The mantra of reform: *The Power to Transform*, Marshall.

234 Intensive cultivation: "Investing in Children: Changes in Parental Spending on Children, 1972 to 2007," by Sabino Kornwich and Frank F. Furstenberg, tinyurl.com/18r

234 My husband and I shelled out a small fortune: "The Escalating Arms Race for Top Colleges," by Jennifer Moses, *The Wall Street Journal*, February 5, 2011.

2. Change the subjects

235 Let our teaching be full of ideas: "Education for an Information Age," by Bernard John Poole and Elizabeth Sky-McIlvain (McGraw-Hill, 2009).

235 No such thing as algebra: quotationspage/Fran_Lebowitz

236 Interactive learning: "A Brief History of Textbooks, or, Why Apple's 'New Textbook Experience' Is Actually Revolutionary," by Megan Garber, *The Atlantic*, January 12, 2012.

236 Inkling: "Sequoia-backed Inkling Updates iPad E-textbook Platform with Collaborative Study Groups and More," by Leena Rao, TechCrunch, August 24, 2011, tinyurl.com/3uetjbp

236 Pearson: "Pearson's New Interactive Textbooks for the iPad," YouTube, tinyurl.com/7vxyoey

236 Study of Cambridge University: *School Subjects and Curriculum Change*, by Ivor F. Goodson (Routledge, 1993).

237 Cambridge: "Intellectual Guru Seeks 'System Redesign' of Secondary Education," by Peter Wilby, *The Guardian* (London), September 21, 2009.

237 Derek Bok: "What You (Really) Need to Know," by Lawrence H. Summers, *The New York Times*, January 20, 2012.

3. Flip the classroom

237 An automated cousin: From a talk by Salman Khan, "Reinventing Our Education Future, at the University of California Santa Barbara, October 10, 2011.

237 Khan Academy: www.khanacademy.org

238 Future of education: "Flipping the classroom," *The Economist*, September 17, 2011.

238 Sage on the stage: "From Sage on the Stage to Guide on the Side," by Alison King, *College Teaching*, volume 41, 1993.

238 Superteachers: *Change.edu: Rebooting for the New Talent Economy*, by Andrew S. Rosen (Kaplan, 2011).

238 Teaching with video: "Virtual and Artificial, but 58,000 Want Course," by John Markoff, *The New York Times*, August 15, 2011.

4. Stop talking, start making

240 Case method of learning: "What They Don't Teach Law Students: Lawyering," David Segal, *The New York Times*, November 19, 2011.

240 Stage theory of child development: *Hare Brain, Tortoise Mind: How Intelligence Increases When You Think Less*, by Guy Claxton, (Harper Perennial, 1999).

240 Creativity is disdained as frivolous: *The Design of Business: Why Design Thinking is the Next Competitive Advantage*, by Roger L. Martin (Harvard Business School Press, 2009).

241 Land Grant College Act: *Change.edu*, Rosen.

241 Gadget Camp: "At This Girls' Camp, Crafts Take a Drill Press," by Motoko Rich, *The New York Times*, August 18, 2011.

242 Trade Tech High School: From a personal interview with Doreen Quinn (2011).

242 The best way to learn is by doing your own projects: From a talk by Ray Kurzweil, "Innovation in an Era of Accelerating Technologies," at the University of California Santa Barbara, March 6, 2012.

243 European Year of Creativity: "The Creativity Crisis," by Po Bronson and Ashley Merryman, *Newsweek*, July 10, 2010.

243 Creative achievement requires an act of courage: *The Grace of Great Things: Creativity and Innovation*, by Robert Grudin (Ticknor & Fields, 1990).

5. Engage the learning drive

243 ADHD is a fake disease: *Out of Our Minds*, Robinson.

243 Aesthetic and anaesthetic: "Changing Education Paradigms," by Sir Ken Robinson with RSA Animate, YouTube, tinyurl.com/376bdv2

243 Decline of creativity: "The Creativity Crisis," Bronson and Merryman.

244 Anat Baniel: *The Hand: How Its Use Shapes the Brain, Language, and Human Culture*, by Frank R. Wilson (Vintage, 1998).

244 Shallow learning vs. deep learning: "Forgetting Curve," Wikipedia, en.wikipedia.org/wiki/Forgetting_curve

244 2010 Gallup poll: "Making Kids Work on Goals (and Not Just in Soccer)," by Sue Shellenbarger, *The Wall Street Journal*, March 9, 2011.

245 I think it's sixth-grade: From a talk by Salman Khan, "Reinventing Our Education Future", at the University of California Santa Barbara, October 10, 2011.

6. Advance beyond degrees

245 Gaming the system: *Academically Adrift: Limited Learning on College Campuses,* by Richard Arum and Josipa Roksa (University of Chicago Press, 2011).

245 Five hours of studying per week: Ibid.

246 The abolishment of grading: *The New Economics,* Deming.

246 Principle of flow: *Flow,* Csikszentmihalyi.

246 Right-answer fixation: From a talk by Donald J. Treffinger, "Creative Problem-solving for Teachers," at the Project Interact Spring Conference, 1984.

247 Block system: "David Helfand's New Quest," by Tamar Lewin, *The New York Times,* January 20, 2012.

Shape the future

247 Mind shaping is world shaping: *The Power to Transform,* Marshall.

248 Cognitive recapitulation: *The Hand,* Wilson.

248 A culture so profound it lasted 20,000 years: *The Cave Painters: Probing the Mysteries of the World's First Artists,* by Gregory Curtis (Knopf, 2006).

INDEX

Eisenhower, Dwight, 121
Eisner, Michael, 8
either/or propositions, 91–94
  "and" thinking, 93–94
  civilizations based on
    opposition, 92
  false dichotomies, 92, 94
The Elements of Style, 72, 188
emotional brain
  animal instincts, 41
  automatic quality, 47
  biases
    confirmation, 84–86
    religious/cultural, 86–87
  versus computers, 39
  confirmation bias, 84–86
  empathy, 43, 45
  during Industrial Age, 39
  morality, 45
  perceptual defenses, 84
  prefrontal cortex, 47
    disassociated activity
      patterns, 139
  psychopathic behavior, 45
  short/long term values, 102
  sociopathic behavior, 87
  Stroop Test, 47–48
Emotional Intelligence, 82
empathy, 78–79, 82–83. *See also*
  feeling metaskill
"The Escalating Arms Race for Top
  Colleges," 234
"An Essay on the Principle of
  Population," 202
Euclid, 57
eudaimonia, 22
evolution. *See* human evolution
Excite network, 183
exformation, 192–193
exponential change. *See also* change

in genetics, 5
  in information technology, 5
  versus linear, 7
  in population, 202
  problems as by-product of, 8
  in robotics, 5
extropy *versus* entropy, 2
eye test of aesthetic judgment,
  195–196

F
Facebook, 139, 183, 224, 227
false dichotomies, 92, 94
Fannie Mae/homeownership, 115
Farnsworth, Philo, 160
feeling metaskill
  drawbacks using only
    feelings, 37, 45–48
  ego and id, 40
  empathy, 78–79, 82–83
  intuition
    and autistics, 43
    biases
      confirmation, 84–86
      limiting use of, 46
    from deep experience, 42
    from emotional learning, 42
Feynman, Richard, 162
Fiat 500, 225
flow in creativity, 49, 211
Ford, Henry, 194
Ford, Tennessee Ernie, 114
Ford Motors, 183, 194, 217
Foursquare, 227
fourth brain, 248
France, Midi-Pyrénées, XIII
France, Anatold, 235
Freud, Sigmund
  ego and id, 40
  horse and rider metaphor, 40, 47